D1559015

# EDUCATION AND EMPLOYMENT

# education
# and
# employment

THE
EARLY CAREERS
OF
COLLEGE GRADUATES

## Laure M. Sharp

THE JOHNS HOPKINS PRESS
BALTIMORE AND LONDON

# ACKNOWLEDGMENTS

This book summarizes findings and interpretations derived from a set of studies initiated in 1959 under the sponsorship of the National Science Foundation through its Manpower Studies Group. I am most grateful to the Foundation, and especially to Thomas Mills and Robert Cain, for their support and encouragement over the years, and for the free hand I was given while engaged in this work. Needless to say, the Foundation is in no way responsible for some of the loftier interpretations and conclusions found here and there in these pages.

Over the ten-year life span of this project, too many of my co-workers at the Bureau of Social Science Research have given counsel and assistance in various phases of this research to enable me to make all appropriate acknowledgments. However, my greatest obligation is to Rebecca Krasnegor, who had a major share in the data analysis, and to Richard Jones, who accomplished the seemingly impossible chore of shepherding the data through two generations of computers. Ira Cisin and Samuel Lyerly provided much-needed statistical wisdom. And throughout the years the study benefited from the supportive and stimulating climate of the Bureau, for which its director, Robert T. Bower, is primarily responsible.

My special thanks are due to Jane Stein, who performed the difficult task of reducing masses of statistics and text to what I hope is a readable volume of manageable size.

# CONTENTS

# LIST OF TABLES

# APPENDIX TABLES

# I

---

## INTRODUCTION

The rising level of educational achievement among the postwar generation of young Americans is one of the basic social phenomena of our time. Although a sizable minority of students, especially in the slums of large cities, have not yet been adequately reached by the educational system, increasing numbers of young people are completing high school, more are enrolling in colleges from which increasing proportions graduate, and more are able to attend professional and graduate schools. Recent student unrest and changes in the organizational structure of many campuses are secondary to this phenomenon and, in many respects, are repercussions of the rapid growth and change.

It is estimated that 70 percent of all those who reached the age of eighteen since 1960 have graduated from high school. About half of this group went on to attend college-level institutions. Seventy percent of those who entered college will eventually obtain a college degree, although it may take some of them many years. In other words, one out of four youngsters born since World War II will be a college graduate, and many others will acquire further academic credentials during their lifetimes. In 1965 500,000 men and women received the bachelor's degree; recent projections put the number of college graduates at 742,000 in 1970 and 927,000 in 1975. The comparable figures for 1956 and 1960 were 287,000 and 366,000, respectively.

It is difficult for some to believe that quantitative change of this magnitude can take place without an adverse qualitative change. The argument is sometimes heard that we are simply witnessing an inflation of the degree structure, rather than a genuine expansion of educational achievement. There are those who argue that in our affluent society the college degree is just one more consumption item acquired by large numbers of persons for status,

1

postponement of entry into the work force, or military deferment. According to this school of thought, many jobs are held today by college graduates that were filled in the past by persons who had no more than a high school education.

This argument, which carried little weight even a few years ago, lacks total conviction now. The growing volume of information — student aptitude data, college curricula, and occupational requirements — suggests that today's academic or preprofessional degrees represent a heavier study investment and a higher level of achievement than their counterparts a generation ago. That is, the growing number of professions, the complexity of professional work roles, and the pace of technological innovation that affects these work roles require more intensive education. The average college-bound student today takes more advanced work in high school than his father did; and today's college graduate is more likely to continue his formal education beyond college. Additionally, several years of training have been added to most professional preparation. Teachers or nurses, who previously held post-high school certificates, now are required to have at least a bachelor's degree for entrance into the profession and often a master's degree for professional advancement. Engineers, who in the past rarely sought advanced degrees and who could break occasionally into the field without a baccalaureate, now often need a master's degree to work in the newest, most challenging, and most lucrative specialties. On college faculties, the Ph.D. has long been a requirement for achieving the top ranks; this trend has accelerated tremendously and now affects the lower ranks, the less prestigious institutions, and fields outside of the arts and sciences.

The growth in the demand for higher education has led to a tremendous increase in the sizes of educational establishments. This is reflected both in the expansion of older institutions and the creation of new ones. The emphasis on degrees for newer occupations has led to a proliferation of new departments, schools, and institutes.

Qualitative differences have always existed among American universities. College rating has been a popular game with at least three generations of Americans, but a more complex differentiation is taking place now. Although the old "prestige" schools are still with us, there exist side by side, often within the same university, graduate departments and professional schools with varying quality-ratings. In short, the effect of the boom in higher education has not been to lower standards for requirements for the college degree, but rather to increase further the tremendous diversification which characterizes the American educational system.[1] In recent years this diversification seems to have been dictated primarily by the self-images and aspirations

---

[1] For a penetrating analysis of the changing educational scene, see Christopher Jencks and David Riesman, *The Academic Revolution* (Garden City, N.Y.: Doubleday & Company, Inc., 1968).

characteristic of various disciplines and preprofessional fields of study. There is little doubt that the educational establishment is turning out a tremendous variety of graduates and that field of study, not the institution attended, accounts for most of this variance.

From the point of view of the student, one major consequence of this tremendous expansion of the educational enterprise is an upheaval of traditional patterns of study. More students attend colleges and universities for longer periods of time, but not necessarily in an orderly, continuous fashion. Study has become a drawn-out process, extending well past the early years of adulthood; there are often no clear boundaries between periods of life devoted to study and work. Educational, employment, and family roles intersect and interact, and at certain points in time, any one of the roles may take precedence. Our campuses are filled with married students, men in uniform, and older men and women preparing for second careers. With the rising costs of education, ways of meeting the tremendous expenses associated with long years of study have multiplied. Graduate study, long treated as a discrete phenomenon, is actually a life-cycle phenomenon. More recently, an interlude devoted to the search for identity – through protest or introspective activities – seems to have become a common interruption in the graduate study cycle. The total process that takes place as college graduates become responsible adults, members of professions, and holders of advanced degrees is better understood through an examination of these relationships. Furthermore, only by realizing the current norms of this life-cycle behavior can rational forms in graduate study patterns be perceived.

It is the purpose of this book to examine some aspects of the new era in education and its effects on work roles through the experiences of a recent cohort of college graduates. Cohort analysis – the charting of the fate of a given group over time – can provide insights into generational patterns. In fact, this methodology is being used increasingly as an essential tool for analyzing the process of change. In the past, the absence of cohort data has plagued those studying various aspects of graduate education in the United States and the relationships between study and subsequent work outcomes. Recently, as a result of large-scale studies of college students and graduates, a considerable body of data has been accumulated, providing a rich source of cohort information in this field for the first time. This book owes its source material to one set of these studies. In 1959, the National Science Foundation (NSF) sponsored a two-year follow-up study of a large cross section of the June 1958 graduating class, including recipients of bachelor's, master's, and professional degrees.[2] In 1963, these same graduates were contacted for a

---

[2]Bureau of Social Science Research, *Two Years After the College Degree: Work and Further Study Patterns* (National Science Foundation Report, NSF 63-26; Washington, D.C.: U.S. Government Printing Office, 1963).

second, more detailed follow-up study, again under NSF sponsorship. It is from the findings of these studies, especially the second, that most of the data discussed in the following chapters are drawn.

The first of the NSF-sponsored surveys yielded data from 32,000 respondents who had received the bachelor's degree in 1958; a subsample of this group was selected for inclusion in the 1963 study. These were men and women selected at random from all colleges and universities in the United States; they represent approximately 16,000 men and 9,000 women who graduated from four-year programs in 1958.[3] Additionally, 3,700 men and 1,700 women who received a master's degree in 1958 were surveyed. It is through their experiences in the five-year period following graduation that we hope to present the answers to some of the questions which preoccupy educators, researchers, policy-makers, and young people: What are the dynamics of career outcomes? What accounts for various patterns of study and employment? How influential are family members when it comes to study and job decisions? How mobile are young college graduates? Does the type of school attended really make a difference? How do the careers of men and women compare with respect to graduate study and employment? What is the part played by military service in the careers of college men?

Obviously, we will not provide definitive answers to these and the many other questions which are of major concern today. Furthermore, because of the fast changes that we are witnessing each passing year, information in the social sciences is often obsolete by the time the latest computer printout becomes available to the researcher. Since 1963, the year when most of the information presented here was collected, there have been events which are significantly affecting the careers of more recent cohorts of college graduates. The Vietnam war and changes in the Selective Service legislation have reduced the availability of college deferments; many men in the 1958 cohort, especially at the graduate level, were able to defer military duty, while today this is not the case. Campus unrest and student militancy, together with the cutback in government support for campus research, may have further contributed to a decline in graduate study, although, generally speaking, the impact of student protest behavior has been important primarily at the undergraduate level. There are also indications of a recent trend toward later campus marriages and family formation, no doubt influenced by the changes in sexual mores facilitated by more acceptable and effective birth control devices. These developments may narrow the differences in graduate enrollment between men and women that were so startling when the 1958 cohort was studied in 1963. The introduction of the War on Poverty and the impetus

---

[3] See Appendix for details on sample selection, response rate, and weighting procedures.

given to finding solutions to related urban and racial problems may have created new types of jobs for some of the college graduates who majored in the social sciences and whose career position appeared marginal in 1963. Elementary and high school teachers, who as a group were most critical of their working conditions in 1963, have experienced some gains in their relative salary and prestige position in recent years.

But it is unlikely that many of the crucial findings reported here have been altered profoundly over the five-year period. In fact, some of the basic trends — the tendency toward early specialization and occupational choice, continuing involvement in graduate study, a high level of occupational stability, interest in teaching, and ambivalence toward business employment on the part of arts and sciences majors — have been reinforced, rather than reversed, during the past few years.

# II

---

## UNDERGRADUATE MAJORS AND EARLY CAREERS

**M**uch of the discussion in the following chapters is based on the assumption that the undergraduate major is probably the most important factor in a student's subsequent career. There is strong evidence in our studies that even for liberal arts students the final choice of a college major represents a strong vocational commitment – whether active or passive – and has far-reaching consequences for the graduates' post-college careers.

When we talk about students who major in different fields, we are talking not only about differences in the course of study, but also about differences in personal background. But at times, the decision to major in a specific field is a fairly casual one, dictated by personal convenience rather than by a long-term occupational objective. This seeming casualness has helped perpetuate the myth, especially in the liberal arts or sciences, that the formal undergraduate major has little to do with subsequent occupational outcome. This myth is based in part on the traditional concept of a liberal education that is devoid of vocational overtones. But it has even been claimed that sizable numbers of preprofessional students – such as engineering or premedicine majors – are quite likely to end up working in fields having relatively little to do with their college major.

As recently as 1954, data on graduate study patterns of 1951 undergraduates were interpreted as demonstrating that "the flexibility of vocational objective traditionally provided by American schools continues all the way up to the graduate school level. A student is free to change his mind and change his course even after the bachelor's degree has been received."[1] Fur-

---

[1] Dael Wolfe, *America's Resources of Specialized Talent* (New York: Harper and Brothers, 1954), p. 40.

thermore, from an examination of the patterns of the occupational history of three cohorts (1930, 1940, and 1951 alumni), it was concluded that despite close correspondences between study major and occupations in many fields, the really significant finding was that "as a consequence of the variety of occupational patterns every profession includes people with a variety of backgrounds."[2]

There is no doubt that, from the standpoint of a free and creative society, the idea of diversity in backgrounds and interests – the scientist who knows economics, the social worker who knows something about engineering, the architect who is well versed in psychology – is attractive and well worth promoting. However, a realistic interpretation of trends since World War II suggests that such cases are rare indeed. Of course, field switches between college majors and graduate school or jobs do occur, but they are more the exception than the rule. When such switches take place, they tend to be either in related fields (from chemistry to chemical engineering) or in fields that are related because of recent trends in the specialization of subfields (from mathematics to economics, or political science to systems development).

The extent to which students enter college with firm study or career objectives varies widely. For those who major in one of the arts or sciences, the choice of a major often can be postponed until the third year of undergraduate study. On the other hand, students in preprofessional fields, such as engineering or premedicine, usually must begin earlier to follow a concentrated program in their major field. In general, however, the amount of switching of majors between the freshman and senior years is very high in all fields.

The most comprehensive study on the subject in recent years was conducted by the National Opinion Research Center (NORC) in 1964. It suggests that students who enter college with a relatively firm occupational choice from which they are not too likely to deviate over the four-year college period are oriented toward careers in education and business and most often come from low socioeconomic backgrounds. Of the students who selected these two fields as their freshman choice, only about 15 percent of the education majors and 27 percent of the business majors had changed their career objective and their major during their four years in college. Conversely, only about one-half of the students in all other fields showed the same consistency between the freshman and senior years.[3] The changes that take place over the four-year period are generally found to have the effect of

[2]*Ibid.*, p. 74.
[3]James A. Davis, *Undergraduate Career Decisions* (Chicago: Aldine Publishing Company, 1965), p. 16.

bringing about both closer congruence between students' values and interests, and the likelihood that these values can be maximized by the future job.[4]

It is clear that early specialization is rewarded in graduate school, and continuity between college field and area of work is rewarded in the labor market. In graduate school, a change of field usually leads to more drawn-out graduate study with less likelihood of financial support. And in the jobs held within the five-year period following graduation, those who work in fields closely related to their major advance more rapidly than those who do not. There are many exceptions to this rule, but it seems necessary to stress that the choice of an undergraduate major will have a profound effect on a student's future, even if the choice — as is usually the case — is made within a fairly well defined cluster of fields. Once a decision is made — no matter how casually — to major in history rather than economics, in English rather than French, a "tagging" process has begun. A consequent channeling into a rather limited number of post-college choices then begins to take place. The chances are that the history major rather than the economics major will become a graduate student or a secondary school teacher.

The extent to which undergraduate specialization promotes vocational or professional commitment is demonstrated by the data on graduate and professional education for the class of 1958. By the end of the summer of 1963, almost 60 percent of the June 1958 college graduates (61 percent of the men and 53 percent of the women) had attended graduate or professional school for at least one term, although not necessarily in pursuit of a graduate or professional degree.[5] Almost one-fourth of all the graduates had received an advanced degree. Differences by field were extremely marked, not only between fields at opposite ends of the academic spectrum — business versus physics, for example — but also within broad areas, such as the humanities. Differences between undergraduate fields tended to follow a similar pattern for both sexes, even though men usually enrolled twice as often as women (Table 2.1).

It can be argued that the graduate enrollment rates for different fields reflect the professional aspirations and interests of graduates in various areas. To some extent this is no doubt the case, but it can also be argued that these enrollment rates reflect the educational requirements of various types of jobs, as well as the occupational opportunities open to college majors in various fields.

---

[4]This is the central theme of much of the recent literature on occupational choice. See, in particular, Morris Rosenberg, *Occupations and Values* (Glencoe, Ill.: The Free Press, 1957); and John L. Holland, "Current Psychological Theories of Occupational Choice and Their Implications for National Planning," *The Journal of Human Resources*, Vol. 2 (Spring 1967), pp. 176-90.

[5]Statistical data supporting this statement can be found in Table 3.7.

Table 2.1.  Graduate or Professional Degree Enrollment, 1958-63 (1958 B.A. Recipients)  *(percentages)*

| Undergraduate Major | Men (N=16,293) | Women (N=9,290) |
|---|---|---|
| *Total* | *41.0* | *22.1* |
| *Natural Sciences* | *60.0* | *29.3* |
| Biological science | 69.0 | 28.9 |
| Premedicine | 83.0 | 50.0 |
| Chemistry | 58.2 | 25.7 |
| Earth science | 36.3 | 11.8 |
| Physics | 62.3 | 47.1 |
| Other physical sciences | 52.4 | 18.5 |
| Mathematics | 45.9 | 30.7 |
| *Engineering* | *30.9* | *24.4* |
| Chemical | 45.2 | a |
| Civil | 22.7 | a |
| Electrical | 37.1 | a |
| Industrial | 24.1 | a |
| Mechanical | 27.9 | a |
| Mining | 28.7 | a |
| Other | 29.8 | a |
| *Social Sciences* | *52.0* | *28.0* |
| Economics | 33.5 | 22.8 |
| History | 61.0 | 34.9 |
| Political science | 57.4 | 29.6 |
| Psychology | 61.0 | 27.4 |
| Sociology and anthropology | 51.6 | 23.1 |
| Other | 51.4 | 26.1 |
| *Humanities and Arts* | *53.3* | *26.3* |
| English and journalism | 54.0 | 26.4 |
| Fine arts | 43.6 | 22.6 |
| Foreign language | 59.2 | 32.0 |
| Philosophy | 67.1 | 22.7 |
| Religion | 57.3 | 34.3 |
| *Health* | *17.5* | *14.3* |
| Pharmacy (nursing for women) | 12.1 | 17.7 |
| Other | 50.0 | 6.8 |
| Agriculture (home economics for women) | 31.5 | 14.2 |
| Business and commerce | 17.3 | 19.5 |
| Education | 50.0 | 12.1 |
| General | 54.5 | 22.8 |

*a* Too few cases for computation.

Students who major rather casually in a field that seems to guarantee an easily available degree may find that they will not have access to professional status without graduate study. As a result, we witness considerable "drifting" into graduate school, as opposed to early Ph.D. commitment.[6] This late enrollment may be the result of the students' post-college discovery that they

[6] Bernard Berelson, *Graduate Education in the United States* (New York: McGraw-Hill Book Company, 1960), p. 143.

are indeed committed. In the eyes of potential employers, they either have a wrong specialty or not enough specialized preparation and are therefore considered ineligible for jobs with the promise of professional status and advancement. Often when there is not an early commitment to graduate study, there is a consequent lack of appropriate undergraduate preparation. In such cases, graduate school functions primarily as a "retread" institution, protecting or enhancing the graduate's investment in his college degree. As one would expect, drifting into graduate school probably means getting into a less prestigious institution, receiving less financial support, and taking a slower and rockier path to professional achievement.

The undergraduate field also influences the types of jobs held. Often graduate or professional education plays an important intervening role, since many jobs require advanced degrees, especially in professional and teaching fields. The data in Table 2.2 are extremely crude, since broad occupational groupings include jobs at many levels. Still, the table conveys some notion of how graduates sort themselves out along occupational lines in relation to the undergraduate field.

The influence of the undergraduate major is perhaps best illustrated by comparing narrowly related fields that are often considered a toss-up by students about to choose a major. Of the men who majored in psychology and who were working five years later, 16 percent were teachers (half of them at the high school level), 24 percent were in business occupations, 17 percent were working as social scientists (mostly psychologists), 9 percent were in humanistic professions (mostly clergymen), and 5 percent were social workers. For the sociology majors, the proportion of teachers was higher (21 percent), of social scientists much lower (3 percent); over 30 percent became social workers and clergymen, and 27 percent entered business occupations. In both fields, high school teaching and business tended to absorb a large proportion of the students who were not seeking advanced degrees. However, looking only at the group which sought to enter a professional field other than high school teaching, we see a fairly sharp divergence between the psychology majors (who became psychologists) and the sociology majors (who became social workers or clergymen). If political science majors are included in this comparison, we find that 25 percent were working as lawyers five years later; the comparable percentages for psychology and sociology majors were around 3 percent.

Data on occupational outcome for women are much more difficult to interpret because of a recurrent finding that the majority of women, regardless of their undergraduate majors, become teachers. However, the data of the 1958 survey do show some differences: The young woman who majors in sociology is more likely to find work in a related field, usually social work, than her classmate who majored in political science. The latter has fewer

Table 2.2.  Undergraduate Major of 1958 College Graduates Who Were Employed Full-Time in 1963

*(percentages)*

| Undergraduate Major | Number Employed Full-Time | Natural scientist | Engineer | Social scientist | Humanistic professional | Health professional | Teacher | Business and managerial | Other professional | Semiprofessional | Clerical and sales | Other nonprofessional | No answer | Total Percent |
|---|---|---|---|---|---|---|---|---|---|---|---|---|---|---|
| | | | | | | | Occupation in 1963 | | | | | | | |
| **Men** | | | | | | | | | | | | | | |
| *Total* | *14,812* | *6.0* | *18.8* | *1.1* | *5.1* | *5.8* | *21.6* | *21.7* | *7.5* | *1.6* | *7.2* | *2.4* | *1.1* | *99.9* |
| Natural sciences | 2,146 | 25.5 | 10.8 | 0.3 | 1.0 | 21.9 | 20.6 | 6.0 | 5.3 | 2.2 | 3.8 | 1.8 | 0.9 | 100.1 |
| Engineering | 2,953 | 2.0 | 77.3 | 0.3 | 0.7 | 0.2 | 3.0 | 7.5 | 3.4 | 0.9 | 2.8 | 1.0 | 1.0 | 100.1 |
| Social sciences | 2,753 | 1.8 | 2.3 | 4.3 | 7.9 | 2.7 | 25.6 | 24.8 | 16.3 | 1.1 | 8.8 | 3.5 | 1.1 | 100.1 |
| Humanities and arts | 1,472 | 1.0 | 1.4 | 1.1 | 28.3 | 1.8 | 34.6 | 14.0 | 7.5 | 2.0 | 4.8 | 2.4 | 1.2 | 100.1 |
| Health | 286 | 4.1 | – | – | – | 87.1 | 4.1 | 0.3 | 0.7 | 0.7 | 2.1 | – | 0.7 | 99.8 |
| Agriculture | 417 | 35.7 | 1.4 | 1.2 | 1.4 | 2.9 | 15.6 | 11.0 | 9.1 | 2.6 | 7.0 | 10.3 | 1.7 | 99.9 |
| Business and commerce | 3,164 | 0.5 | 4.7 | 0.2 | 1.2 | – | 5.3 | 58.7 | 6.8 | 1.9 | 16.8 | 2.6 | 1.2 | 99.9 |
| Education | 1,545 | 2.4 | 1.9 | 0.7 | 2.5 | 0.8 | 75.9 | 4.3 | 5.0 | 1.7 | 1.7 | 1.9 | 1.1 | 99.9 |
| General courses | 76 | 5.3 | 10.5 | – | 3.9 | 14.5 | 43.4 | 6.6 | 10.5 | 1.3 | 2.6 | 1.3 | – | 99.9 |
| **Women** | | | | | | | | | | | | | | |
| *Total* | *4,334* | *1.2* | *0.3* | *0.7* | *5.3* | *6.2* | *67.2* | *3.6* | *6.2* | *2.8* | *4.2* | *1.1* | *1.1* | *99.9* |
| Natural sciences | 395 | 11.6 | 1.8 | 0.8 | 3.0 | 9.1 | 44.8 | 2.0 | 3.5 | 17.0 | 2.5 | 2.0 | 1.8 | 99.9 |
| Engineering | 23 | – | 17.4 | – | – | – | 52.2 | 4.3 | 17.4 | – | 8.7 | – | – | 100.0 |
| Social sciences | 622 | 0.5 | 0.2 | 3.2 | 6.4 | 2.6 | 55.8 | 6.1 | 14.8 | 1.9 | 6.3 | 0.8 | 1.4 | 100.0 |
| Humanities and arts | 884 | 0.1 | – | 1.0 | 14.0 | 0.3 | 64.4 | 3.8 | 4.2 | 0.5 | 8.9 | 1.6 | 1.1 | 99.9 |
| Health | 283 | 0.4 | – | – | 0.7 | 65.7 | 18.0 | 0.7 | 1.4 | 10.2 | 0.4 | 0.4 | 2.1 | 100.0 |
| Home economics | 222 | 0.9 | – | – | – | 4.1 | 57.7 | 2.7 | 28.4 | 3.2 | 0.9 | 0.5 | 1.8 | 100.2 |
| Business and commerce | 212 | – | 1.4 | – | 3.3 | 0.5 | 45.3 | 20.8 | 4.7 | 0.5 | 20.3 | 2.8 | 0.5 | 100.1 |
| Education | 1,667 | – | – | – | 2.6 | 0.7 | 90.8 | 1.4 | 2.6 | 0.1 | 0.5 | 0.7 | 0.7 | 100.1 |
| General courses | 27 | 3.7 | – | – | – | 14.8 | 66.7 | – | 7.4 | 3.7 | – | – | 3.7 | 100.0 |

professional alternatives to teaching than the sociology major and is more likely to take a nonprofessional job as a saleswoman or secretary.

An important consequence of taking a job unrelated to one's training has to do with the kind of job this will be. It is likely that it will be a nonprofessional job rather than a job in another profession. For example, the engineering major who does not work as an engineer rarely works as a social scientist or humanist; he is more likely to be employed as a businessman, a salesman, or in a clerical job. It is especially noteworthy to look at the social science majors, among whom relatively large proportions were employed in business and in professionally marginal jobs (clerical, sales, and other nonprofessional positions). While business may actually be a satisfactory or deliberately chosen occupation, evidence from other studies suggests that a business career is a reluctant choice for many students who were not business or economics majors.[7] This is suggested by the lower incidence of business employment among natural science majors than among social science majors. In 1963, a chemistry or mathematics major with just the bachelor's degree was much sought after for employment in his field, whereas those in the social sciences who had no advanced training were often unable to find employment in their own fields.

A college graduate who chooses or is forced to make a radical field switch after graduation either has a fairly lengthy retreading operation ahead, or else he will end up in a professionally marginal position. The smoothest careers, in terms of graduate study and jobs, are enjoyed by those who do not deviate from the area which they selected for themselves during their undergraduate years. Of course, what happens over a lifetime may well be a different story. We can predict, however, that college graduates who move into nonprofessional occupations or into the world of business are unlikely to return later to a profession.

[7]Rose K. Goldsen et al., What College Students Think (Princeton, N.J.: D. Van Nostrand Company, Inc., 1960), pp. 39-42.

# III

---

## GRADUATE STUDY

The typical graduate student most often is viewed as the recent B.A. recipient off to full-time graduate school, perhaps first enrolled for the M.A. and later definitely for the Ph.D. This student receives some financial aid along the way, perhaps gets married at some point, and finally, obtains his advanced degree. Such a student exists and even dominates in some universities and departments. Indeed, we can say that he is found most often in the natural sciences, where the combination of early commitment to the field and the availability of funds for financial support leads to fairly regular study patterns, although even here the proportion of part-time students is quite high.[1]

Side by side with this "typical" graduate student is another who is much harder to classify. For this student, academic activities and study patterns are more erratic; even receiving a degree is not necessarily an early, well defined goal. The university, nevertheless, performs an important function for such a student, giving him considerable academic exposure and training. In fact, one cannot ignore this "deviant" graduate student; in many fields, he and fellow "deviants" probably outnumber those who are thought to be the norm.

In the case of our 1958 cohort, graduate schools were filled with a mixture of full-time and part-time students, early and late enrollers, and those only taking courses. Two dominant impressions of graduate and professional school education emerge from a study of this group. One is the tremendous amount of activity past the bachelor's degree: there is a lot of course-taking

---

[1] See National Science Foundation, *Graduate Student Support and Manpower Resources in Graduate Science Education (Fall 1965, Fall 1966)* (NSF 68-13; Washington, D.C.: U.S. Government Printing Office, June 1968).

and degree enrollment, and a modest amount of degree completion. The second is the unpatterned, slow, and discontinuous way in which much of this advanced education takes place.

The recent growth and popularity of graduate study has been anticipated for some time by those who follow educational trends at close range. This high interest in advanced study is reflected among the present cross section of 1958 graduates. Within five years of college graduation nearly 60 percent attended graduate or professional school for at least one term, and almost one-fourth of all graduates had received an advanced degree. The National Opinion Research Center found that the class of 1961 indicated remarkably corresponding intentions. More than 60 percent of those college seniors had definite plans for advanced studies within two years of their graduation.[2] A more recent study of the class of 1965 showed even higher expectations: 70 percent of all graduates planned to go to graduate school, 26 percent to the doctoral level.[3]

Educators also have noted the slow and seemingly wasteful nature of our system of graduate study. Shifting between full-time and part-time study, between degree enrollment and nondegree enrollment, as well as dropping studies for one or more semesters is common. Students are increasingly interspersing study periods with travel or work. It is not surprising, therefore, to find that only half of the 1958 graduates who enrolled for advanced degrees studied full-time and continuously. In fact, part-time students who combined study and a career or homemaking constituted slightly over one-third of the group. A sizable group of college graduates – nearly 25 percent – took courses without being degree enrolled. It would seem that these students, whose education has gone beyond the bachelor's degree, will not receive an advanced degree or will receive it only many years later.

## Enrollment and Timing Patterns

A general finding of our study is that the undergraduate major unmistakably emerges as the best predictor of post-college enrollment for professional and graduate studies. This is partially explained by the fact that graduate study is usually in the same field as the undergraduate major or in a related field. Data from the 1958 cohort show that majoring in premedicine, biological science, philosophy, physics, history, and psychology most often results in graduate degree enrollment; majoring in pharmacy, business ad-

---

[2] James A. Davis, *Great Aspirations* (Chicago: Aldine Publishing Company, 1964), p. 43.

[3] Alexander W. Astin and Robert J. Panos, *The Educational and Vocational Development of American College Students* (Washington, D.C.: American Council on Education, 1969).

ministration, and some' branches of engineering least often leads to it. Of course, the undergraduate fields of premedicine, biological sciences, and political sciences are heavily preprofessional for doctors and lawyers.

In the undergraduate fields where graduate or professional school enrollment is frequent, graduate degree completion rates are higher than in other undergraduate fields. The highest proportions of degree recipients were found in premedicine (77 percent of all men who had majored in this field held a graduate or professional degree five years after graduation), biological science (56 percent), and philosophy (55 percent). Similarly, continuous full-time graduate study is characteristic of those who majored in premedicine, biological sciences, chemistry, and philosophy. Alternating periods of full-time and part-time study are followed mostly by graduates in the humanities and arts, while those with engineering and education backgrounds show a tendency toward part-time study.

The types of degrees sought – professional or academic – as well as fields of study are vital determining factors of full-time or part-time enrollment patterns. Doctors, dentists, and, to a lesser extent, lawyers seldom have the option of part-time or prolonged study. Accordingly, nearly all of the M.D. and D.D.S. candidates and about four-fifths of the LL.B. and J.D. candidates studied full-time. In graduate schools, in spite of the option for part-time study in a certain number of institutions and fields, Ph.D. candidates and recipients tend to study full-time and continuously, although somewhat less regularly than those in professional schools. Table 3.1 indicates that 62 percent of the men seeking Ph.D.'s and 49 percent of the women were engaged in continuous full-time studies. These students, living in the full-time study-oriented subculture of the graduate school, seem to have a serious commitment to their respective fields from the outset.

It is the student whose terminal goal is the M.A. or a degree in education who most often alternates between study and nonstudy periods, or who follows part-time study programs. As many as 60 percent of the M.A. and Ed.D. candidates in our study fell into these categories. Furthermore, study patterns differ for men and women. Women more often study part-time, while men show a tendency to study full-time.

Once the M.A. is received, the patterns vary again. Our five-year follow-up study included a total of 5,442 respondents who received a master's degree in 1958. At this time, only one-fourth of the 1958 M.A. recipients were pursuing further studies. In this group graduate work was undertaken most often in the natural and social sciences, whereas the master's degree was usually the terminal degree in engineering, business, and education. In the post-master's phase of graduate study, fewer than half of the men and one-third of the women in this group studied full-time (Table 3.2). Only the few men and women who pursued professional degrees (excluding doctorates in education)

Table 3.1. Pattern of Graduate Study and Graduate Degree Sought (1958 B.A. Recipients)

*(percentages)*

| Degree Sought or Received | Number Enrolled | Pattern of Graduate Study | | | | | Total Percent |
|---|---|---|---|---|---|---|---|
| | | Full-time[a] | Alternated[b] | Part-time[c] | Discontinued[d] | No answer | |
| **Men** | | | | | | | |
| *Total* | *6,672* | *50.9* | *10.2* | *32.6* | *4.5* | *1.9* | *100.1* |
| B.A. | 13 | 53.8 | 7.7 | 38.5 | – | – | 100.0 |
| M.A. | 3,301 | 33.1 | 14.1 | 46.4 | 5.8 | 0.5 | 99.9 |
| Ph.D. | 886 | 61.7 | 8.6 | 24.6 | 4.2 | 0.9 | 100.0 |
| Ed.D. | 63 | 31.7 | 11.1 | 49.2 | 7.9 | – | 99.9 |
| M.D. | 489 | 98.0 | 0.8 | 0.8 | 0.4 | – | 100.0 |
| D.V.M. | 27 | 96.3 | 3.7 | – | – | – | 100.0 |
| D.D.S. | 98 | 100.0 | – | – | – | – | 100.0 |
| LL.B., J.D. | 611 | 83.5 | 2.3 | 13.4 | 0.7 | 0.2 | 100.1 |
| Divinity degrees | 354 | 79.9 | 9.6 | 7.3 | 3.1 | – | 99.9 |
| Other | 807 | 39.8 | 9.0 | 33.0 | 5.8 | 12.4 | 100.0 |
| No answer | 23 | 52.2 | 8.7 | 39.1 | – | – | 100.0 |
| **Women** | | | | | | | |
| *Total* | *2,051* | *31.8* | *16.4* | *40.3* | *8.4* | *3.0* | *99.9* |
| B.A. | 3[e] | | | | | | |
| M.A. | 1,635 | 30.0 | 17.2 | 42.8 | 8.9 | 1.1 | 100.0 |
| Ph.D. | 96 | 49.0 | 16.7 | 25.0 | 9.4 | – | 100.1 |
| Ed.D. | 30 | 20.0 | 6.7 | 66.7 | 3.3 | 3.3 | 100.0 |
| M.D. | 30 | 100.0 | – | – | – | – | 100.0 |
| D.D.S. | – | – | – | – | – | – | – |
| D.V.M. | 1[e] | | | | | | |
| LL.B., J.D. | 18 | 72.2 | 22.2 | 5.6 | – | – | 100.0 |
| Divinity degrees | 12 | 66.7 | 8.3 | 16.7 | – | 8.3 | 100.0 |
| Other | 225 | 24.0 | 14.2 | 35.6 | 7.6 | 18.7 | 100.1 |
| No answer | 1[e] | | | | | | |

[a] Continuous, full-time study.
[b] Alternated study and nonstudy periods.
[c] Completed all or some graduate work as part-time study.
[d] Enrolled for degree which was not obtained.
[e] Too few cases to compute percent.

fit the image of the graduate student who studies full-time until receiving the degree; this included 93 percent of the M.D. candidates and 82 percent of the LL.B. and J.D. candidates. The pursuit of a doctorate in education, on the other hand, was a full-time activity for only 19 percent of the men and 5 percent of the women. For Ph.D. candidates continuous full-time study is the usual pattern in the natural sciences (except for mathematics) and chemical engineering. In the social sciences only about half of the Ph.D. candidates were continuously engaged in full-time work toward the degree. And in most fields of engineering, the humanities, arts, and education, graduate studies were more frequently on a part-time or an on-and-off basis.

Table 3.2. Pattern of Graduate Study and Graduate Degree Sought (1958 M.A. Recipients)

*(percentages)*

| Degree Sought or Received | Number Enrolled | Pattern of Graduate Study | | | | | Total Percent |
|---|---|---|---|---|---|---|---|
| | | Full-time[a] | Alternated[b] | Part-time[c] | Discontinued[d] | No answer | |
| **Men** | | | | | | | |
| *Total* | *1,144* | *44.6* | *12.5* | *37.4* | *4.8* | *0.7* | *100.0* |
| M.A. | 150 | 32.7 | 12.7 | 47.3 | 6.7 | 0.7 | 100.1 |
| Ph.D. | 704 | 48.9 | 11.6 | 36.1 | 3.3 | 0.1 | 100.0 |
| Ed.D. | 91 | 18.7 | 15.4 | 48.4 | 17.6 | – | 100.1 |
| M.D. | 15 | 93.3 | 6.7 | – | – | – | 100.0 |
| D.D.S. | 2[e] | | | | | | |
| LL.B., J.D. | 27 | 81.5 | 3.7 | 11.1 | 3.7 | – | 100.0 |
| Divinity degrees | 13 | 84.6 | – | 15.4 | – | – | 100.0 |
| Other and degree unknown | 142 | 35.9 | 18.3 | 38.0 | 3.5 | 4.2 | 99.9 |
| **Women** | | | | | | | |
| *Total* | *216* | *31.9* | *12.0* | *45.8* | *9.3* | *0.9* | *99.9* |
| M.A. | 52 | 23.1 | 11.5 | 63.5 | 1.9 | – | 100.0 |
| Ph.D. | 106 | 43.4 | 13.2 | 39.6 | 3.8 | – | 100.0 |
| Ed.D. | 22 | 4.5 | 13.6 | 18.2 | 63.6 | – | 99.9 |
| M.D. | 1[e] | | | | | | |
| LL.B., J.D. | 1[e] | | | | | | |
| Divinity degrees | 1[e] | | | | | | |
| Other and degree unknown | 33 | 21.2 | 9.1 | 60.6 | 3.0 | 6.1 | 100.0 |

[a] Continuous, full-time study.
[b] Alternated study and nonstudy periods.
[c] Completed all or some graduate work as part-time study.
[d] Enrolled for degree which was not obtained.
[e] Too few cases to compute percent.

The enrollment picture is indeed complex. We have noted already the common occurrence of shifts between full-time and part-time study, between degree enrollment and nondegree enrollment, and the dropping of studies for a semester or more. The picture is further confused by university regulations because some schools grant formal degree and candidacy only after a certain number of graduate courses have been completed.

In general, fields with a tendency toward full-time enrollment also show a tendency toward early enrollment. Early enrollment, in fact, is a particular characteristic of intensive students. Of the 1958 college graduates who had received advanced degrees by 1963, nearly 90 percent had enrolled within two years of their college graduation. There can be little doubt from these findings that students who start their graduate careers shortly after they

obtain their undergraduate degree are committed to their field and are potentially successful in terms of degree completion (Table 3.3).

Table 3.3. Time of First Enrollment for Degree Recipients and Degree Candidates
(1958 B.A. Recipients)

| Time of First Enrollment | Total | | Current[a] Candidates | | Degree[b] Recipients | |
|---|---|---|---|---|---|---|
| | Total Number | Percent | Number | Percent | Number | Percent |
| **Men** | | | | | | |
| First enrolled 1958-60 | 5,201 | 78.0 | 1,751 | 62.4 | 4,126 | 89.4 |
| First enrolled 1960-63 | 1,290 | 19.3 | 931 | 33.2 | 427 | 9.3 |
| Nonspecified | 181 | 2.7 | 121 | 4.3 | 60 | 1.3 |
| Total | 6,672 | 100.0 | 2,803 | 99.9 | 4,613 | 100.0 |
| **Women** | | | | | | |
| First enrolled 1958-60 | 1,442 | 70.3 | 481 | 51.9 | 1,071 | 86.2 |
| First enrolled 1960-63 | 509 | 24.8 | 353 | 38.1 | 165 | 13.2 |
| Nonspecified | 100 | 4.9 | 92 | 9.9 | 8 | 0.6 |
| Total | 2,051 | 100.0 | 926 | 99.9 | 1,244 | 100.0 |

[a]"Current Candidates" includes M.A. and Ph.D. and professional degree candidates as well as M.A. recipients who were candidates for another degree at the time of the survey.

[b]"Degree Recipients" includes M.A. recipients, professional degree recipients, as well as M.A. recipients who are candidates for another degree. This last group, "M.A. recipients who are candidates," is included in both categories.

But for many others, the path toward the first graduate degree is characterized by a late start, interruptions, and slow progress in several fields. Our
data show that as many as one-fourth to one-third of those seeking graduate
degrees in engineering, economics, and education wait several years following
college graduation before becoming degree enrolled (Appendix Table A).
Clearly these students made relatively late decisions to embark upon, or drift
into, graduate study.

Once a decision to enroll is made, there seems to be satisfaction with the
choice of field, or at least a determination to stick it out, given the losses
entailed in changing fields. As previously mentioned, many students have
made a firm choice of field by the time they enter college, while others
switch a good deal at the undergraduate level. But by the time they earn their
undergraduate degree, their broad area of interest is well established, although
there may be some further switching into related fields. By the time students
are working toward their first graduate degree, they usually are fully committed to a specific field of study. Only 6 percent of the 1958 graduates were
dissatisfied enough with their field to change it while working toward a

master's degree or doctorate; less than 1 percent of the M.A. holders made a change while working on the latter.

The most frequent type of change is between fields within the same broad subject area: for example, from history to economics, or earth science to physics. But when changes from one subject area to another occur, education proves to gain the most. This switching into the field of education, which accounted for close to half of all changes at the master's level, partially explains why it is a late enrollment field. Additionally, students who have taught for a few years perhaps find it necessary or desirable to obtain a graduate degree in the field; or maybe they decide belatedly to enter teaching as a result of changes in their occupational plans.

### Do the Best Students Go to Graduate School?

Before answering this question, it is necessary to define "the best students." Most educational researchers would probably agree that performance on a standardized test at the time of high school or college graduation would be the best single measure to use. Such tests are the standardized aptitude and achievement tests designed by the College Entrance Examination Board and by the American College Testing Program, the National Merit Scholarship Tests, or the Graduate Record Examinations. However, not all college graduates take these tests, and for the cohort under study here, most of whom graduated from high school in 1954 or earlier, standardized testing was much less common than is the case for the current generation of high school graduates. It was therefore necessary to devise a cruder measure of academic achievement and ability for purposes of this study. As part of the study design, the undergraduate colleges were asked to indicate the four-year grade-point average (GPA) for graduates in the survey. In the vast majority of cases, this information was made available. An adjustment was made to improve the comparability of this GPA between schools of different quality.[4]

Whether the students who received the best grades are necessarily and always the "best" students is far from clear. We have no data, for example, to judge the extent to which students who obtained the highest scores in high school tests complete college and graduate study programs. What recent research findings demonstrate time and again is the importance of grades, both

---

[4] The method used follows the same general lines as the construction of the API (Academic Performance Index) developed by NORC in their study of the class of 1961 (see Davis, *Great Aspirations*, pp. 27-29). Schools were classified into four groups, based on a combination of criteria involving test scores of undergraduates on the National Merit Scholarship test, library expenditures, the presence of a Phi Beta Kappa chapter, etc. Grade point averages then were increased by selected factors to allow for school differences. (The adjusted categories are as follows: high – 3.2 and over, medium – 2.7-3.1, low – 2.6 and below.)

as an instrument used by students for self-appraisal and career decision, and as a screening mechanism by employers and graduate schools.[5]

Over-all, we found that 38 percent of the men in the high GPA group (with an adjusted GPA of 3.2 or better) had not sought a graduate degree in the five-year period since they left college, compared to 73 percent of their classmates in the lowest group (GPA 2.6 or below). For women, the difference was considerably smaller, for the simple reason that both groups included few degree seekers.

At the risk of oversimplification, we can say that we do not know if the most able students go on to graduate study, but clearly the most successful ones do — although of course there are a good many exceptions.

In Chapter VI we will show that those students who received the best grades at the undergraduate level are most likely to go on to graduate school, regardless of the quality of the undergraduate institution attended. Thus, there is no doubt that the best students from the highly selective schools will be well represented in graduate schools. The pattern becomes less clear-cut for academically talented students whose undergraduate record was undistinguished. The student who graduates from a nonselective college with an A average is more likely to go to graduate school than the C+ student from an Ivy League school, although in terms of academic ability the latter may be at least as capable as the former. As the system operates, the graduate school is creaming off primarily those students who made the best academic adjustment in high school and college, while possibly failing to recruit other equally talented ones.

### Financial Support

The problem of finances is one that besets students throughout their academic life. Despite the large amounts of aid spent by public and private sources on graduate support, most students finance themselves while pursuing their advanced degrees. Over-all, fewer than 30 percent of the degree-enrolled graduates reported that they were helped to meet half or more of their annual living and study expenses during any given year.

It may seem paradoxical that fewer than 30 percent of those who eventually pursued advanced studies even applied for funds, although financial problems posed the greatest obstacles to continued study for the 1958 cohort. This may be attributed to the students' realistic view of themselves, to their perceived inability to qualify for funds, and — in fields other than the sciences — to their knowledge of the paucity of resources available. Neverthe-

---

[5]On the first point, see Howard S. Becker, Blanche Greer, and Everett Hughes, *Making the Grade — The Academic Side of College Life* (New York: John Wiley & Sons, Inc., 1968).

less, it is one of the surprising findings of our survey that fewer than 3 percent of the students who applied for graduate financial suppport were turned down.[6]

Rejection rates were somewhat higher in the humanities and social sciences (4 percent) than in the natural sciences and engineering (3 percent and 2 percent, respectively), but in no single discipline did they exceed 6 percent for either men or women.

The self-screening mechanism at work here is obviously of a very high order, since the availability of funds is limited. Furthermore, we found that the rejected applicants more often than not went on to graduate school in spite of this rejection. The most frequent consequence of not receiving funds was a slowdown of the study process; rejected applicants were relatively numerous among students who had not yet obtained a graduate degree.

It is clear that students seeking the higher academic degrees receive the greatest proportion of financial support. Those who had obtained the Ph.D. by 1963 and students who had one graduate degree and who were candidates for a second (usually M.A.'s working toward the Ph.D.) were the favored groups. Most striking is the high incidence of support for the most successful group — those who received the Ph.D. since 1958. As Table 3.4 indicates,

Table 3.4. Financial Support by Degree Enrollment (1958 B.A. Recipients)

| Degree Enrolled | Total Respondents | | | Men | | | Women | | |
|---|---|---|---|---|---|---|---|---|---|
| | Number | All or some support *(percent)* | No support *(percent)* | Number | All or some support *(percent)* | No support *(percent)* | Number | All or some support *(percent)* | No support *(percent)* |
| *Total* | *8,723* | *26.6* | *73.4* | *6,672* | *27.9* | *72.1* | *2,051* | *22.4* | *77.6* |
| Ph.D. recipient | 353 | 77.9 | 22.1 | 335 | 78.2 | 21.8 | 18 | 72.2 | 27.8 |
| M.A. recipient and a candidate | 863 | 56.7 | 43.3 | 744 | 58.5 | 41.5 | 119 | 45.4 | 54.6 |
| M.A. recipient, not a candidate | 3,024 | 28.6 | 71.4 | 1,980 | 29.2 | 70.8 | 1,044 | 27.5 | 72.5 |
| Degree candidate[a] | 2,866 | 15.8 | 84.2 | 2,059 | 17.6 | 82.4 | 807 | 11.3 | 88.7 |
| Professional degree recipient | 1,617 | 14.6 | 85.4 | 1,544 | 14.2 | 85.8 | 63 | 23.8 | 76.2 |

[a] Includes M.A., Ph.D., and professional degree candidates who hold only the bachelor's degree.

[6] The actual incidence of rejection is minimized because of the priority system established in processing the data. A respondent who experienced several rejections but who was successful during any given year and received assistance was classified as "grant received." The only "rejected" respondents are those who never received any form of assistance. However, given the prevalence of multiple applications for aid, this seemed to us the most rational approach, although it tends to underestimate the impact of rejection in a given year.

nearly 80 percent of the Ph.D. recipients received some support, compared with less than 30 percent of those whose advanced studies terminated with the master's degree, and less than 60 percent of those who were working for post-master's degrees. Whether the Ph.D. recipients complete their work more quickly because they are financially able to do so, or whether they receive help because they are more promising and more highly motivated cannot be determined from these data. One suspects it is a rather complex interrelation between the two.

Much attention has recently focused on the favorable situation of graduate students in the natural sciences in terms of availability of financial aid. There is further evidence of this in the survey findings: Nearly three-quarters of the men and only a slightly lower percentage of the women who obtained a degree between 1958 and 1963 received some support for at least one year while doing graduate work in the natural sciences. There is considerable variation among disciplines. Chemistry placed highest, earth science the lowest. Support for engineering also ran high, with close to half of all students receiving some financial help. Here, too, we see some variation, with greater frequency of support for chemical and mining engineers (Table 3.5).

Social science students fared next best, with more than two-fifths of the degree recipients receiving aid while working on the M.A. or Ph.D. In the humanities and arts, on the other hand, the over-all support level was much lower. Strangely enough, women in this group received more than double the support of men. This may be the result of greater acceptance of women in these areas or of the high academic caliber of the women who engage in graduate study in these fields.

It is in education that graduate aid was not available to the majority of our students. More than 80 percent of the recipients of advanced degrees in education did not get support as compared with 29 percent in the natural sciences. Clearly, the resources are not there, nor is there the commitment to the traditional graduate study pattern. A vicious circle is in operation. The education degree seekers — with their tendency for late enrollment, part-time study, and greater switching of fields — clearly have trouble establishing a claim to a support system. In the absence of heavy infusions of funds, the pattern is unlikely to change.

Another comparison by graduate fields shows that those working for professional degrees are much less likely to obtain financial support than those pursuing academic degrees. The lesser availability of funds for the professional degree students is, of course, the paramount reason; however, we also know that more of the men and women in these fields are of higher socioeconomic origin, with greater personal or family resources for study.

It is important to realize that the data presented here represent only crude and general indicators of graduate support. They tell us nothing about the

Table 3.5.  Graduate or Professional Degree Recipients: Field of First Degree Received and
Financial Support (1958 B.A. Recipients)

| Field of First Graduate Degree Received | Men | | | Women | | |
|---|---|---|---|---|---|---|
| | Number of degree recipients[a] | Some or total support (percent) | No support[b] (percent) | Number of degree recipients[a] | Some or total support (percent) | No support[b] (percent) |
| Total | 4,559 | 32.4 | 67.6 | 1,245 | 29.2 | 70.8 |
| Natural Sciences | 556 | 72.7 | 27.3 | 100 | 69.0 | 31.0 |
| Biological science | 173 | 74.0 | 26.0 | 42 | 76.2 | 23.8 |
| Chemistry | 124 | 85.5 | 14.5 | 17 | 82.4 | 17.6 |
| Earth science | 52 | 53.8 | 46.2 | 1[c] | | |
| Physics | 78 | 76.9 | 23.1 | 5[c] | | |
| Other physical sciences | 16 | 62.5 | 37.5 | 2[c] | | |
| Mathematics | 113 | 63.7 | 36.3 | 33 | 51.5 | 48.5 |
| Engineering | 453 | 47.5 | 52.5 | – | – | – |
| Chemical | 48 | 68.7 | 31.2 | – | – | – |
| Civil | 55 | 50.9 | 49.1 | – | – | – |
| Electrical | 160 | 43.7 | 56.2 | – | – | – |
| Industrial | 44 | 29.5 | 70.5 | – | – | – |
| Mechanical | 72 | 44.4 | 55.6 | – | – | – |
| Mining | 21 | 71.4 | 28.6 | – | – | – |
| Other | 53 | 45.3 | 54.7 | – | – | – |
| Social Sciences | 329 | 46.2 | 53.8 | 104 | 38.5 | 61.5 |
| Economics | 54 | 57.4 | 42.6 | 2[c] | | |
| History | 102 | 39.2 | 60.8 | 41 | 34.1 | 65.9 |
| Political science | 48 | 50.0 | 50.0 | 9[c] | | |
| Psychology | 80 | 45.0 | 55.0 | 24 | 54.2 | 45.8 |
| Sociology and anthropology | 21 | 47.6 | 52.4 | 14 | 28.6 | 71.4 |
| Other | 24 | 45.8 | 54.2 | 14 | 28.6 | 71.4 |
| Humanities and Arts | 633 | 30.6 | 69.4 | 213 | 61.0 | 39.0 |
| English and journalism | 104 | 33.7 | 66.3 | 62 | 56.5 | 43.5 |
| Fine arts | 102 | 46.1 | 53.9 | 96 | 28.1 | 71.9 |
| Foreign language | 42 | 76.2 | 23.8 | 26 | 42.3 | 57.7 |
| Philosophy | 24 | 54.2 | 45.8 | 2[c] | | |
| Religion | 361 | 18.6 | 81.4 | 27 | 29.6 | 70.4 |
| Health | 659 | 17.0 | 83.0 | 95 | 52.6 | 47.4 |
| Nursing | – | – | – | 47 | 80.9 | 19.1 |
| Other | – | – | – | 48 | 25.0 | 75.0 |
| Agriculture | 88 | 72.7 | 27.3 | – | – | – |
| Home economics | – | – | – | 23 | 65.2 | 34.8 |
| Business and commerce | 321 | 15.9 | 84.1 | – | – | – |
| Education | 910 | 20.7 | 79.3 | 560 | 10.2 | 89.8 |
| Other fields | 610 | 15.7 | 84.3 | 150 | 33.3 | 66.7 |

[a] Excludes respondents who have not yet earned a degree as well as recipients of degrees in fields unknown.
[b] Includes nonresponse to the question of support.
[c] Too few cases to compute percent.

actual amounts of money granted or the duration of support. We feel, however, that more refined information would merely further emphasize the gap
between the affluent and nonaffluent fields.

As was previously shown, students who undertake graduate studies by and
large have done better as undergraduates than those who did not enroll.
Similarly, those who obtain financial aid are those who had obtained the
highest grades, although once more the relationship does not hold consistently. Our data show that the higher the GPA the more often the enrolled
graduate studies full-time and the more financial aid he received. Of the group
under study, 37 percent of the men and 27 percent of the women with high
GPA's received some graduate support, in contrast to 18 percent and 9 percent, respectively, from the low GPA group. In general, barring the exceptions presented by doctors and lawyers for whom aid is uniformly low, the
better students tend to receive the limited resources for financial assistance;
but even in the high GPA group, the majority are excluded from assistance,
and more so in some fields than in others.

Financial obstacles, then, may be in some cases synonymous with ineligi-
bility for financial support because of undergraduate achievement. It is interesting to observe that the high GPA group complained less often than others
about financial obstacles when asked to account for slow progress in graduate
school (Table 3.6).

Students in the best-supported fields are probably the more talented ones,
since a direct relationship has been observed between financial support,
academic aptitude, and career field. We have just seen that graduate students
in the sciences received the most aid, whereas those in education received the
least. A National Opinion Research Center survey revealed that, excluding the
professional fields of law and medicine, those in science had the highest
academic aptitude and Academic Performance Index (API), while those in
education scored much lower.[7] For doctors and lawyers, however, this
relationship between financial support, career field, and academic aptitude is
not valid. The highest academic aptitude was noted in a professional grouping
that includes medicine and law, but as previously noted and explained, financial aid for this group was low.

It would be hasty, however, to conclude that all is indeed for the best,
with the most capable students going into the fields where most of the aid is
available. As mentioned before, chances are high that a number of talented
students stop their education at the undergraduate level because they were
relatively unsuccessful in a highly selective and competitive undergraduate
institution. But even among those who did well at the undergraduate level,

[7]John K. Folger, "Some Relationships Between Ability and Self-Reported Grades,"
*Sociology of Education*, Vol. 40 (Summer 1967), p. 273.

Table 3.6.  Reason for Thinking Study Completion "Too Slow" by Grade Point Average (GPA)
of Degree-Enrolled Graduates (1958 B.A. Recipients)

*(percentages)*

| GPA | Number of Degree-Enrolled Students[a] | Could Not Afford It | Course Difficulty | Faculty Pressure | Inability To Push Oneself | Inconvenient Schedule | Language Requirement | Thesis Requirement | Unaware of Routine | No Answer | Total Percent |
|---|---|---|---|---|---|---|---|---|---|---|---|
| | | | | | **Men** | | | | | | |
| *Total* | *2,630* | *56.1* | *2.1* | *3.3* | *14.1* | *5.6* | *2.0* | *4.6* | *2.1* | *10.3* | *100.2* |
| Low GPA | 729 | 62.7 | 1.5 | 1.9 | 11.9 | 4.0 | 0.3 | 3.6 | 2.1 | 12.1 | 100.1 |
| Medium GPA | 752 | 62.8 | 2.4 | 1.7 | 13.0 | 6.1 | 2.0 | 3.5 | 1.5 | 7.0 | 100.0 |
| High GPA | 870 | 44.9 | 2.6 | 4.7 | 17.0 | 6.9 | 3.3 | 6.2 | 3.0 | 11.3 | 99.9 |
| GPA not available | 279 | 55.6 | 0.7 | 6.5 | 13.3 | 3.9 | 2.5 | 5.0 | 1.4 | 11.1 | 100.0 |
| | | | | | **Women** | | | | | | |
| *Total* | *776* | *53.4* | *3.9* | *3.7* | *15.1* | *6.4* | *0.8* | *1.9* | *2.7* | *12.1* | *100.0* |
| Low GPA | 141 | 59.6 | – | – | 17.0 | 5.7 | 1.4 | 1.4 | 8.5 | 6.4 | 100.0 |
| Medium GPA | 214 | 57.0 | 3.7 | 3.3 | 13.6 | 8.4 | 0.9 | 0.9 | 1.4 | 10.7 | 99.9 |
| High GPA | 329 | 45.9 | 6.7 | 5.5 | 13.4 | 6.1 | 0.6 | 3.3 | 1.2 | 17.3 | 100.0 |
| GPA not available | 92 | 62.0 | – | 4.3 | 21.7 | 4.3 | – | – | 2.2 | 5.4 | 99.9 |

[a]This table is limited to degree-enrolled students who felt study completion "too slow."

there is considerable slippage in terms of graduate enrollment and progress. Without going into the complex subject of early career motivation, which in turn affects the career field choices made by college students and graduates, it is quite clear from the data at hand that there is an abundance of capable students whose graduate studies would be greatly speeded up and facilitated if more aid were available. And even in the high support fields, it does not look as though we have reached the point where most of the better students can count on support through the long years of graduate work.

## The Road to the Ph.D.

For the great majority of Ph.D.'s, graduate study is a slow process. After receiving the master's degree in 1958, only 10 percent of the men and 3 percent of the women pursuing Ph.D.'s had received them five years later. Ph.D. candidates greatly outnumbered Ph.D. recipients. Moreover, women Ph.D. candidates outnumbered recipients by two to one. One would think that the highly select group of women who go beyond the master's degree would be able to progress as fast as the men. It is evident that the social obstacles that initially delay women's entrance into graduate education are operative even at this advanced level.

More meaningful conclusions about the rate of study involve an examination of degree completion rates by type of degree and by field; these significant differences tend to be obscured by the over-all findings. Clearly, the long and erratic pattern leading to degree completion is more prevalent among those oriented toward academic degrees than among those seeking professional and more job-oriented degrees. Of the graduates on the bachelor level in 1958, only 1 percent had earned a Ph.D. within the five-year period under study; 77 percent of those whose undergraduate field was premedicine had received an advanced degree — presumably the M.D. — within the same period of time. In terms of speed and continuity then, the professional schools clearly do a more efficient job of supplying manpower to their respective professions.

Another fundamental characteristic of graduate education that our study confirmed is the split of different fields of study into rapid and slow degree completion fields. While the slow degree completion fields primarily show increases in the number of candidates in the years following receipt of the undergraduate degree, the rapid fields show gains in degrees received. The rapid fields are the natural sciences, psychology, philosophy, sociology, and anthropology; the slow fields are English, economics, political science, history, and foreign languages.[8] In chemistry, which is the most outstanding of the fast fields, 42 percent of the men who received an M.A. in 1958 had received a Ph.D. by 1963. In great contrast, fewer than 20 percent of those studying history, English, and foreign languages had received doctorates within the five-year period. This contrast is sharpened when one realizes that these three fields are areas in which more than half of the men with M.A.'s enrolled for further study (Appendix Tables D and E). The doctorate in education is also slow on the completion scale. This fact, of course, is well known and has been confirmed extensively by this cohort of M.A. recipients. The data show that only 12 percent of the men and 5 percent of the women who received the M.A. in 1958 were Ph.D. or Ed.D. recipients by 1963.

The time lag between receipt of a degree and enrollment for subsequent academic work turns out to be as great for the M.A.'s as it is for the B.A.'s. This is rather surprising. Since the M.A. in many instances is merely an automatic requirement to be fulfilled on the way to a Ph.D., it might have been assumed that men and women who ultimately seek the Ph.D. are committed to continuous study. The exception is in the field of education, where the M.A. is often the terminal degree; as many as 60 percent of the women

---

[8] For a comprehensive discussion of this issue, see Kenneth W. Wilson, *Of Time and the Doctorate* (SREB Research Monograph, No. 9; Atlanta: Southern Regional Education Board, 1965). The ranking of fields in terms of length of study reported by Wilson corresponds exactly to the above findings for the 1958 cohort.

postponed work beyond the M.A. and enrolled for the doctorate only after a three- to five-year hiatus. But in other fields too, procrastination is prevalent. Over-all, 18 percent of the men and 37 percent of the women in the 1958 M.A. group waited at least two years before enrolling for another academic degree – usually the Ph.D. This compares closely with 19 percent of the men and 25 percent of the women who put off enrollment for their first graduate degree by at least two years after receiving the bachelor's degree.

The long road to the Ph.D. has many obstacles. Most students, we have already noted, see financial reasons as the overwhelming deterrent to speedier degree completion. This finding is most apt to come from degree candidates rather than from recipients. Nevertheless, more than two-fifths of the 1958 master's recipients en route to a further degree found that their studies were proceeding too slowly because they could not afford to study full-time. Another reason for slow progress, most often reported by students with higher grade point averages, was that they did not push themselves hard enough.

Other obstacles often cited by critics of the present system of graduate education seemed less important to our graduates. There are complaints about thesis and language requirements and faculty pressure to participate in research work or teaching which further postpones thesis completion; but these complaints are voiced by a minority of respondents. This is important in light of earlier reports, particularly Berelson's 1963 study. He found that over one-third of all recent Ph.D. recipients (in the sciences the percentage was even higher) agreed with the statement that "major professors often exploit doctoral candidates by keeping them as research assistants too long, by subordinating their interest to departmental or the professor's interest in research programs, etc."[9] The difference between the findings reported by Berelson and those from the Bureau of Social Science Research's (BSSR) 1963 survey can probably be largely explained by the fact that Berelson's study concentrated on elite universities where research projects loom large in the lives of faculty and administration. The 1958 graduates included in the studies discussed here were a national cross section including many Ph.D. candidates in the lower-prestige graduate schools, where the pressures are of a different order. For the faculty in these institutions, awarding doctorates, rather than managing research projects, is perhaps still the area of greatest interest and professional accomplishment.

Educators can ponder whether our graduate system is wasteful and whether it takes too long to usefully complete degrees, especially the Ph.D., but it is the students themselves who hold the most illuminating answers. As

---

[9] Bernard Berelson, *Graduate Education in the United States* (New York: McGraw-Hill Book Company, 1960), p. 162.

one might have anticipated, the degree recipients tend to consider their rate of study completion just right, while the candidates feel they are proceeding too slowly (Appendix Table F). However, on balance it appears that in the eyes of most graduate students the situation is not perceived as an overly disturbing one. There is some feeling that it would be helpful if more aid were available; but it also seems that relatively few students find themselves forced to abandon their plans because of lack of financial aid. One feels that while it would be good to get through school faster, it is not really too uncomfortable to combine some work, part-time study, and a family life. In fact, in terms of life style, this may be preferable to the prolonged, aided graduate student status that seldom provides a truly comfortable way of living.

It appears that the continuing slow pace of degree completion, despite exhortation and increased financial assistance, represents a basic adaptation to the current academic situation. Perhaps it provides, even for the career-oriented student, the slower pace toward adult role commitment for which current generations show a strong predilection. Graduate study has become an accepted and adequate way of life for many young married couples. There may be a positive quality in the longer but less intensive exposure to the university, which proponents of drastic reform will have to consider. In a time of rapid technological and social change, keeping in touch with one's field is essential for continued professional competence; the confines of the university provide such contact. Whether slow degree completion rather than frequent refresher contacts is the answer is, of course, debatable, but meanwhile, at a time when university resources already are strained, this may be a positive adaptation.

At the same time, while this slow-paced academic system may adequately serve the traditional function of supplying manpower to the universities, it serves the research needs of industry and government far less.

The degree-granting institutions find themselves under severe cross pressures. On the one hand, more rapid degree completion is urged by planners and recruiters who seek to staff expanding fields, such as research and teaching in smaller and newer institutions outside of universities. On the other hand, in many fields more flexible study arrangements for part-time and special students are desired. It is not an easy task for universities to adapt their procedures to the increasingly large student bodies and, at the same time, to satisfy the diversity of demands. The universities seem to be reluctant to make basic changes in their traditional structures at this time. The uncertainties introduced by changes in draft policies add to the confusion. Perhaps slow degree completion with prolonged exposure to the university, which was the pattern followed by the class of 1958, represents the best adaptation under these circumstances.

## Family Influences on Graduate Students

Life-cycle situations – in particular, marital status and parenthood – play an important role in the analysis of the graduate study picture. The presence of children, for example, makes study not only less likely for the mothers, but also for the fathers. There is strong evidence that male degree recipients are more often single or are married without children (Table 3.7).[10] Since men with children tend to be enrolled somewhat less often than those without, it can be hypothesized that it is the date of birth of the first child rather than marriage per se which is most crucial in terms of graduate study. Further, it would appear that for men the most propitious combination for

Table 3.7. Marital Status in 1963 and Graduate School Attendance since Graduation in 1958 (1958 B.A. Recipients)

*(percentages)*

| Marital Status | Number | Never in school | Some school | Degree candidate | M.A. recipient and not a candidate | Professional degree recipient | M.A. recipient and candidate | Ph.D. recipient | Total Percent |
|---|---|---|---|---|---|---|---|---|---|
| **Men** | | | | | | | | | |
| *Total* | *16,293* | *39.3* | *19.7* | *12.6* | *12.2* | *9.5* | *4.6* | *2.1* | *100.0* |
| Never married | 2,706 | 29.7 | 19.8 | 14.3 | 15.3 | 11.9 | 6.9 | 2.1 | 100.0 |
| Married, no children | 2,477 | 30.8 | 19.3 | 14.7 | 12.4 | 12.9 | 6.9 | 2.9 | 99.9 |
| Married, children | 10,652 | 44.0 | 19.5 | 11.8 | 11.2 | 8.1 | 3.5 | 1.9 | 100.0 |
| Widowed, separated, divorced | 191 | 26.2 | 25.1 | 17.8 | 15.7 | 11.0 | 3.7 | 0.5 | 100.0 |
| No answer | 267 | 39.0 | 27.0 | 8.2 | 12.7 | 9.4 | 1.9 | 1.9 | 100.1 |
| **Women** | | | | | | | | | |
| *Total* | *9,290* | *47.2* | *30.7* | *8.7* | *11.2* | *0.7* | *1.3* | *0.2* | *100.0* |
| Never married | 1,836 | 22.8 | 36.7 | 14.1 | 21.5 | 1.6 | 3.0 | 0.4 | 100.1 |
| Married, no children | 1,474 | 37.0 | 34.3 | 11.1 | 15.3 | 0.5 | 1.2 | 0.5 | 99.9 |
| Married, children | 5,492 | 58.5 | 27.7 | 5.7 | 7.0 | 0.4 | 0.7 | 0.1 | 100.1 |
| Widowed, separated, divorced | 290 | 27.9 | 39.0 | 17.2 | 12.1 | 1.7 | 2.1 | – | 100.0 |
| No answer | 198 | 66.2 | 18.7 | 11.6 | 1.5 | – | 2.0 | – | 100.0 |

[10]This is a consistent finding in recent studies of graduate students. Alan S. Berger, in his survey of 1961 science graduates found that fathers were less often enrolled. When they were enrolled, it was less often on a continuous basis. See his *Longitudinal Studies on the Class of 1961: The Graduate Science Students* (Chicago: National Opinion Research Center, January 1967), pp. 14-18.

speedy degree completion is marriage with postponement of the birth of the first child. Because of the wife's earnings, immediate financial pressures are not so great, while pressures for earnings in the fairly near future are strong. One can also hypothesize that the same personality characteristics are associated with early marital decisions and the drive to complete graduate study. In any event, the data show that married men tend to complete their studies faster than those who remain single. Of the 1958 M.A. group, 16 percent of the husbands without children, 11 percent of those with children, and only 7 percent of the single men received their Ph.D. by 1963.

It is more difficult to analyze these data for women. Marriage rather than motherhood clearly constitutes the major dividing line between study and nonstudy for the 1958 M.A. recipients; for the B.A. graduates, motherhood is more of a determining factor. The predominance of education majors, many of whom took the terminal M.A. only, further complicates the picture.

Over and beyond the role played by marital status is that of the values or feelings of one's spouse or parents about the necessity and desirability for graduate school. It is difficult to say whether these feelings bring about degree enrollment, or whether degree enrollment bolsters one's feelings about support from parents or spouses. Whatever the dynamics, perception of marital or parental support for advanced study is important in the enrollment decision. When spouses or parents think advanced study is very important, the proportion of students enrolled is higher than in situations where parents and spouses do not feel it important (Appendix Tables B and C).

The question asked of the cohort of 1958 B.A. recipients was "How important does your spouse (or parents) think it is for you to study for an advanced degree?" More than one-third of the men felt that their wives considered it very important, whereas only 16 percent of the women felt their husbands considered it very important. Additionally, husbands — and wives to a lesser degree — perceived increasing moral support from their spouses according to the level of degree candidacy or attainment. Nearly three-quarters of the men who received Ph.D.'s by 1963 felt that their wives thought it was very important for them to obtain the degree. Only three of the ten women in a similar academic position reported this high degree of support.

Parents apparently show similar emotions concerning graduate education for their children as do husbands and wives. Not surprisingly, parents are seen as giving slightly greater stress to its importance for sons rather than for daughters. Having friends who go to graduate or professional school also correlates closely with graduate enrollment. The more friends one has who attend graduate school, the more likely he or she is to continue studying.

In the graduate study decision-making process, the prevalence of strong reinforcing influences from parents, marriage partners, and friends is well documented by these data. What is not known, however, and what could be learned only through the use of more intensive study devices, is the extent to which parental interest is the early, dominant influence, which in turn affects the selection of friends and marriage partners. Other research on graduate study motivation suggests that institution and peer-group influences in the undergraduate environment are stronger determinants of graduate study decision than parental influences.[11] However, it can be concluded from the data presented here that everyone is in favor of some graduate study, certainly for men, and that the male graduate school student can find considerable psychological support in his environment.

### The Status of Women Graduate Students

It has long been known that women are less likely to enroll in graduate school than men. This is well documented through various national follow-up studies as well as through studies conducted by women's and coeducational schools.[12] Our data confirm this, showing that about half of the women graduates terminated their contact with higher education at the time they received their bachelor's degree, in contrast to about two-fifths of the men.

Our study confirms what other recent studies had led one to expect. Women generally get better grades than men, but in spite of their unquestioned ability, they are still less likely to enroll in graduate school. In the 1958 cohort, 35 percent of the women and only 23 percent of the men were in the high GPA group. Yet of this group, 64 percent of the women and only 32 percent of the men did not enroll for any kind of graduate or professional degree (Appendix Table G).

Trends show that women who attend graduate school are more likely to take courses without being degree candidates; men are more likely to be working toward a degree (Table 3.8). Even after receiving a graduate or professional degree, women's proclivity to take courses continues. It can be speculated that the greater predilection for this activity is a sex-linked characteristic which women share — for a variety of psychological and sociological reasons — regardless of educational attainment and professional activity. Women tend to go to graduate school for academic and intellectual reasons, while men are more interested in furthering their education vis-à-vis career objectives and better job opportunities (Table 3.9).

[11] See, for example, Walter L. Wallace, *Student Culture* (Chicago: Aldine Publishing Company, 1966), Chapter IV.

[12] For example, of the class of 1961, 42 percent of the male graduates were enrolled in degree programs in each of the first two years following graduation. The comparable percentages for women were 25 and 26 percent. Joe L. Spaeth and Norman Miller, *Trends in the Career Plans and Activities of the 1961 College Graduates* (Chicago: National Opinion Research Center, March 1965).

Table 3.8.  Graduate and Professional School Attendance since 1958 (1958 B.A. Recipients)

| Attendance | Total | | Men | | Women | |
|---|---|---|---|---|---|---|
| | Number | Percent | Number | Percent | Number | Percent |
| Never Enrolled | 10,795 | 42.2 | 6,406 | 39.3 | 4,389 | 47.2 |
| Took Courses Only | 6,065 | 23.7 | 3,215 | 19.7 | 2,850 | 30.7 |
| Degree Enrolled | 8,723 | 34.1 | 6,672 | 41.0 | 2,051 | 22.1 |
| Total | 25,583 | 100.0 | 16,293 | 100.0 | 9,290 | 100.0 |

Table 3.9.  Most Important Reason for Graduate or Professional School Enrollment
(1958 B.A. Recipients)

*(percentages)*

| Undergraduate Major | Total Degree Enrolled | Better Job[a] | Intellectual Interest[b] | Career Objectives[c] | Never Occurred[d] | No Answer | Total Percent |
|---|---|---|---|---|---|---|---|
| **Men** | | | | | | | |
| *Total* | *6,672* | *33.7* | *26.0* | *34.8* | *2.7* | *2.8* | *100.0* |
| Natural sciences | 1,564 | 25.6 | 29.8 | 37.4 | 4.7 | 2.5 | 100.0 |
| Engineering | 965 | 44.2 | 28.1 | 24.0 | 0.9 | 2.7 | 99.9 |
| Social sciences | 1,595 | 29.0 | 22.6 | 42.3 | 2.9 | 3.1 | 99.9 |
| Humanities and arts | 929 | 23.1 | 32.8 | 38.4 | 1.9 | 3.7 | 99.9 |
| Business and commerce | 568 | 44.0 | 23.6 | 31.2 | 1.2 | – | 100.0 |
| Education | 807 | 49.2 | 17.5 | 26.8 | 2.2 | 4.3 | 100.0 |
| All other | 244 | 40.2 | 24.6 | 32.0 | 2.9 | 0.4 | 100.1 |
| **Women** | | | | | | | |
| *Total* | *2,051* | *27.0* | *42.0* | *24.5* | *3.7* | *2.8* | *100.0* |
| Natural sciences | 235 | 21.7 | 46.4 | 26.0 | 4.3 | 1.7 | 100.1 |
| Engineering | 11 | 27.3 | 72.7 | – | – | – | 100.0 |
| Social sciences | 397 | 22.9 | 37.5 | 35.5 | 1.8 | 2.3 | 100.0 |
| Humanities and arts | 529 | 18.3 | 44.8 | 30.6 | 5.5 | 0.8 | 100.0 |
| Business and commerce | 58 | 32.8 | 41.4 | 13.8 | 6.9 | 5.2 | 100.1 |
| Education | 632 | 36.2 | 39.6 | 15.7 | 3.8 | 4.7 | 100.0 |
| All other | 189 | 33.9 | 44.4 | 16.9 | 1.1 | 3.7 | 100.0 |

[a] Better job and salary opportunities with an advanced degree.
[b] Satisfying my academic or intellectual interests.
[c] Could not fulfill my career objectives with just an undergraduate degree.
[d] It just never occurred to me not to go to graduate or professional school.

The trend toward part-time study has been cited already, showing that more than one-third of the students enrolled for graduate and professional degrees studied part-time at some point during their graduate studies. The percentage of women studying part-time versus full-time, however, was far greater than for men. Forty percent of the women were part-time students, while only 33 percent of the men fell into this category. In terms of graduate fields, women in education and history tended most often to study part-time; those in chemistry, religion, and health fields were usually full-time students.

The women, as the men, study part-time mostly for financial reasons. But as one might expect, family considerations also affect the decision for women to study part-time or full-time. These considerations become nearly as important a factor as finances for women pursuing post-master's degrees. Of the 1958 B.A. graduates, 59 percent of the women who had children by 1963 never attended graduate school, while only 37 percent of the married women without children did not continue their education. The 1958 M.A. group, however, shows a different picture. Here, marriage rather than motherhood constitutes the major dividing line between graduate study and nonstudy. Single women were candidates for an additional academic degree twice as often as married women — with or without children. It is revealing that large numbers of the 1958 M.A. cohort (32 percent) were still single five years after they received their advanced degree. Even in this generation, there is a residue of the correlation between higher education and spinsterhood that was so characteristic of earlier periods.[13]

In line with women's greater predilection for course-taking, having children does not prevent taking courses to the same extent as it inhibits graduate degree enrollment. Clearly degree enrollment represents a kind of conflicting commitment which mothers do not feel free to undertake; taking courses is a legitimate "cultural" activity which a mother can undertake without limiting her other roles. Nearly 30 percent of the 1958 graduates with children took courses; only a slightly higher percentage of the married women without children followed the same pattern (Table 3.7).

When analyzing the woman's position in the graduate school situation, it must be remembered that our five-year span is insufficient for evaluating the long-term picture. Although it is now advocated that women should be encouraged and helped financially to combine professional careers with marriage, the emphasis is primarily on the post-childbearing period. Conceivably, a fair number of these 1958 graduates will enter graduate or professional school within as many as fifteen years of graduation. It is also possible that the recent emphasis on graduate study for women, as well as improvements in the total opportunity structure as it affects women, are already reflected in our findings. This includes greater academic flexibility and availability of more student aid. One may assume from this that still further growth in enrollment can be expected in the future; of course, the draft of male graduate students may alter the picture even faster than is presently the case.

---

[13] Many of the women in this group were older teachers who sought the M.A. relatively late in life. Among younger women, the proportion married and pursuing graduate studies is probably higher, although the differential persists.

But that is speculation. What is documented in the survey data are the expectations of the women themselves. They plan to partake in additional and late-starting studies even to a greater extent than men. Many women (10 percent) have plans to enroll in graduate school after 1970. This highlights the contrast between the different life situations of women and men. The women postpone their plans for family reasons; yet they clearly have career aspirations for later in life. The men, on the other hand, are facing the necessity of building careers within a more short-range time period and of reconciling the claims of graduate study, military service, and family support in the immediate post-college years.

## The Process of Continuing Education

There is no doubt that the idea of continuing education has made tremendous inroads among the educated. In fact, the intentions of the 1958 cohort indicate that the concept of a lifetime of work-study continuity and interchangeability has been fully accepted. When questioned five years later, one-third of those who received their B.A. in 1958 indicated plans to begin work at some future time on an academic or professional degree. This proportion is all the more outstanding when one considers that at the time of our survey 15 percent of the group were then degree candidates and 23 percent already had received at least one advanced degree. Even taking into account the overlap between the latter groups as well as allowing for some wishful thinking or lip-service to the cause of higher education, we can expect considerable increments in graduate enrollment after a relatively long nonenrollment period. It is clear that the graduate careers of this group are far from complete. Thus, it is likely that over a period of time as many as 20 to 25 percent of the graduates will obtain a degree for which they were not enrolled five years after graduation. An examination of educational plans, as tabulated in Table 3.10, reveals that students in fields of previous high degree enrollment (especially the natural sciences), as well as in those with previous low degree enrollment (business, commerce, and engineering), have little intention of beginning graduate work in the future. Expectations for future graduate work are highest in the "in-between groups": mathematics, fine arts, religion, education, history, and foreign languages. The bulk of this work is in the field of education; more than half of the future students in this field are women. This indicates a continuation of the trend for late degree initiation and completion in this field.

There seems to be relatively little likelihood that large numbers of degrees will be granted in the sciences for which enrollment did not take place within the first five years of graduation. This takes on a new significance for women when it is remembered that most of the men with high GPA's in these fields already are enrolled in graduate studies. It can be conjectured — although our

Table 3.10.  Do You Expect To Begin Work on One or More Graduate Degrees Sometime in the Future?
(1958 B.A. Recipients)

*(percentages)*

| Undergraduate Major Field | Men | | | | Women | | | |
|---|---|---|---|---|---|---|---|---|
| | Number | No | Yes | No Answer | Number | No | Yes | No Answer |
| *Total* | *16,293* | *64.2* | *30.2* | *5.6* | *9,290* | *60.7* | *33.1* | *6.1* |
| *Natural Sciences* | *2,607* | *65.8* | *28.0* | *6.2* | *803* | *65.6* | *28.9* | *5.5* |
| Biological science | 689 | 64.4 | 28.4 | 7.1 | 322 | 66.8 | 27.3 | 5.9 |
| Premedicine | 305 | 78.7 | 15.1 | 6.2 | 30 | 63.3 | 33.3 | 3.3 |
| Chemistry | 562 | 71.4 | 22.8 | 5.9 | 156 | 75.0 | 20.5 | 4.5 |
| Earth science | 245 | 72.2 | 23.7 | 4.1 | 17 | 41.2 | 58.8 | – |
| Physics | 252 | 57.9 | 36.1 | 6.0 | 17 | 41.2 | 35.3 | 23.5 |
| Other physical sciences | 103 | 58.3 | 36.9 | 4.9 | 27 | 63.0 | 37.0 | – |
| Mathematics | 451 | 54.8 | 38.6 | 6.7 | 234 | 62.0 | 32.9 | 5.1 |
| *Engineering* | *3,127* | *67.3* | *28.5* | *4.0* | *45* | *60.0* | *35.6* | *4.4* |
| Chemical | 257 | 71.6 | 24.9 | 3.5 | – | – | – | – |
| Civil | 429 | 71.6 | 24.7 | 3.7 | – | – | – | – |
| Electrical | 827 | 63.5 | 33.4 | 3.1 | – | – | – | – |
| Industrial | 342 | 67.5 | 26.0 | 6.4 | – | – | – | – |
| Mechanical | 834 | 65.5 | 30.2 | 4.3 | – | – | – | – |
| Mining | 136 | 72.8 | 23.5 | 3.7 | – | – | – | – |
| Other | 302 | 70.9 | 25.8 | 3.3 | – | – | – | – |
| *Social Sciences* | *3,070* | *62.2* | *31.5* | *6.2* | *1,417* | *60.6* | *32.5* | *6.8* |
| Economics | 677 | 72.2 | 22.6 | 5.2 | 83 | 65.1 | 30.1 | 4.8 |
| History | 736 | 58.3 | 35.5 | 6.2 | 320 | 60.3 | 30.9 | 8.7 |
| Political science | 435 | 62.1 | 30.6 | 7.4 | 138 | 59.4 | 36.2 | 4.3 |
| Psychology | 395 | 63.0 | 32.2 | 4.8 | 274 | 61.7 | 30.7 | 7.7 |
| Sociology and anthropology | 263 | 60.1 | 33.8 | 6.1 | 307 | 62.2 | 33.2 | 4.6 |
| Other | 564 | 55.9 | 36.3 | 7.8 | 295 | 57.6 | 34.2 | 8.1 |
| *Humanities and Arts* | *1,743* | *55.7* | *36.6* | *7.7* | *2,014* | *57.0* | *36.8* | *6.3* |
| English and journalism | 734 | 59.7 | 30.7 | 9.7 | 1,001 | 52.7 | 41.6 | 5.7 |
| Fine arts | 505 | 55.0 | 40.2 | 4.8 | 631 | 60.7 | 33.1 | 6.2 |
| Foreign language | 135 | 53.3 | 36.3 | 10.4 | 243 | 59.7 | 33.3 | 7.0 |
| Philosophy | 219 | 51.1 | 41.5 | 7.3 | 31 | 61.3 | 25.8 | 12.9 |
| Religion | 150 | 46.7 | 46.7 | 6.7 | 108 | 66.7 | 25.0 | 8.3 |
| *Health* | *302* | *81.5* | *12.3* | *6.3* | *676* | *71.3* | *25.3* | *3.3* |
| Pharmacy | 258 | 85.3 | 9.3 | 5.4 | – | – | – | – |
| Nursing | – | – | – | – | 470 | 68.5 | 27.4 | 4.0 |
| Other | 44 | 59.1 | 29.5 | 11.4 | 206 | 77.7 | 20.9 | 1.5 |
| Agriculture | 456 | 69.7 | 24.6 | 5.7 | – | – | – | – |
| Home economics | – | – | – | – | 574 | 65.7 | 27.5 | 6.8 |
| Business and commerce | 3,287 | 74.1 | 23.2 | 2.7 | 478 | 70.7 | 25.3 | 4.0 |
| Education | 1,612 | 44.2 | 45.8 | 10.0 | 3,239 | 57.4 | 35.8 | 6.8 |
| General | 88 | 56.8 | 36.4 | 6.8 | 44 | 59.1 | 34.1 | 6.8 |

analysis has not been refined to the point where it can be documented — that most men science majors who performed well at the undergraduate level go on to graduate study in their field or in a closely related one. Women in the same circumstances, however, do not go on with their studies, at least not immediately. When they do go to graduate school at a later stage in their life, it is more likely to be in the field of education, rather than in their original scientific field.

The conclusive fact remains that graduate study is very much an integral part of the educational scene — whether it is started immediately after receiving a B.A. or several years later. However, in spite of this growing emphasis on graduate work, the point has not yet been reached where a sizable proportion of college graduates take it for granted that their education would be incomplete without a higher degree. As an indication of this, the majority of the cohort of 1958 graduates chose career objectives and better job and salary opportunities as the most important reasons for continuing their education. It has been concluded by others[14] that colleges fail to sell students hard enough and early enough on the advantages of graduate study. Perhaps what is really involved, however, is that, for status as well as job reasons, the need for an undergraduate degree is now taken for granted by educators and by the public, while the same belief with respect to a graduate degree is only slowly taking hold. What seems to be more generally accepted is the need for some graduate education — started directly after college graduation or perhaps at a later point in life.

## Geographic Influences

A final look at the cohort of 1958 college graduates as they move through graduate schools shows a clear relationship between geographic mobility and educational careers. One finds that the most academically minded students are also the most mobile. (Mobility here is defined in terms of change of residence between regions, states or different size cities within states.) They have high grades and most often enroll in graduate school. There is strong evidence that enrollers tend to move more than nonenrollers. Furthermore, the proportion of movers increases with each additional degree received. For example, the 1963 data show that Ph.D. recipients who were nonmovers constituted only 5 percent of the total group; nonmovers made up 25 percent of the group that never enrolled in graduate school. Furthermore, the men who seek advanced degrees are much more likely to make a more significant move (including a different state) than those who are only taking courses or are candidates for master's degrees. These findings are in line with those of detailed migration studies which show considerable interregional moves made by advanced graduate degree seekers.[15]

[14] Davis, *Great Aspirations,* p. 140.

[15] See in particular Abbott L. Ferriss, "Graduate Student Migration and Regional Loss of Talent" (unpublished working paper; Washington, D.C.: Russell Sage Foundation, 1968). For a comprehensive analysis of student migration, see Charles S. Gossman

A striking finding revealed in the data is that women are more likely to attend graduate school in their home state (the state in which they attended high school) than are men. Of the women Ph.D. candidates, 41 percent studied in their home state in contrast to 30 percent of the men. Similarly, a high proportion of women seeking advanced degrees did not change the size of their city. It appears that these women reside in areas where opportunities exist for graduate study and where they are able to take courses and become degree candidates without moving. It would seem that educational facilities at hand attract many women who would otherwise never enroll in further studies.

The importance of the undergraduate major in a student's career already has been indicated. We also have seen that majoring in certain fields most likely leads to graduate school attendance, which in turn leads to more geographic movement. Our analysis of the data reveals a further relationship between geography and the undergraduate major. There are indications that growing up in a particular region affects the students' selection of a major field. Men from the Northeast and Pacific coast areas were more likely to major in the social sciences than those from the Mountain region; the latter were more likely to major in engineering. A partial explanation is that most college students — 82 percent of all undergraduates enrolled in 1963 — attend college in their home state.[16] Since an area's economic development or traditions are often reflected in the schools, especially state universities, educational programs may concentrate on particular fields of study. This not only restricts the choice of possible major fields, but also emphasizes study areas for which the student has been conditioned by his environment. It is not surprising to find concentrations of engineering graduates from regions where mining is an important part of the economy.

Similarly, the size of the community where one lives at the time of high school graduation is a factor in the choice of an undergraduate major. As one would expect, rural youths majored in agriculture in greater proportion than urban youths; the latter were more likely to major in business and commerce. Smaller cities, with fewer than 10,000 people, produced higher proportions of education majors. The likelihood that women will major in the social sciences or humanities and arts increases with the size of the population of the original place of residence, while the proportion of those entering education decreases. This suggests that living in larger cities awakens women to educational and occupational possibilities beyond the traditionally approved teaching careers.

*et al., Migration of College and University Students in the United States* (Seattle: University of Washington Press, 1968).

[16]Mabel C. Rice and Paul L. Mason, *Residence and Migration of College Students, Fall 1963* (Washington, D.C.: U.S. Government Printing Office, 1965), p. 3.

There are further differences by region and city. College graduates from certain areas of the country, specifically the Northeast and the East North Central states, proved more likely to go to graduate school than students from the rest of the country. A small-town background did not prevent graduate school enrollment, but as shown by our group, it inhibited seeking professional degrees. As the city size increased, the proportion of professional degree recipients also rose.

This geographic analysis contributes to the evidence — which will be discussed further in Chapter IV — that the population of the 1958 college graduates may be splitting into two distinct subpopulations: a cosmopolitan group and a local group. The cosmopolitan group tends to undertake graduate training and, because of long-distance moves, probably acquires a national rather than a regional outlook. The local group, on the other hand, tends to spend much of its life in the same region. Although various professions are in both groups, the cosmopolitans generally include more scientists, engineers, and humanists, while the locals include more teachers and businessmen. Cosmopolitans settle down to marriage and parenthood later in life than the locals do. Parenthood, it is well known, is a stabilizing factor, cutting down the amount and incidence of geographic movement. It can be reasoned from this evidence that different life styles are emerging for subgroups of college graduates, and that these life styles often are associated with the selection of one's undergraduate field of study.

# IV

## EMPLOYMENT

The new career men and women, working either full- or part-time, represent nearly three-quarters of the 1958 group. The proportion employed full-time five years after college is extraordinarily high; it includes almost the entire group (91 percent) of the men graduates and almost half of the women graduates. When men are not working, it is usually because they are full-time graduate students, while women most often do not work because they are housewives. Family responsibilities, particularly early parenthood, tend to polarize the situation further. Men come increasingly under pressure to engage in full-time work, and women become more committed to the role of housewife and mother. In spite of this, many — whether for career reasons or because of financial pressures — succeed in combining various family, professional, and educational roles (Appendix Table H).

### Relationship between Jobs and the Undergraduate Major

As stressed throughout this book, occupational choice is integrally related to the choice of the undergraduate major. It is not possible to judge whether this close correspondence between college major and later employment results primarily from the graduate's own choice of an occupation, or whether employers show a preference for students who have majored in a field related to the job to be filled. Obviously, both elements are involved.

Nevertheless, it seems that there are few transient occupational roles. Those committed to a profession, which dates back to the choice of the undergraduate major, have entered it; those who engage in nonprofessional work after graduation are unlikely to negotiate later professional entry. The exceptions are found among semiprofessionals, many of whom were research assistants employed by universities at the time of our study.

Judging from the men in our cohort, the more preprofessional the undergraduate major, the more likely employment will be in a corresponding or related occupation (Table 4.1). For example, natural science majors worked as natural scientists, as professionals in the health field, or as teachers. And more than three-quarters of the engineering majors were employed as engineers.[1] Even in the business, managerial, clerical, and sales groups — by tradition the most open occupations in terms of undergraduate preparation —

Table 4.1. Undergraduate Major of Full-Time Employed B.A. Recipients by Occupation

*(percentages)*

| Undergraduate Major | Number Employed Full-Time | Natural scientist | Engineer | Social scientist | Humanistic professional | Health professional | Teacher | Business and managerial | Other professional | Semiprofessional | Clerical and sales | Other nonprofessional | No answer | Total Percent |
|---|---|---|---|---|---|---|---|---|---|---|---|---|---|---|
| **Men** | | | | | | | | | | | | | | |
| *Total* | *14,812* | *6.0* | *18.8* | *1.1* | *5.1* | *5.8* | *21.6* | *21.7* | *7.5* | *1.6* | *7.2* | *2.4* | *1.1* | *99.9* |
| Natural sciences | 2,146 | 25.5 | 10.8 | 0.3 | 1.0 | 21.9 | 20.6 | 6.0 | 5.3 | 2.2 | 3.8 | 1.8 | 0.9 | 100.1 |
| Engineering | 2,953 | 2.0 | 77.3 | 0.3 | 0.7 | 0.2 | 3.0 | 7.5 | 3.4 | 0.9 | 2.8 | 1.0 | 1.0 | 100.1 |
| Social sciences | 2,753 | 1.8 | 2.3 | 4.2 | 7.9 | 2.7 | 25.6 | 24.8 | 16.3 | 1.1 | 8.8 | 3.5 | 1.1 | 100.1 |
| Humanities and arts | 1,472 | 1.0 | 1.4 | 1.1 | 28.3 | 1.8 | 34.6 | 14.0 | 7.5 | 2.0 | 4.8 | 2.4 | 1.2 | 100.1 |
| Health | 286 | 4.1 | - | - | - | 87.1 | 4.1 | 0.3 | 0.7 | 0.7 | 2.1 | - | 0.7 | 99.8 |
| Agriculture | 417 | 35.7 | 1.4 | 1.2 | 1.4 | 2.9 | 15.6 | 11.0 | 9.1 | 2.6 | 7.0 | 10.3 | 1.7 | 99.9 |
| Business and commerce | 3,164 | 0.5 | 4.7 | 0.2 | 1.2 | - | 5.3 | 58.7 | 6.8 | 1.9 | 16.8 | 2.6 | 1.2 | 99.9 |
| Education | 1,545 | 2.4 | 1.9 | 0.7 | 2.5 | 0.8 | 75.9 | 4.3 | 5.0 | 1.7 | 1.7 | 1.9 | 1.1 | 99.9 |
| General courses | 76 | 5.3 | 10.5 | - | 3.9 | 14.5 | 43.4 | 6.6 | 10.5 | 1.3 | 2.6 | 1.3 | - | 99.9 |
| **Women** | | | | | | | | | | | | | | |
| *Total* | *4,334* | *1.2* | *0.3* | *0.7* | *5.3* | *6.2* | *67.2* | *3.6* | *6.2* | *2.8* | *4.2* | *1.1* | *1.1* | *99.9* |
| Natural sciences | 395 | 11.6 | 1.8 | 0.8 | 3.0 | 9.1 | 44.8 | 2.0 | 3.5 | 17.0 | 2.5 | 2.0 | 1.8 | 99.9 |
| Engineering | 23 | - | 17.4 | - | - | - | 52.2 | 4.3 | 17.4 | - | 8.7 | - | - | 100.0 |
| Social sciences | 622 | 0.5 | 0.2 | 3.2 | 6.4 | 2.6 | 55.8 | 6.1 | 14.8 | 1.9 | 6.3 | 0.8 | 1.4 | 100.0 |
| Humanities and arts | 884 | 0.1 | - | 1.0 | 14.0 | 0.3 | 64.4 | 3.8 | 4.2 | 0.5 | 8.9 | 1.6 | 1.1 | 99.9 |
| Health | 283 | 0.4 | - | - | 0.7 | 65.7 | 18.0 | 0.7 | 1.4 | 10.2 | 0.4 | 0.4 | 2.1 | 100.0 |
| Home economics | 222 | 0.9 | - | - | - | 4.1 | 57.7 | 2.7 | 28.4 | 3.2 | 0.9 | 0.5 | 1.8 | 100.2 |
| Business and commerce | 212 | - | 1.4 | - | 3.3 | 0.5 | 45.3 | 20.8 | 4.7 | 0.5 | 20.3 | 2.8 | 0.5 | 100.1 |
| Education | 1,667 | - | - | - | 2.6 | 0.7 | 90.8 | 1.4 | 2.6 | 0.1 | 0.5 | 0.7 | 0.7 | 100.1 |
| General courses | 27 | 3.7 | - | - | - | 14.8 | 66.7 | - | 7.4 | 3.7 | - | - | 3.7 | 100.0 |

[1] Similar findings pertain to all engineering graduates in the labor force. See Mildred A. Schwartz, *The United States College-Educated Population: 1960* (Chicago: National Opinion Research Center, 1965), p. 104.

more than half of the incumbents had majored in the field of business and commerce.

On the other hand, social science majors, perhaps the least preprofessional group, were scattered throughout occupational fields. They were clustered in unrelated fields of business, management, teaching, and a variety of other professions. In fact, less than 5 percent of the male social science majors had positions as social scientists. This essentially is due to the lack of jobs in this field, especially jobs for which a graduate with only a B.A. would be qualified.[2] The small, heterogeneous group of semiprofessionals also drew from many of the undergraduate fields. This is partly explained by the fact that men in this group were working as research assistants in diverse fields.

The picture for women is dramatically different. Regardless of their undergraduate major, women tend to be teachers. As many as 67 percent of our employed women were full-time teachers five years after they graduated. As is to be expected, most of the education majors (91 percent) went into teaching, but the same pattern is repeated for the great majority of women. We see that in all fields, except those in the health area, women more often teach than go into jobs more directly related to their undergraduate major. For example, as many as 56 percent of the women who had majored in the social sciences became teachers, while only 3 percent held jobs as social scientists; among the natural science majors, 45 percent became teachers and 12 percent became natural scientists. Some of the reasons for this high concentration of women − both B.A. and M.A. recipients − in teaching will be discussed at length in a later section.

### Importance of the Master's Degree

While the choice of the undergraduate major remains the single most influential determinant of occupational outcome, graduate study is also a vital element. In many fields, the graduate degree often becomes the great divider between those who become true professionals and those who do not. By comparing Tables 4.1 and 4.2, it can be seen that employment as a "scientist" is much more frequent at the master's level and that M.A. recipients tend to be employed in related occupations to a greater extent than the B.A.'s. For example, at the M.A. level, 34 percent of the biology graduates were employed as biologists; 27 percent as college teachers, in all probability teaching biology or doing research in the field; 8 percent as high school teachers, hopefully teaching biology or science; 5 percent in the health occupations; and 1 percent as physicists. The picture in most of the social sciences is

[2]This may be one area where the survey data, although recent, are somewhat obsolete. The recent growth in social and urban welfare planning and research activities at the federal and local levels may have improved the opportunities for those with training in the social sciences at the bachelor's level.

Table 4.2.  Graduate Field of Full-Time Employed M.A. Recipients by Occupation

*(percentages)*

| 1958 Graduate Field | Number Employed Full-Time | Natural scientist | Engineer | Social scientist | Humanistic professional | Health professional | Teacher | Business and managerial | Other professional | Semiprofessional | Clerical and sales | Other nonprofessional | No answer | Total Percent |
|---|---|---|---|---|---|---|---|---|---|---|---|---|---|---|
| | | | | | | | | Occupation | | | | | | |
| **Men** | | | | | | | | | | | | | | |
| *Total* | *3,445* | *10.3* | *15.3* | *3.3* | *3.0* | *1.3* | *44.5* | *13.2* | *5.3* | *0.3* | *1.7* | *1.0* | *0.8* | *100.0* |
| Natural sciences | 495 | 52.3 | 10.7 | 0.4 | 0.8 | 2.8 | 27.5 | 0.4 | 1.8 | 0.8 | 1.0 | 1.0 | 0.4 | 99.9 |
| Engineering | 533 | 4.7 | 75.3 | 0.6 | 0.4 | 0.2 | 8.6 | 4.1 | 3.9 | 0.6 | 0.4 | 0.4 | 0.6 | 99.8 |
| Social sciences | 353 | 1.4 | 2.0 | 23.5 | 2.3 | 1.7 | 42.2 | 15.0 | 8.5 | 0.3 | 2.0 | 0.8 | 0.3 | 100.0 |
| Humanities and arts | 268 | – | 0.7 | 1.1 | 18.3 | – | 67.9 | 4.5 | 3.7 | – | 1.5 | 0.7 | 1.5 | 99.9 |
| Health | 54 | 9.3 | 7.4 | – | – | 37.0 | 11.1 | 25.9 | 3.7 | 1.9 | – | – | 3.8 | 100.1 |
| Agriculture | 72 | 65.3 | 2.8 | – | – | – | 22.2 | 2.8 | 4.2 | 1.4 | – | 1.4 | – | 100.1 |
| Business and commerce | 485 | 1.0 | 9.9 | 2.3 | 0.6 | – | 9.7 | 64.9 | 3.5 | 0.4 | 5.4 | 2.1 | 0.2 | 100.0 |
| Education | 1,067 | 0.7 | 0.5 | 0.9 | 1.9 | 0.3 | 87.6 | 2.6 | 2.1 | – | 1.1 | 0.9 | 1.3 | 99.9 |
| Other fields | 118 | 0.8 | 2.5 | – | 16.1 | 0.8 | 13.6 | 5.1 | 58.5 | – | 1.7 | – | 0.8 | 99.9 |
| **Women** | | | | | | | | | | | | | | |
| *Total* | *1,229* | *2.4* | *0.3* | *1.7* | *6.9* | *6.0* | *66.9* | *0.7* | *9.1* | *2.0* | *0.8* | *0.9* | *2.3* | *100.0* |
| Natural sciences | 59 | 27.1 | 3.4 | – | 1.7 | 3.4 | 44.1 | – | 1.7 | 16.9 | – | – | 1.7 | 100.0 |
| Engineering | 1[a] | | | | | | | | | | | | | |
| Social sciences | 100 | 1.0 | – | 17.0 | 8.0 | 4.0 | 44.0 | 3.0 | 12.0 | 4.0 | 2.0 | 3.0 | 2.0 | 100.0 |
| Humanities and arts | 131 | – | – | 0.8 | 14.5 | 1.5 | 75.6 | – | 1.5 | 0.8 | 1.5 | 1.5 | 2.3 | 100.0 |
| Health | 51 | 7.8 | – | – | – | 64.7 | 21.6 | – | 5.9 | – | – | – | – | 100.0 |
| Home economics | 40 | – | 2.5 | – | 2.5 | – | 57.5 | – | 30.0 | 2.5 | – | – | 5.0 | 100.0 |
| Education | 729 | 0.8 | – | 0.1 | 3.4 | 4.5 | 82.6 | 0.1 | 3.3 | 1.0 | 0.8 | 0.8 | 2.5 | 99.9 |
| Other fields | 118 | 1.7 | – | 1.7 | 26.3 | – | 14.4 | 4.2 | 49.2 | 0.8 | – | – | 1.7 | 100.0 |

[a] Too few cases to compute percents.

similar. For economists, much of the employment is in business occupations, which is related employment for men in this field.

But the differences in occupational patterns between the natural and social scientists, which were apparent at the B.A. level, persist for the M.A. group. Table 4.2 shows that men M.A. recipients in the natural sciences are most frequently employed as natural scientists, whereas the social scientists are most often teachers. Men who have specialized in the social sciences teach twice as often at the college level as in high schools; women are more often high school teachers (Appendix Table I).

The differences in occupations between B.A. and M.A. holders are least marked in those professional fields where correspondence between the under-graduate major and occupation is high, such as business and commerce, education, or engineering. Nevertheless, a master's degree in these fields generally leads to employment in the corresponding occupation even more often than a bachelor's.

One must remember that many M.A. holders, especially in the natural and social sciences, have completed a great deal of additional graduate or professional work since 1958. In many cases, they have earned another degree. For example, one-third of the male M.A. natural scientists and one-fourth of the social scientists earned a Ph.D. by 1963, and in the social sciences, another 23 percent were Ph.D. candidates. On the other hand, those in business, clerical, and other nonprofessional occupations seldom undertook further studies. Thus, the greater correspondence between field of study and occupation on the M.A. level — particularly for natural and social scientists — is due not only to the passage of time since the M.A. was earned but also to advanced degrees subsequently received.

## Women Who Hold the M.A.

Women master's holders in fields other than education are working predominantly in their chosen field. Of course, the great majority still become teachers, but they teach more often at the college and secondary school level, while women with only B.A.'s teach more often at the elementary school level. Of the thirty-three master's in psychology, for example, eleven teach and fourteen work as psychologists. This suggests that the competitive position of women who hold an advanced degree is quite strong.

It seems that there is considerable professional payoff from the advanced degree for women. In fact, 44 percent of the women with master's degrees found their graduate education valuable in the performance of their work in all occupations, compared with 39 percent of the men (Table 4.3). This

Table 4.3. How Important Were Your Undergraduate and Graduate Backgrounds as Prerequisites for Your Current Job? (1958 M.A. Recipients, in 1963)

*(percentages)*

| Current Degree and Job | Men | | Women | |
|---|---|---|---|---|
| | Undergraduate degree | Graduate degree | Undergraduate degree | Graduate degree |
| Degree in my field a prerequisite for job | 42.8 | 39.4 | 55.8 | 44.1 |
| Degree in this or related field prerequisite for job | 24.2 | 13.7 | 16.0 | 10.7 |
| Degree in any field prerequisite for job | 24.9 | 4.8 | 17.4 | 7.0 |
| No degree needed | 5.5 | 40.0 | 3.0 | 34.6 |
| No answer | 2.6 | 2.0 | 7.7 | 3.6 |
| Total percent | 100.0 | 99.9 | 99.9 | 100.0 |
| (Total number) | (3,445) | (3,445) | (1,229) | (1,229) |

evaluation perhaps reflects women's greater belief in the value of education, which seems to be a sex-linked characteristic. But it is also clear from our survey data that for women – perhaps more than for men – an advanced degree represents the ticket to higher professional status.

## Degrees as a Job Prerequisite

In light of the growing popularity of graduate school attendance, it is interesting to observe that for our cohort undergraduate rather than graduate education was of greater importance in obtaining jobs. For the group who received their master's in 1958, there is considerable emphasis on the importance of the graduate degree as a job prerequisite and as a tool for work performance; yet even they feel that the undergraduate degree and not the graduate degree is of greater importance. As can be seen in Table 4.3, about 40 percent of the men and 35 percent of the women did not think that the graduate degree that they held was a prerequisite for their current job, but only 4 percent thought that an undergraduate degree was not necessary.

While the advanced degree is often not a necessary requirement for job entry or advancement, it is apparent that the M.A. is an extremely useful degree. More than 80 percent of the graduates reported that they make considerable use of graduate school knowledge on their jobs. With the exception of those in semiprofessional and nonprofessional jobs, only some groups of engineers and businessmen found their graduate work of little relevance to their occupations; but even in these fields, over three-fifths had positive feelings about the value of their graduate studies in relation to their job performance (Appendix Table J). In brief, there seems to be little doubt that the M.A. enhances the feeling of professional competence for job holders in most occupations. Health professionals and social scientists, for example, most consistently see a need for a graduate degree.

On the other hand, those natural scientists who did not pursue graduate education saw little need for it in connection with their current jobs (Appendix Table K). Of those natural scientists who did not get an advanced degree, nearly three-fourths said it was not necessary, whereas only 55 percent of the social scientists with the terminal bachelor's degree thought that they did not need an advanced degree. This seems surprising at first glance, since the natural science majors tend to go on to graduate school more often than any other group.

But once more, it is necessary to remember that not all natural science majors, and certainly only a minority of social science majors, made their careers specifically in their fields. However, among those men who became professional scientists, the highest proportion with graduate degrees were social scientists rather than natural scientists. Five years after college graduation, the B.A. was the terminal degree for 65 percent of the natural scientists and for only 42 percent of the social scientists. Table 4.4 shows that close to 30 percent of the social scientists, as compared to 18 percent of the natural scientists, either have a Ph.D. or are Ph.D. candidates.

One can assume that natural scientists have many more employment opportunities where formal education requirements are less rigid. This suggests that natural scientists are developing what might be termed a nonacademically oriented segment, largely located in industry and to some extent in government where advanced degrees apparently are not needed for an orderly career progression. A comparable situation does not exist in the social sci-

Table 4.4.  Full-Time Occupation and Graduate Study (1958 B.A. Recipients)

*(percentages)*

| Occupation | Number Employed Full-Time | Graduate Study | | | | | | | Total Percent |
|---|---|---|---|---|---|---|---|---|---|
| | | Never in school | Some school | Degree candidate | M.A. recipient and not candidate | Professional degree recipient | M.A. recipient and candidate | Ph.D. recipient | |
| **Men** | | | | | | | | | |
| *Total* | *14,812* | *41.8* | *20.7* | *10.8* | *12.9* | *9.0* | *2.7* | *2.1* | *100.0* |
| Natural scientist | 887 | 36.2 | 20.3 | 8.3 | 16.6 | 0.5 | 4.1 | 14.1 | 100.1 |
| Engineer | 2,792 | 48.4 | 25.6 | 12.2 | 11.0 | 0.2 | 1.9 | 0.7 | 100.0 |
| Social scientist | 169 | 11.2 | 14.2 | 16.6 | 28.4 | - | 15.4 | 14.2 | 100.0 |
| Humanistic professional | 761 | 27.5 | 16.2 | 6.8 | 9.1 | 38.6 | 1.6 | 0.3 | 100.1 |
| Health professional | 861 | 30.5 | 7.3 | 1.7 | 1.7 | 56.7 | 1.5 | 0.5 | 99.9 |
| Teacher | 3,195 | 12.1 | 23.5 | 24.1 | 27.9 | 1.4 | 7.1 | 3.9 | 100.0 |
| Business and managerial | 3,213 | 63.6 | 22.3 | 4.9 | 8.2 | 0.7 | 0.3 | - | 100.0 |
| Other professional | 1,113 | 33.8 | 12.7 | 4.8 | 7.2 | 40.5 | 0.8 | 0.3 | 100.1 |
| Semiprofessional | 233 | 59.2 | 21.9 | 7.3 | 2.6 | 2.6 | 4.3 | 2.1 | 100.0 |
| Clerical and sales | 1,073 | 75.1 | 16.8 | 4.9 | 2.9 | 0.2 | 0.1 | - | 100.0 |
| Other nonprofessional | 354 | 54.5 | 29.9 | 6.5 | 6.2 | 1.7 | 1.1 | - | 99.9 |
| No answer | 161 | 49.7 | 14.3 | 11.2 | 15.5 | 6.2 | 1.2 | 1.9 | 100.0 |
| **Women** | | | | | | | | | |
| *Total* | *4,335* | *32.0* | *35.7* | *12.2* | *16.9* | *1.1* | *1.7* | *0.3* | *99.9* |
| Natural scientist | 54 | 42.6 | 24.1 | 1.9 | 18.5 | - | 9.3 | 3.7 | 100.1 |
| Engineer | 15 | 53.3 | 26.7 | 13.3 | 6.7 | - | - | - | 100.0 |
| Social scientist | 32 | 25.0 | 25.0 | 18.7 | 21.9 | - | 9.4 | - | 100.0 |
| Humanistic professional | 228 | 29.4 | 25.9 | 10.1 | 28.5 | 1.8 | 4.4 | - | 100.1 |
| Health professional | 267 | 55.8 | 19.5 | 4.9 | 8.2 | 10.1 | 1.5 | - | 100.0 |
| Teacher | 2,912 | 24.4 | 39.6 | 15.6 | 18.3 | 0.1 | 1.7 | 0.3 | 100.0 |
| Business and managerial | 156 | 62.8 | 28.2 | 0.6 | 8.3 | - | - | - | 99.9 |
| Other professional | 269 | 30.1 | 33.8 | 6.3 | 25.3 | 4.1 | 0.4 | - | 100.0 |
| Semiprofessional | 122 | 56.6 | 31.1 | 3.3 | 6.6 | 0.8 | 0.8 | 0.8 | 100.0 |
| Clerical and sales | 184 | 66.3 | 28.8 | 3.3 | 1.1 | 0.5 | - | - | 100.0 |
| Other nonprofessional | 47 | 65.9 | 19.1 | 4.3 | 4.3 | 2.1 | 4.3 | - | 100.0 |
| No answer | 49 | 42.9 | 42.9 | 4.1 | 6.1 | 4.1 | - | - | 100.1 |

ences. Perhaps this is because social scientists are more degree conscious, or because the two level system – academic and nonacademic careers – has not yet developed for them. It is relevant that our earlier studies showed that natural science majors received considerably more training in their field at the undergraduate level than did social science majors.[3] Concern with inadequacies of the undergraduate curriculum, in fact, has been a subject of considerable interest to sociologists in recent years.[4] If in years to come nonacademic or applied social scientists emerge as a new professional category – and there are straws in the wind that such an occupation may well become established in response to social and technical needs – strengthening of the undergraduate curriculum will become especially important.

## Teaching Careers

The tremendous growth of the education sector is fully reflected in the occupational experiences and aspirations of recent graduates. Teaching is one of the most popular occupations and is favored by those who contemplate a future career change. Among our cohort, women working full-time are employed predominantly (67 percent) as teachers; for men, teaching is the most popular occupation (22 percent) after business. Since the master's degree in the field of education is an important credential, it is not surprising that teaching is an even more popular occupation for the 1958 M.A. recipients. Teachers, in fact, constitute the largest sector of that group: Close to half of all the men and more than two-thirds of the women master's recipients were teachers.

### The Teaching Hierarchy

All levels of teaching – elementary, high school, and college – are careers frequently sought by men as well as women. We know that women are attracted to teaching at the grade school levels for a variety of sociocultural and psychological reasons, some relating to job availability. But elementary and high school teaching are also important career channels for men for several reasons. Education majors are often region-bound; they are trained locally and are perhaps less mobile than men in other fields. Others have school administrative ambitions on the local level. Teaching is also increasingly attractive to social science and humanities majors as a stopgap solution for those who are undecided about their careers and others who seek draft

---

[3] Laure M. Sharp, "The Meaning of the Bachelor's Degree," *Sociology of Education*, Vol. 37 (Winter 1963), pp. 93-109.

[4] Elbridge Sibley, *The Education of Sociologists in the United States* (Washington, D. C.: Russell Sage Foundation, 1963).

deferment for which certain teaching jobs may make them eligible. Others are interested in ghetto teaching or experimental programs for idealistic or intellectual reasons.

At the college level, the attraction of teaching is very high for both men and women in comparison to previous generations. The field has grown enormously, its image has changed, salaries have improved, and in general, there seems to be a higher prestige associated with college teaching. In part, the profession has become more attractive because of the greater amount of interchange between college and community. Teachers are recruited for consulting work and are increasingly being used to help solve local and national problems. Teaching at the college level also becomes more accessible to graduates of various backgrounds and interests as the growth and expansion of the university complexes open up new opportunities. Junior colleges may appeal for those who are not motivated to aim for the top, or for whom the Ph.D., usually required at the college level, is a more remote possibility.

A general finding of our study is that teachers aspire to climb within the system — from elementary school to high school, from high school to junior college, and on to a four-year college or the university. To move from one level to the next often requires the completion of graduate work. A comparison of the B.A. and M.A. groups indicates that there were fewer elementary and high school teachers and a larger proportion of college teachers among the men who were M.A. holders (Table 4.5). For the women, a slightly

Table 4.5. Teachers by Type of Institution

*(percentages)*

| Institution | 1958 B.A. Recipients | | 1958 M.A. Recipients | |
|---|---|---|---|---|
| | Men | Women | Men | Women |
| Elementary school | 14.8 | 59.5 | 7.6 | 40.6 |
| Secondary school | 68.7 | 35.4 | 50.9 | 42.3 |
| College | 16.4 | 5.1 | 41.6 | 17.0 |
| Total percent | 99.9 | 100.0 | 100.1 | 99.9 |
| (Total number) | (2,837) | (2,802) | (1,109) | (699) |

different pattern developed: M.A. holders made up a larger proportion of high school and college teachers and a correspondingly smaller proportion at the elementary level. The desirability of college teaching as a long-range career objective is apparently well embedded in the minds of some college students by the time they graduate. A more recent study found that 8 percent of college seniors expected to find their first job in higher education, compared to 14 percent who chose this as their "career employer."[5]

The differences between men's and women's teaching patterns persist throughout their careers. Women teach at the elementary school level more often than men, as indicated by the experiences of both the B.A. and M.A. group. Furthermore, women tend to teach at the college or university level much less often than men. By 1963, more than 16 percent of the men in the 1958 B.A. cohort were teaching at colleges versus only 5 percent of the women (Table 4.5). Of those who were college teachers, both men and women were usually instructors, but more men had reached the assistant professor level (Table 4.6). For the master's group, the pattern was repeated: Only 17 percent of the women teachers were at the college level, compared to

Table 4.6.  Occupational Titles of College Teachers, 1963 (1958 B.A. Recipients)

*(percentages)*

| College Teachers | Number | Title | | | | | Total Percent |
| | | Teaching Assistant | Instructor | Assistant Professor | Associate Professor | Professor | |
| --- | --- | --- | --- | --- | --- | --- | --- |
| Total[a] | 584 | 0.7 | 62.0 | 34.8 | 1.4 | 1.2 | 100.1 |
| Men | 448 | 0.9 | 59.4 | 37.3 | 1.8 | 0.7 | 100.1 |
| Women | 136 | – | 70.6 | 26.5 | – | 2.9 | 100.0 |

[a] Other and no answer eliminated.

42 percent of the men. Five years after receiving the master's, ten men were employed as full professors, while only one woman had that distinction.[6]

This employment pattern among teachers – the move from lower to higher grade levels – is indicative of future trends. The greater influx into college teaching five years after receiving the B.A. probably coincides with progress toward the Ph.D., commonly a requirement for university teaching. One can assume that there will be greater movement into college teaching from this cohort as more and more advanced degrees are received.

[5] Alexander W. Astin and Robert J. Panos, *The Educational and Vocational Development of American College Students* (Washington, D. C.: American Council on Education, 1969), Table 15.

[6] It may well be that this difference in rank is largely due to more frequent and more rapid Ph.D. completion among men. A recent study of college teachers in the science fields suggests that women Ph.D.'s tend to have equal or higher ranks than their male colleagues, but lower salaries. Alan E. Bayer and Helen S. Astin, "Sex Differences in Academic Rank and Salary Among Science Doctorates in Teaching," *Journal of Human Resources*, Vol. 3 (Spring 1968), pp. 191-200.

Over time it appears that there is an increase in college employment for those in natural sciences, social sciences, and humanities. It is interesting that the male natural scientists do not flock to college teaching to the same extent as social scientists. In part this may be due to the higher level of graduate degree completion by social scientists, which would make them more eligible for better college teaching positions. However, it may also reflect the better career opportunities for young natural scientists in industrial employment.

## Career Commitment

Teachers are strongly committed to their occupation, as indicated by anticipated life-time work plans. Nearly 80 percent of the B.A. group and 90 percent of the M.A. group want to remain within the field of education, although not at their present level of teaching. Many hope to switch to teaching higher grades or to educational administration.

It is often said that teaching is a stopgap occupation for men, which they leave as they encounter better paying opportunities or become better qualified for other types of work as a result of graduate study. There is little evidence in our data to confirm this hypothesis, certainly with respect to college teaching but also at other levels. Of the 1958 men B.A. graduates who were teachers in 1960, 80 percent were still teachers in 1963. In fact, it appears that in some occupations, nonteaching jobs were really the stopgap measures until the respondents were qualified for college positions. For example, 20 percent of the M.A. humanistic professionals and nearly 25 percent of the social scientists switched into teaching at the college level within five years after receiving their master's.

In general, the teaching profession is composed of an extremely stable group. Over 61 percent of the B.A. education majors did not change their occupation or employer during the five-year period covered by our study. It is true that small numbers of men transferred out of teaching into other occupations. Thirteen percent of the social scientists and 10 percent of those in the humanistic professions in 1963 had been teaching three years earlier. Table 4.7 indicates that these defections occurred most often at the secondary school level. But looking at the young men and women who expect to change employers in the future, we see that potential new recruits outnumber defectors. For would-be changers, the greatest interest is generated in employment by a college or university (Appendix Table L), although there is some indication of moves from college to industrial employers, presumably by graduate students employed as assistants and instructors whose careers have not yet crystallized. But college teaching is the goal for most of those who plan moves, either from other levels of teaching or from industrial and other employers. For women the trend is even clearer than for men: University employment is the major field that attracts women now working for other

Table 4.7. Distribution of Teachers by School Level, 1960 and 1963
(1958 B.A. Recipients)

*(percentages)*

| Teachers | 1960 | | 1963 | |
|---|---|---|---|---|
| | Men | Women | Men | Women |
| *College* | *3.9* | *1.1* | *14.6* | *4.9* |
| *Secondary* | *73.2* | *36.6* | *61.0* | *34.0* |
| With major in education | 38.9 | 37.1 | 38.3 | 38.0 |
| With other major | 61.1 | 62.9 | 61.7 | 62.0 |
| *Elementary* | *17.5* | *58.4* | *13.2* | *57.3* |
| With major in education | 61.3 | 67.0 | 62.2 | 66.6 |
| With other major | 38.7 | 33.0 | 37.8 | 33.4 |
| *Other* | *5.3* | *3.9* | *11.2* | *3.8* |
| Total percent | 99.9 | 100.0 | 100.0 | 100.0 |
| (Total number) | (2,752) | (4,235) | (3,195) | (2,912) |

employers. For the M.A. group, among both men and women, college teaching is the only field that gains employees.

For those who switched into teaching between 1960 and 1963, the most important reasons for the change were that the new occupation better suited their talents, aptitude, and interests. By contrast when businessmen, salesmen, and engineers changed occupations, they chose "better future" prospects (which implied career advancement) as the most frequent reason for changing their occupations (Appendix Table M).

### Professional Problems

In spite of the heavy commitment to teaching, there is a serious problem which affects the teaching profession at the elementary and high school levels and seems to be so widespread that it may augur trouble. This problem for teachers, unmatched by any other group, is an extreme dissatisfaction with income. Perhaps this dissatisfaction is heightened by the fact that teachers are so seriously committed to their profession.

It is relevant to point out that income was a central factor in the value system of our teachers. For men, income ranked third in importance as a career objective, after the opportunity to do interesting work and the opportunity to be helpful to others and to society.[7]

In our group, as many as 39 percent of the male teachers were dissatisfied with their salaries. The median income of male teachers was $6,220 in 1963,

[7]Other career-related values for teachers as well as other professions are discussed in detail in a later section of this chapter.

or about $1,300 lower than that of the total cohort of male graduates. This initial differential is maintained over the years. Although teachers more than any other group report earnings in addition to their salaries, these earnings fail to close the gap. Women teachers do not share this resentment. Their median income five years after college graduation was $5,710 versus $5,660 for the total group of women. This is, however, a matter of relative deprivation for women, since their median income is nearly $2,000 a year lower than that of men.

It is noteworthy that among the more committed members of the profession — the M.A. recipients — concern about income remains high, in comparison to members of other professions. Nearly 30 percent of the men were dissatisfied with their income, the highest dissatisfaction percentage for any occupation in the M.A. group. This further confirms our finding that teachers are considerably more concerned with salaries than one might have anticipated. Considering recent improvements in teachers' salaries, one might speculate that the dissatisfaction expressed by teachers on the subject of income reflects other grievances, in particular the struggle for full professional recognition and autonomy as well as higher social status. It may also be caused more by public discussion and spotlighting of this issue than by personal experience with low pay. It should be noted that in spite of dissatisfaction with their level of income, the high rate of occupational retention indicates that few teachers seek alternatives in other occupations. Because of their loyalty to their chosen work, many teachers engage in determined efforts to improve the status of their profession. The recent rash of teacher strikes for more pay and more authority could have been predicted from these findings. For others, the search for a more personal solution centers around moves to other school systems or to higher steps on the educational ladder.

If the high demand for teachers persists, and this is likely to be the case for male teachers, the effect might be a considerable drifting of the younger men between school systems and levels in search of better financial rewards. But even more likely is the prospect that elementary and high school teachers will experience some of the remarkable improvements in salary and prestige levels that have characterized the field of higher education over the past two decades.

### Business, Science, and Government Careers

#### Who Goes into Business?

There has been considerable talk in recent years about the business community's inability to attract and retain college graduates. The practice of frequent job changing by recent graduates is one of concern to some employers, especially large corporations.[8] It may well be, however, that the lack of enthusiasm for business is primarily found among Ivy League graduates recruited into the largest and most prestigious corporations. Looking at a broad cross section of graduates from all types of schools, we found that business careers were still the most popular occupation for the men in our cohort who had been out of college five years.[9] Business careers included varied positions at all levels of the executive hierarchy. There were bankers, buyers, accountants, business trainees and executives, managers, office clerks, salesmen, secretaries, and operators of office machines such as computers. For a large segment of this group, business was a planned and desired occupation.

Our data show that teaching — the most popular career for men in 1960, two years out of college — fell to second place in 1963, yielding to the dominance of business careers. Since teaching had a relatively high retention rate, it is probable that this change was caused by an upgrading of those in sales and clerical work and the recruitment of men who first entered the labor force after 1960 — most often because they had been in the military at the time of the 1960 survey (Table 4.8).

Given the relationship between the undergraduate major and subsequent life patterns, it is not surprising that the greater majority (59 percent) of men in business were business majors. Another 25 percent of the businessmen were social science majors. There is a tendency for some social science majors to move toward business careers. In fact, for economists and political scientists, certain types of business careers are an expected outcome. By 1963, 28 percent of those who in 1960 worked in a social science field had transferred into business. Unfortunately, our data are too crude to permit us to distinguish between managerial, career-type outcomes, and less professional business occupations. Even on the post-graduate level, looking at our M.A. cohort, we see that social scientists gravitated toward business careers. More than one-quarter of the M.A. holders who changed occupations between 1960 and 1963 went into business. Many of these were probably economists, for whom "management" is often the ultimate career goal.

The majority of businessmen in our cohort majored in business or in a related area. In contrast, one often hears that Ivy League and other prestigious schools find that business employers favor liberal arts graduates over the graduates of business curricula. What is true for the Ivy League should not be seen as characteristic for a broad cross section of American colleges and universities.

---

[8] See, for example, Edgar H. Schein, "The First Job Dilemma," *Psychology Today* (March 1968), pp. 27-37.

[9] Business and managerial occupations attracted less than 4 percent of the women graduates. We have therefore excluded data on women in this section on business careers.

Table 4.8. Occupational Recruitment of Men, 1960-63 (1958 B.A. Recipients)

*(percentages)*

| 1963 Occupation | Number | Natural scientist | Engineer | Social scientist | Humanistic professional | Health professional | Teacher | Business and managerial | Other professional | Semiprofessional | Clerical and sales | Other nonprofessional and no answer | Not employed full-time in 1960 | Total Percent |
|---|---|---|---|---|---|---|---|---|---|---|---|---|---|---|
| *Total* | *16,293* | *3.7* | *14.5* | *0.5* | *2.5* | *1.9* | *16.9* | *15.2* | *1.3* | *2.5* | *6.9* | *3.4* | *30.7* | *100.0* |
| Natural scientist | 887 | *40.1* | 3.3 | 0.1 | 0.2 | 0.2 | 4.1 | 3.5 | 0.5 | 4.5 | 1.7 | 3.6 | 38.2 | 100.0 |
| Engineer | 2,792 | 1.9 | *70.9* | 0.3 | 0.3 | 0.2 | 0.6 | 5.0 | 0.5 | 1.6 | 0.8 | 2.4 | 15.5 | 100.0 |
| Social scientist | 169 | 2.4 | 1.8 | *15.4* | 2.4 | 1.8 | 13.0 | 5.9 | 0.6 | 5.9 | 1.2 | 3.6 | 46.2 | 100.2 |
| Humanistic professional | 761 | 0.1 | 1.2 | – | *36.0* | 0.1 | 10.0 | 2.1 | 0.7 | 1.6 | 2.2 | 2.0 | 44.0 | 100.0 |
| Health professional | 861 | 1.4 | – | – | 0.2 | *29.3* | 1.0 | 0.6 | – | 2.0 | 2.1 | 1.0 | 62.4 | 100.0 |
| Teacher | 3,195 | 0.7 | 0.8 | – | 0.5 | 0.3 | *68.7* | 4.1 | 0.8 | 0.7 | 1.3 | 1.9 | 20.2 | 100.0 |
| Business and managerial | 3,213 | 1.1 | 4.0 | 0.7 | 1.2 | 0.3 | 3.3 | *54.2* | 0.5 | 1.3 | 11.4 | 3.4 | 18.5 | 99.9 |
| Other professional | 1,113 | 2.3 | 2.2 | 0.9 | 0.8 | 0.2 | 2.5 | 3.1 | *9.1* | 4.2 | 3.2 | 7.5 | 64.0 | 100.0 |
| Semiprofessional | 233 | 5.2 | 3.0 | – | 1.7 | – | 4.3 | 1.7 | 1.7 | *32.6* | 3.4 | 11.2 | 35.2 | 100.0 |
| Clerical and sales | 1,073 | 1.5 | 3.4 | 0.3 | 1.1 | 0.3 | 3.1 | 17.8 | 1.0 | 2.3 | *48.2* | 0.8 | 20.1 | 99.9 |
| Other nonprofessional and no answer | 515 | 6.6 | 9.5 | 1.2 | 1.7 | 0.4 | 5.6 | 15.9 | 3.5 | 8.5 | 6.0 | *20.4* | 20.6 | 99.9 |
| Not employed full-time in 1963 | 1,481 | 2.5 | 4.7 | 0.5 | 1.8 | 0.8 | 12.9 | 5.8 | 0.5 | 2.1 | 3.0 | 2.3 | *63.0* | 99.9 |

While industry clearly has no problem recruiting among business majors and certain groups of social science majors, there is less interest in business careers on the part of arts and science majors, either immediately after receiving a college or advanced degree or even several years later. Only B.A. graduates employed in semiprofessional, technical, clerical, and other nonprofessional jobs indicated long-term aspirations centered around business occupations.

Early identification as a businessman seems high for the 1958 cohort, as measured by occupational retention. Nearly three-quarters of the businessmen stayed within their field during the five-year period under study. Moreover, planned shifts usually involve movement into other branches of industry rather than into other types of employment. For example, the main shift for businessmen is expected to be from manufacturing to nonmanufacturing or vice versa.

Looking at long-term gains and losses, business seems to be holding its own with the male B.A. holders, although it runs a poor second to that great magnet, the university. Later recruits, except for those who plan to move from clerical and sales positions and from one type of business occupation to another, are supplied mainly from the engineering profession (Table 4.9). It is

Table 4.9.  Expected Life-Time Occupation and Current Occupation—Men
(1958 B.A. Recipients)

| Occupation in 1963 | Number | Expected Life-Time Occupation | | | | | | | | | | | |
|---|---|---|---|---|---|---|---|---|---|---|---|---|---|
| | | Natural scientist | Engineer | Social scientist | Humanistic professional | Health professional | Teacher, college | Teacher, other | Business and managerial | Other professional | Semiprofessional | Clerical and Sales | Other, no answer |
| *Total[a]* | *2,219* | *93* | *126* | *48* | *96* | *116* | *264* | *283* | *681* | *157* | *7* | *76* | *272* |
| Natural scientist | 100 | 20 | 5 | 2 | 1 | 4 | 33 | 2 | 11 | 3 | – | 2 | 17 |
| Engineer | 396 | 19 | 102 | 3 | 2 | 3 | 25 | 6 | 159 | 21 | 2 | 5 | 49 |
| Social scientist | 23 | – | – | 7 | 1 | – | 10 | 1 | 3 | – | – | – | 1 |
| Humanistic professional | 79 | – | – | 4 | 25 | 1 | 13 | 15 | 11 | 2 | – | – | 8 |
| Health professional | 117 | 7 | – | 2 | – | 91 | 1 | 3 | 10 | 1 | – | – | 2 |
| Teacher | 471 | 20 | 10 | 8 | 19 | 2 | 110 | 194 | 29 | 21 | 1 | 8 | 49 |
| Business and managerial | 441 | 1 | 1 | 5 | 20 | 3 | 41 | 19 | 234 | 30 | – | 46 | 41 |
| Other professional | 134 | 7 | 2 | 9 | 11 | 1 | 15 | 9 | 19 | 29 | 1 | – | 31 |
| Semiprofessional | 81 | 13 | 3 | – | 4 | 1 | 11 | 3 | 23 | 11 | 2 | 3 | 7 |
| Clerical and sales | 217 | – | 1 | 2 | 9 | 9 | 1 | 22 | 124 | 24 | – | 10 | 15 |
| Other, no answer | 160 | 6 | 2 | 6 | 4 | 1 | 4 | 9 | 58 | 15 | 1 | 2 | 52 |

[a] This table is limited to men who, in answer to the question "Do you expect to have your current occupation for the major part of your working life?" chose the third answer: "No, expect to have other occupation."

relevant to mention here that career values for businessmen and managers center on income, and many engineers work in settings where the highest rewards go to executive and managerial personnel. For many career-minded engineers, the executive office rather than the senior engineer's office is the ultimate goal.

We feel that what concerns industrial employers is not a general lack of interest in business employment, but rather a lack of interest on the part of the best-qualified graduates from "high quality" institutions. With the possible exception of certain specialized fields, like accounting and systems analysis, employers do not face a quantitative problem. For most managerial and business occupations, there are large numbers of business majors who wish to remain in the same region. They are ready recruits for local employers. Altogether, there is not enough evidence to suggest that business has valid complaints about its current lack of high-quality recruits in sufficient numbers. Given the total growth of the college-trained segment and the strengthening of middle-level institutions, it would appear that the business community continues to have access to large numbers of competent graduates. Furthermore, data presented in Chapter VI show that among our cohort, a relatively high proportion of graduates from the most selective and prestigious colleges were recruited for employment by business firms. This group, however, may not have included the top students, who were more likely to go on to graduate school.

## Choices of Engineers and Natural Scientists

Engineering was the third most popular career after business and teaching. Nearly 20 percent of the men worked as full-time engineers.

Engineers worked in their field more often than graduates in other occupations (except women teachers). Five years after college graduation 77 percent of the men engineering majors were working as engineers. They also had the highest retention rate of all occupations (84 percent) and the highest salaries ($9,540 versus $7,570 for the norm).

Yet engineers plan to change their field of occupation more than any other group. The profession apparently has a long-term career satisfaction problem. This finding has interesting implications, given the successful early career outcomes for engineering graduates. It appears that the engineers' lack of long-term professional attachment is related to their personal value systems; they tend to put higher emphasis on career advancement and income-related factors than on factors associated with professional identification and creativity. In addition, more than three-quarters of the young engineers worked in industry, in contrast to many other young professionals; this no doubt reinforces the values that characterize business, thus exposing young engineers to cross pressures between professional and business life styles.[10]

Although at the undergraduate level students in engineering and the natural sciences display many similarities, their early employment histories are quite different. Surprisingly, the proportion of natural science majors employed full-time five years after receiving the B.A. is still comparatively low — 82 percent versus 95 percent for men who majored in engineering. This may be, in part, because of the large number in this field who attended graduate school full-time; by 1963 their graduate deferments may have expired, which is suggested by the relatively high contingent (10 percent) of natural science majors on military duty. Unlike engineers, natural science majors are not concentrated in the business world; only half of them worked for industry, while the other half worked for educational or nonprofit institutions and government agencies.

The professional orientation of women who majored in the natural sciences, as for women in all fields, is overwhelmingly toward the field of education. Only 12 percent of the women natural science majors worked as

[10]See James A. Davis, *Undergraduate Career Decisions* (Chicago: Aldine Publishing Company, 1965), pp. 180-90, for a related discussion of the characteristics of undergraduates who major in engineering.

scientists; 17 percent as semiprofessionals and technicians, such as research or laboratory assistants; and 45 percent as full-time teachers. Men natural science majors, on the other hand, worked more often in their field: 26 percent of the men in this group were full-time natural scientists by 1963 (Table 4.1). Apparently many women who specialize in the natural sciences make early decisions to become teachers, and not necessarily at the college level. A recent study of graduate students in the sciences showed that, in these fields, as many women aspired to academic careers (working in colleges and universities) as were oriented toward elementary and secondary school teaching. In other fields, the proportion with academic aspirations is much lower. Still, women in the natural sciences are much more likely than men to consider teaching at the elementary or secondary level; the men ranked colleges (48 percent) or private industry (30 percent) as their top choices.[11]

### Work Roles of Young Scientists and Engineers

The tremendous demand for talent in science and engineering was reflected dramatically by the specialized nature of the work performed by young scientists and engineers in all fields of employment. There is little evidence that these young professionals were being underutilized in nonprofessional or routine tasks, a not infrequent complaint in the past. Today the largest number of jobs are in research and development work. This field accounted for 51 percent of the jobs male natural scientists held. This was the predominant assignment for the chemists (74 percent), physicists (82 percent), and biologists (62 percent). Agricultural scientists were more prone to administrative and operational work; earth scientists most often had operational duties (Table 4.10). For engineers, the work most often reported depended on the specialty: civil and industrial engineers worked primarily in operations and administration; electrical and mechanical engineers worked in research and development.

Compared to scientists and engineers who received the B.A. in 1958, the M.A. recipients engaged more often in research and development and less often in operational work. Over-all, more than half of the male scientists and engineers combined (70 percent of the natural scientists, 47 percent of the engineers) who held the M.A. were in research and development. The difference in jobs performed by B.A. and M.A. holders is especially noteworthy for engineers in several specialties: about two-thirds of the chemical, electrical, and mechanical engineering graduates with the master's degree were engaged in research and development work versus less than half of the bachelor recipients in the same fields.

[11] Alan S. Berger, *Longitudinal Studies on the Class of 1961: The Graduate Science Students* (Chicago: National Opinion Research Center, January 1967).

Table 4.10. Type of Work Performed in 1963 by Natural Scientists and Engineers—Men
(1958 B.A. and M.A. Recipients)

*(percentages)*

| Job Title | B.A. | | M.A. | | Type of Work Performed | | | | | | | | | |
|---|---|---|---|---|---|---|---|---|---|---|---|---|---|---|
| | | | | | Research and development | | Administration and management | | Operations | | Other | | No answer | |
| | Total Number | Total Percent | Total Number | Total Percent | B.A. | M.A. | B.A. | M.A. | B.A. | M.A. | B.A. | M.A. | B.A. | M.A. |
| *Total* | *3,848* | *100.0* | *994* | *99.8* | *35.7* | *53.5* | *13.0* | *14.1* | *27.8* | *10.4* | *17.0* | *14.8* | *6.5* | *7.0* |
| *Natural Scientist* | *887* | *99.9* | *355* | *99.9* | *50.5* | *70.4* | *9.0* | *6.8* | *19.7* | *8.7* | *13.3* | *10.1* | *7.4* | *3.9* |
| Agricultural scientist | 248 | 100.0 | 52 | 100.0 | 13.7 | 50.0 | 24.2 | 13.5 | 22.6 | 11.5 | 24.6 | 17.3 | 14.9 | 7.7 |
| Biological scientist | 115 | 100.0 | 59 | 100.1 | 61.7 | 81.4 | 3.5 | 8.5 | 12.2 | 1.7 | 13.9 | 6.8 | 8.7 | 1.7 |
| Chemist | 243 | 99.9 | 76 | 100.0 | 74.1 | 88.2 | 1.6 | 1.3 | 18.5 | 6.6 | 2.4 | - | 3.3 | 3.9 |
| Physicist | 89 | 99.8 | 49 | 99.8 | 82.0 | 81.6 | 1.1 | 2.0 | 7.9 | 2.0 | 7.7 | 10.1 | 1.1 | 4.1 |
| Earth scientist | 75 | 99.9 | 54 | 100.1 | 30.7 | 51.9 | 4.0 | 1.9 | 42.7 | 29.6 | 17.2 | 13.0 | 5.3 | 3.7 |
| Other physical scientist | 32 | 99.9 | 22 | 100.0 | 50.0 | 68.2 | 9.4 | 18.2 | 6.2 | - | 18.7 | 13.6 | 15.6 | - |
| Mathematician | 85 | 100.1 | 43 | 100.1 | 60.0 | 60.5 | 5.9 | 11.6 | 22.4 | 4.7 | 10.6 | 18.6 | 1.2 | 4.7 |
| *Engineer* | *2,792* | *99.8* | *527* | *100.0* | *31.7* | *47.1* | *14.6* | *20.7* | *31.7* | *12.0* | *17.3* | *14.9* | *4.5* | *5.3* |
| Chemical | 203 | 100.0 | 57 | 100.1 | 40.4 | 66.7 | 3.9 | 10.5 | 32.5 | 14.0 | 21.2 | 5.4 | 2.0 | 3.5 |
| Civil | 398 | 100.1 | 46 | 100.0 | 7.5 | 8.7 | 17.6 | 17.4 | 38.4 | 17.4 | 26.5 | 54.3 | 10.1 | 2.2 |
| Electrical | 707 | 99.9 | 136 | 99.9 | 48.1 | 66.9 | 11.6 | 19.1 | 27.0 | 4.4 | 10.7 | 6.6 | 2.5 | 2.9 |
| Mechanical | 587 | 100.1 | 91 | 100.0 | 46.5 | 61.5 | 8.9 | 17.6 | 24.4 | 9.9 | 15.0 | 7.7 | 5.3 | 3.3 |
| Mining | 98 | 99.8 | 20 | 100.0 | 36.7 | 45.0 | 6.1 | 10.0 | 41.8 | 30.0 | 9.1 | 15.0 | 6.1 | - |
| Industrial | 322 | 100.1 | 48 | 99.9 | 2.5 | 6.2 | 33.9 | 50.0 | 54.7 | 27.1 | 6.2 | 10.4 | 2.8 | 6.2 |
| Other | 477 | 100.1 | 129 | 99.9 | 24.5 | 36.4 | 17.0 | 20.9 | 24.1 | 10.1 | 30.5 | 20.9 | 4.0 | 11.6 |

[a] "Other" includes (1) sales, promotion, and public relations; (2) writing; (3) consulting; (4) training; and (5) other. Total percents for the B.A.'s were 3.2, 1.1, 3.8, 0.4 and 8.5 respectively; for M.A.'s 1.2, 1.8, 5.3, 0.3 and 6.2.

The concentration of young scientists and engineers in research and development is partly a function of age, since administrative and managerial jobs usually are not open to newcomers. Thus, the proportion of men in this survey who are in research and development work is higher than it was for all the scientists and engineers in the United States in 1962, one year before our study was made. The patterns, however, are similar. A National Science Foundation study shows that 72 percent of all physicists and close to half of all mathematicians, biologists, and chemists worked in research and development in 1962.[12] The similarity between the job distribution of this cohort and their respective professions as a whole was sufficiently close to contribute to the impression suggested by our findings: that jobs taken in the earliest part of men's careers are good indicators of long-term occupational outcome, and that specific entry jobs, if they exist at all, are quite uniformly distributed within functional specialties.

[12] National Science Foundation, *Scientific and Technical Manpower Resources* (NSF 64-28; Washington, D. C.: U.S. Government Printing Office, 1964).

*The Influence of Federal Government Programs*

Our follow-up studies have shown that fairly large numbers of recent graduates enter or leave government service during the early years of their career. Are there any set patterns in this movement? The major finding is that federal government employment was more popular five years after graduation than it was immediately after college. The federal government employed 8 percent of the B.A. men and 3 percent of the women in 1960; government employment increased to 11 percent and 4 percent respectively in 1963. Yet, as time progresses, it appears that government employment does not have a lasting appeal; in fact, the government is the major projected long-term loser, chiefly to industry. Both the B.A. and M.A. data show that when an expected employer shift relates to government workers, the defectors outnumber the recruits.

It is not surprising that government is the chief employer of social scientists. We know that even today jobs for social scientists do not exist abundantly in the private sector, and in 1963 they were even more scarce. In federal and local agencies, on the other hand, the need for specialists in public administration, economics, social welfare, and the newer interdisciplinary fields, such as urban planning and social science research, is becoming increasingly recognized.

Between 1960 and 1963 social scientists employed by the federal government increased rather dramatically. In 1960, 18 percent of the men and 19 percent of the women social scientists were working for the government; just three years later, 31 percent of the men and 50 percent of the women in this group were federal civil servants, reflecting the growth of opportunities in many newly created agencies in the early 1960's. The increasing employment of social scientists in the government is attributable to the fact that by 1963 more of them had obtained advanced training and were eligible for the opportunities in their fields that the government was offering. Under civil service regulations, many professional jobs require several years of experience or an advanced degree.

Although the younger social scientists seem to be gravitating toward government employment, it must be noted that social scientists show a low level of job retention. This might lead them to shift from government to academic or other nongovernment careers as new opportunities open up. They may then follow the example of men natural scientists, for whom federal government employment declined from 29 percent in 1960 to 25 percent in 1963.

For women in the natural sciences, the shift is definitely toward the government: 14 percent worked for the government in 1960, 25 percent in 1963. Although the data are rather thin, one might speculate that federal employment, in spite of recent attempts to upgrade salary and status, is still second choice for young men who can write their own job tickets. Women, specifically natural and social scientists, seem to encounter better opportunities in government service then in any other nonteaching field.

In summary, it appears that in today's job market the business community has some problems in recruiting young arts and sciences majors and that the government faces problems of retaining the more experienced young professionals. Only the educational establishment is relatively immune to recruitment and retention problems. At the lower grade levels, it relies heavily on women and on the growing number of men who elect to spend their lives in an educational milieu. At the upper levels, the attraction of college careers has become so widespread as to almost guarantee the university its pick among young professionals.

### Special Problem Areas

*Work Patterns of Women*

The early careers of young women graduates merit special consideration. Their post-college work patterns are totally different from men's not only because they cluster in the field of teaching, but also because so many leave the labor force to become housewives. Two years after college graduation, the proportion of men and women employed was roughly the same — 75 percent. Just three years later, only 56 percent of the women worked versus 91 percent of the men (Table 4.11). Even the more committed women, those

Table 4.11.  Employment Status in 1960 and 1963 of 1958 B.A. and M.A. Recipients

*(percentages)*

| Employment Status | Men | | | | Women | | | |
|---|---|---|---|---|---|---|---|---|
| | 1960 | | 1963 | | 1960 | | 1963 | |
| | B.A. | M.A. | B.A. | M.A. | B.A. | M.A. | B.A. | M.A. |
| *Employed* | *74.4* | *87.8* | *91.4* | *94.6* | *75.5* | *85.5* | *55.7* | *78.3* |
| Full-time | 67.8 | 81.1 | 88.8 | 91.8 | 69.9 | 78.7 | 46.2 | 70.4 |
| Part-time | 6.6 | 6.7 | 2.6 | 2.8 | 5.6 | 6.8 | 9.5 | 7.9 |
| *Not employed* | *25.6* | *12.2* | *8.6* | *5.4* | *24.5* | *14.5* | *44.3* | *21.7* |
| Student | 10.1 | 6.0 | 3.4 | 2.3 | 3.4 | 2.7 | 1.7 | 2.2 |
| In military | 13.2 | 5.4 | 4.2 | 2.1 | 0.3 | 0.1 | 0.3 | 0.2 |
| Housewife | – | – | – | – | 19.1 | 10.3 | 40.7 | 18.3 |
| Other[a] | 1.1 | 0.3 | 0.8 | 0.6 | 0.5 | 0.5 | 1.0 | 0.5 |
| No answer | 1.2 | 0.5 | 0.2 | 0.4 | 1.2 | 0.9 | 0.6 | 0.5 |
| Total percent | 100.0 | 100.0 | 100.0 | 100.0 | 100.0 | 100.0 | 100.0 | 100.0 |
| (Total number[b]) | (20,399) | (4,905) | (16,293) | (3,706) | (11,723) | (2,234) | (9,290) | (1,736) |

[a] Includes unemployed, disabled, retired, ill, etc.

[b] Only one employment status is reported here; priorities were established in the order shown in the table. For example, a respondent employed full-time who is also a student is shown only as "employed full-time"; a respondent who is a housewife and employed part-time is shown only in the "employed part-time" column.

who received their M.A. in 1958, started their exodus from the employment field within five years after receiving their advanced degree. In 1960, 86 percent were at work; in 1963, 78 percent. Nevertheless it should again be stressed that, given the age distribution of this cohort, the proportion of full-time employed women was extraordinarily high: Five years after graduation almost half (46 percent) were full-time employees. Furthermore, while there was a drop in over-all female employment by 1963, some increase took place in part-time work; 10 percent of the women worked part-time in 1963 in contrast to 6 percent in 1960. Married women with children account for this increase. When women attempt to play more than one role, they tend to combine household responsibilities and work. The overlap of student status and employment is rare and accounted for only 5 percent of the women in our cohort. Our analysis further shows that 82 percent of the married women without children worked, either full- or part-time, and as many as 35 percent of the mothers worked.

Data for the group of women master's degree holders disclose that women were least likely to be single or childless if their degree was in the field of education. This is, of course, contrary to the stereotype of the spinster school teacher. For those who take an advanced degree in the natural sciences, arts, and nursing, the combination of marriage or motherhood with a career seems hardest to achieve. Since the presence of children is a deterring factor to employment (and graduate study as we saw in Chapter III), it is not surprising that there are decreases in employment of women as time passes after college graduation.

The women in our cohort who were employed full-time most often have backgrounds in education, the sciences, and engineering. For education majors, this seems to be partly related to age: They include the highest proportions of older graduates, whose children are of school age. For science majors, the incidence of full-time employment may be attributed to high career commitment and to marital status; the proportion of single women is largest in this field, thus allowing them greater career involvement.

Family considerations may be an important factor in employment for women, but there are other, more fundamental problems of advancement and income ranges that are created by discrimination. Measured in our survey by the three years between the 1960 and 1963 studies, the initial salary differential between men and women clearly grows over time. For the women with bachelor's degrees, salaries increased by 31 percent during this period while men's salaries increased 38 percent (Table 4.12). Breaking it down by occupations, median salaries for men chemists increased by 40 percent; women chemists' salaries increased only 11 percent. Even in teaching the differential grows: The salaries of men high school teachers increased by 34 percent, those of women only 23 percent.

Table 4.12. Median Salary in 1960 and 1963 by Selected Occupations (1958 B.A. Recipients)

| Occupations | Men | | | Women | | |
|---|---|---|---|---|---|---|
| | 1960 | 1963 | Percent change | 1960 | 1963 | Percent change |
| Total | $5,490 | $7,570 | +38 | $4,330 | $5,660 | +31 |
| Natural Scientist | 5,825 | 7,960 | +37 | 5,300 | 7,140 | +35 |
| Agricultural scientist | 5,290 | 7,110 | +34 | - | - | - |
| Biologist | 5,000 | 7,020 | +40 | 5,145 | 6,375 | +24 |
| Earth scientist | 6,230 | 8,880 | +43 | - | - | - |
| Physicist | 6,760 | 9,930 | +47 | - | - | - |
| Chemist | 6,075 | 8,520 | +40 | 5,325 | 5,815 | +11 |
| Mathematician | 6,220 | 8,950 | +44 | 5,460 | 7,500 | +37 |
| Engineer | 6,955 | 9,540 | +37 | 6,250 | 9,250 | +48 |
| Chemical | 6,795 | 9,130 | +34 | - | - | - |
| Civil | 6,465 | 8,780 | +36 | - | - | - |
| Electrical | 7,255 | 10,210 | +41 | - | - | - |
| Mechanical | 7,260 | 9,750 | +34 | - | - | - |
| Mining | 6,780 | 9,190 | +36 | - | - | - |
| Industrial | 6,590 | 8,730 | +32 | - | - | - |
| Social Scientist | 5,690 | 7,810 | +37 | 4,605 | 6,875 | +49 |
| Psychologist | 5,400 | 8,450 | +56 | 4,800 | 5,735 | +19 |
| Health Professional | 6,895 | 7,340 | + 6 | 4,370 | 5,440 | +25 |
| Pharmacist | 7,320 | 9,170 | +25 | - | - | - |
| Nurse | - | - | - | 4,340 | 5,525 | +27 |
| Therapist | - | - | - | 4,355 | 5,320 | +22 |
| Teacher | 4,535 | 6,220 | +37 | 4,390 | 5,710 | +30 |
| College | 4,660 | 6,745 | +45 | 4,415 | 6,130 | +39 |
| High school | 4,510 | 6,055 | +34 | 4,325 | 5,585 | +23 |
| Elementary | 4,540 | 5,995 | +32 | 4,415 | 5,725 | +30 |
| Other | | | | | | |
| Accountant | 5,430 | 7,730 | +42 | - | - | - |
| Clergyman | 3,715 | 4,995 | +34 | - | - | - |
| Social worker | 4,780 | 6,310 | +32 | 4,190 | 5,820 | +39 |
| Lawyer | 6,375 | 7,360 | +15 | - | - | - |
| Research assistant | 4,795 | 6,425 | +34 | 4,225 | 5,315 | +26 |
| Salesman | 5,665 | 7,990 | +41 | - | - | - |

To a large extent these differentials can be accounted for by the relative levels of graduate study achieved. The double standard, however, remains a factor since differentials generally widened at the M.A. level, even in fields where the M.A. was the terminal degree for the majority of graduates. Men teachers increased their salary by 39 percent, for example, compared to 29 percent for women. In other fields, the gap was slightly bridged. Women social scientists had increased their salary by 32 percent five years after receiving the master's, while men in the same group saw only a 21 percent increase; yet, women social scientists earned $7,500 versus $9,525 for men social scientists. In fact, there was a $2,000 salary differential between the men and women who hold master's degrees, in spite of the fact that the women's median salaries increased by 57 percent between 1960 and 1963 and the men's increased by only 39 percent (Table 4.13). It is evident that the income differential persists even for the more dedicated and work-committed group.

Table 4.13. Median Salary in 1960 and 1963 by Occupation (1958 M.A. Recipients)

| Occupation | Men | | | Women | | |
|---|---|---|---|---|---|---|
| | 1960 | 1963 | Percent change | 1960 | 1963 | Percent change |
| Total | $6,460 | $ 8,990 | +39 | $4,425 | $6,950 | +57 |
| Natural scientist | 7,205 | 10,030 | +39 | 5,830 | 7,900 | +36 |
| Engineer | 7,995 | 12,225 | +53 | a | a | – |
| Social scientist | 7,520 | 9,525 | +21 | 5,665 | 7,500 | +32 |
| Humanistic professional | 5,360 | 5,960 | +11 | 4,945 | 6,600 | +33 |
| Health professional | 6,715 | 8,500 | +27 | 5,540 | 6,800 | +23 |
| Teacher | 5,710 | 7,910 | +39 | 5,420 | 7,000 | +29 |
| Business and managerial | 7,810 | 10,730 | +37 | 6,365 | a | – |
| Other professional | 5,910 | 9,470 | +60 | 5,280 | 7,170 | +36 |
| Semiprofessional | 5,920 | 8,000 | +35 | 5,625 | 6,435 | +14 |
| Clerical and sales | 7,030 | 10,400 | +32 | 3,770 | 4,585 | +22 |
| Other nonprofessional | 6,535 | 7,125 | + 9 | 5,810 | 9,080 | +56 |

[a]Too few cases to compute median salary.

The gap in occupational status between women and comparably educated men is evident in all fields and at all levels, but it is less sharp for master's holders than for those who only have a bachelor's degree. A graduate degree gives women a better foothold in what are otherwise predominantly male occupations, albeit at lower salaries. In fact, the lack of a graduate degree may explain why so many women leave their undergraduate major field when they enter the working world: They are not able to obtain jobs on a competitive basis with men who have had more graduate training.

There can be little doubt that the employment situation of college women is far from satisfactory. The data presented here dispel one of the myths which serves as a justification for this treatment of women in the labor force. It is apparent that commitment to a continuous work role is higher among young college women than is often assumed. Another often heard allegation is that women are not seriously concerned about professional equality, since their primary life goals are in the area of family life and their psychological needs call for supportive rather than competitive roles in the world of work. Given their nature, our studies could only touch superficially on some of these points, but it would seem that status, reward, and advancement are of real concern to many young women professionals. Thus, women with advanced degrees appear to have serious grievances about their lack of opportunity for advancement. As many as 24 percent of the women natural scientists and 19 percent of the social scientists with a master's degree thought this lack of advancement to be the least satisfactory part of their job.

Compared to other professional women, teachers appear to find their total working experience most satisfying, as witnessed by the number of women in teaching. Not only can they combine professional and family roles with greater ease, but the opportunities for advancement and compensation are better in teaching than women can find in other occupations, where they are a distinct minority. The income differential between men and women is smaller in teaching than in all other occupations. Women teachers out of college five years had annual earnings in 1963 of $5,710 as compared to $6,220 for men.

There are however several reasons for challenging the appropriateness of this occupational choice pattern of women. Most experts question the desirability of having the teaching profession a predominantly female one. And there is the very real talent loss that occurs in many occupations because of the nonentrance of gifted women: as a result of the selection and retention processes at the undergraduate level, women graduates are the better students.[13]

Many experts believe that the unprecedented expansion in teaching jobs available to young graduates is unlikely to continue at the same rate in the next decade. Higher retention rates, re-entry of older teachers, utilization of sub-professionals, restructuring of curricula and methods may lead to fewer openings in years to come. Higher salaries may lead to more judicious use of teachers. Clearly, it seems desirable for young women to explore other career lines. This will require considerable rethinking by the women themselves and by employers, who, judging from our findings, do not provide the same opportunities for young professional women as they do for men. But perhaps the most active role must be played by the colleges and universities which in the past – through their formal and informal policies – have been most instrumental in channeling college women into selected fields and occupations.

## The Employment Experience of Negro College Graduates

The 1963 Survey of 1958 B.A. recipients contained data for a small number of Negro graduates; only 247 men and 338 women had identified them-

---

[13]In our cohort, for example, there were more women (35 percent) than men (23 percent) in the high Grade Point Average group. Whether women graduates are really more academically talented than male graduates is of course open to question; they are clearly better gradegetters, but this is believed to reflect personality characteristics rather than greater knowledge or ability. See, for example, Charles E. Werts, "A Comparison of Male vs. Female College Attendance Probabilities," *Sociology of Education*, Vol. 41, No. 1 (Winter 1968), pp. 103-10. But even assuming that the girls are merely equally talented, their failure to enter fields other than teaching constitutes a talent loss.

selves as Negro in answer to a specific question asking for racial background.[14] Because the number of Negroes is so small, comparisons between
the employment experience of Negroes and whites are hazardous at best;
however, some of the differences are so striking that they seem worth pre-
senting here, if only to point out that even as recently as five years ago, the
average Negro college graduate could expect much less favorable career experiences than his white fellow graduates.

It is necessary to take into account the fact that most Negro college
graduates included in the 1963 survey were graduates of predominantly Negro colleges, most of them located in the South. These colleges enroll graduates whose high school education is frequently deficient; their college faculty
and programs are weak in many areas, especially in the sciences and engineering. Furthermore, then as now, Negro students failed to enter certain
fields — especially business administration — because of a strong belief in the
continued prevalence of discriminatory practices.[15]

Negro men work somewhat less often on a full-time basis than white men,
although the differences are not very great (Table 4.14). The alternatives for
Negroes are most often part-time work or service in the armed forces; white
men are more often graduate students if they are not in the labor force. For
the women the differences between whites and Negroes are much more
striking: The female Negro graduate is almost twice as likely to be working
full-time. Eighty-three percent of the Negro graduates — compared to 45 percent of the white college women — classified themselves as employed full-
time in 1963. And almost two-thirds of the white women reported themselves
as housewives whereas only 30 percent of the Negro graduates did.

Differences in occupational outcome between Negro and white graduates
are shown in Table 4.15. Employment in engineering and business — which
together accounted for 40 percent of all jobs held by white men — was
reported by only 16 percent of the Negroes. Conversely teaching was a much
more frequent occupation among Negro than among white men. More dis-
tressing is the finding that a higher percentage of Negroes than whites ended
up in nonprofessional occupations, such as semi-skilled, technical, clerical,
and sales jobs.

There is much less of a gap between jobs held by white and Negro women;
both groups are predominantly teachers. In fact the data suggest that Negro
women who are college graduates are somewhat more likely than whites to

[14] There was a fairly large number of respondents (321 men and 56 women) who
failed to answer this question, and we have reason to assume that Negroes constituted
the largest segment of this group; the employment data for this group is very similar to
that reported here for Negroes.

[15] Joseph H. Fichter, *Graduates of Predominantly Negro Colleges, Class of 1964*
(Washington, D. C.: U.S. Government Printing Office, 1967), p. 174.

Table 4.14. Employment Status in 1963 by Student Status and Race
(1958 B.A. Recipients)

*(percentages)*

| Employment Status | Negro | White | Other | No Answer |
|---|---|---|---|---|
| | | **Men** | | |
| Employed full-time | 87.0 | 91.0 | 88.8 | 91.5 |
| Employed part-time | 4.6 | 3.9 | 4.9 | 4.0 |
| Armed forces | 5.6 | 4.2 | 2.1 | 2.8 |
| Unemployed | 1.1 | 0.6 | 0.7 | 0.3 |
| Full-time student | 3.2 | 5.2 | 9.1 | 4.8 |
| Part-time student | 10.9 | 8.6 | 4.9 | 9.4 |
| Retired | 0.4 | 0.6 | – | 1.1 |
| Total percent[a] | 112.8 | 114.1 | 110.5 | 113.9 |
| (Total number) | (284) | (15,515) | (143) | (351) |
| | | **Women** | | |
| Employed full-time | 83.0 | 44.6 | 65.6 | 59.6 |
| Employed part-time | 6.1 | 10.0 | 5.1 | 24.5 |
| Armed forces | – | – | – | – |
| Unemployed | 0.7 | 0.7 | 2.0 | 4.3 |
| Full-time student | 0.5 | 1.4 | – | – |
| Part-time student | 2.7 | 5.7 | 1.0 | 5.3 |
| Housewife | 30.0 | 62.6 | 61.6 | 20.2 |
| Other (retired, armed forces) | 0.4 | 0.6 | – | – |
| Total percent[a] | 123.4 | 125.6 | 135.3 | 113.9 |
| (Total number) | (407) | (8,690) | (99) | (94) |

[a]Percentages add to more than 100 because some graduates reported more than one status.

seek full-fledged professional status: Negro women who did not become teachers were more often in the health field or other professions, such as social work, than white college women. The unmistakable career orientation of female Negro graduates — already suggested by their higher full-time employment rate — is further borne out by these data.

It is often said by government and private spokesmen that the Negro's chief handicap is an educational one, and that he is basically hindered in competing for better jobs because his educational background is inadequate. Comparing the salaries earned by white and Negro graduates after five years in the labor market, it is hard to escape the conclusion that other factors are still at play.

In 1963, the median earnings of Negro men five years out of college was over $2,000 lower than that of the white members of the same cohort — $5,520 as compared to $7,635 (Table 4.16). Of course, this partly reflects the differences in occupations held, but even when comparing salaries within occupations, a constant differential persists. Again, if we had enough cases, we might look at the differences in terms of geographic area (many Negroes are employed in the South) and graduate training (whites were more likely to

Table 4.15.  Full-Time Occupation in 1963 of 1958 B.A. Graduates by Race

*(percentages)*

| Occupation | Negro | White | Other | No Answer | Total |
|---|---|---|---|---|---|
| **Men** | | | | | |
| Natural scientist | 8.1 | 5.9 | 8.7 | 8.1 | 6.0 |
| Engineer | 4.5 | 19.2 | 26.8 | 12.8 | 18.8 |
| Social scientist | 1.2 | 1.1 | 0.8 | 1.9 | 1.1 |
| Humanistic professional | 3.2 | 5.2 | 4.7 | 5.0 | 5.1 |
| Health professional | 5.3 | 5.9 | 6.3 | 3.7 | 5.8 |
| Teacher | 34.8 | 21.2 | 12.6 | 31.2 | 21.6 |
| Business and managerial | 11.7 | 22.1 | 29.1 | 10.3 | 21.7 |
| Other professional | 9.7 | 7.4 | 6.3 | 10.6 | 7.5 |
| Semiskilled and technical | 4.5 | 1.6 | – | 0.9 | 1.6 |
| Clerical and sales | 9.7 | 7.2 | 2.4 | 8.7 | 7.2 |
| Other nonprofessional and no answer | 7.3 | 3.3 | 2.4 | 6.9 | 3.5 |
| Total percent | 100.0 | 100.0 | 100.0 | 100.0 | 99.9 |
| (Total number) | (247) | (14,117) | (12) | (321) | (14,812) |
| **Women** | | | | | |
| Natural scientist | 1.2 | 1.3 | 1.6 | – | 1.2 |
| Engineer | – | 0.4 | – | 1.8 | 0.3 |
| Social scientist | – | 0.8 | – | 1.8 | 0.7 |
| Humanistic professional | 3.0 | 5.6 | 1.6 | 1.8 | 5.3 |
| Health professional | 9.2 | 5.8 | 14.1 | 7.1 | 6.2 |
| Teacher | 64.8 | 67.2 | 67.2 | 78.5 | 67.2 |
| Business and managerial | 0.9 | 3.9 | – | 3.6 | 3.6 |
| Other professional | 12.7 | 5.7 | 4.7 | 3.6 | 6.2 |
| Semiskilled and technical | 1.5 | 2.9 | 6.2 | – | 2.8 |
| Clerical and sales | 1.8 | 4.6 | 1.6 | – | 4.2 |
| Other nonprofessional and no answer | 5.0 | 2.0 | 3.1 | 1.8 | 2.2 |
| Total percent | 100.1 | 100.2 | 100.1 | 100.0 | 99.9 |
| (Total number) | (338) | (3,877) | (64) | (56) | (4,335) |

have done graduate work or obtained an advanced degree). But the magnitude of the gap leaves little doubt that the Negro college graduates still have a long way to go before their rewards equal those of comparably qualified whites — and this despite the spectacular individual breakthroughs that have been much publicized in recent years.

For women, the data in fields other than teaching are very thin (Table 4.16); yet they point in the same direction, except in the health field (mostly nursing), where earnings for Negroes exceeded those for whites. Over-all, the median income in 1963 for Negro women five years out of college was $4,810 compared to $5,520 for Negro men, $5,700 for white women, and $7,635 for white men. These gradations are familiar to those looking at earnings for various groups of Americans. That they should be present among young college graduates is a commentary on the continued presence of selective economic opportunities — by race and sex — in today's world of work.

Table 4.16. Median Salary by Occupation and Race, 1963 (1958 B.A. Recipients)

| Full-Time Occupation | Negroes | | Whites | |
|---|---|---|---|---|
| | Number[a] | Median salary | Number[a] | Median salary |
| **Men** | | | | |
| *Total* | *229[b]* | *$5,520* | *13,558[b]* | *$7,635* |
| Natural scientist | 20 | 6,400 | 828 | 7,990 |
| Engineer | 11 | 9,250 | 2,699 | 9,535 |
| Social scientist | 3 | 5,500 | 158 | 6,940 |
| Humanistic professional | 8 | 5,000 | 720 | 5,720 |
| Health professional | 13 | 6,900 | 820 | 7,320 |
| Teacher | 86 | 5,380 | 2,970 | 6,280 |
| Business and managerial | 29 | 4,710 | 3,104 | 7,880 |
| Other professional | 24 | 5,630 | 1,042 | 7,490 |
| Semiskilled and technical | 11 | 5,170 | 217 | 6,960 |
| Clerical and sales | 24 | 5,560 | 1,000 | 7,900 |
| **Women** | | | | |
| *Total* | *303[b]* | *$4,810* | *3,767[b]* | *$5,700* |
| Natural scientist | 4 | 6,000 | 47 | 7,250 |
| Engineer | – | | 14 | 9,500 |
| Social scientist | – | | 31 | 6,930 |
| Humanistic professional | 10 | 3,630 | 215 | 5,380 |
| Health professional | 31 | 6,170 | 220 | 5,560 |
| Teacher | 202 | 4,590 | 2,583 | 5,740 |
| Business and managerial | 3 | 4,500 | 148 | 5,680 |
| Other professional | 42 | 5,410 | 220 | 6,070 |
| Semiskilled and technical | 5 | 5,250 | 113 | 5,540 |
| Clerical and sales | 6 | 4,000 | 176 | 4,590 |

[a] In order to present all available data, we have deviated in this table from our usual practice of not showing medians for groups of fewer than twenty respondents. Obviously, data for such groups are suggestive rather than authoritative.
[b] Excludes graduates employed in other fields and no answers.

## How Good A Fit between College Learning and Careers?

Since most college graduates find jobs related to their studies, one can assume that they subsequently utilize skills and knowledge acquired in college. This good correspondence between education and job requirements and performance is not surprising. Recent cohorts of college graduates have entered careers under exceptionally propitious conditions. Not only has the economic climate been favorable, but also technical and social changes have put a premium on college education and on those most recently exposed to new knowledge. This is true in the sciences, as well as in education, management, and even the arts and humanities.

How do the graduates themselves judge the suitability of their college learning for job requirements? The 1960 survey concluded that the great majority of B.A. recipients felt that they made considerable use of their college education on their job. There were variations, of course, which can be attributed to the extent to which specific degrees were necessary to qualify for a given job, or the extent to which course material coincided with what was needed on the job. In general, the teachers tended to see the closest connections between their undergraduate background and their job requirements; business majors at work on business or administrative jobs most often saw little or no connection between their education and job.[16]

The 1963 follow-up study tested whether a longer time perspective would lead to different perceptions of the value of a college education. Most likely the 1960 and 1963 responses would be similar, given the relative absence of occupational turnover. However, it was conceivable that a greater value might be placed on college studies because of the more demanding and responsible jobs held three years later by many of the graduates.

The data indicate a slight increase in the proportion of degree-required jobs and a slight decrease in the value put on college-acquired knowledge in relation to job performance. The increase in degree requirement is only partly the result of the decline in nonprofessional employment. More meaningful changes took place, for example, in the business and humanistic professions. Although many respondents in these occupations still report that a degree is not really required to perform their job, there is a marked decline in this negative response over the three-year period. In 1960, 39 percent of the men in humanistic professions and 29 percent of the businessmen thought that a degree was not necessary; three years later, the respective proportion was 23 percent for each group. It is not unreasonable to assume that this shift is related to professional advancement of many men in these occupations over the three years. Of course, one can also not rule out greater rationalization over the time span.

The experiences of the M.A. group reconfirm the finding that the importance of the graduate degree varies by occupation. The utility of graduate studies is rated very high in all fields, but most highly in the social sciences, followed by the natural sciences. It will be recalled that in the social sciences, undergraduate training seldom led to jobs in a related field, whereas men with undergraduate degrees in one of the natural sciences often found employment as natural scientists and were able to progress in this occupation without obtaining a graduate degree. Our data thus suggest that natural scientists – and to a lesser degree teachers – most often find high convergence between undergraduate studies, graduate studies, and employment. It is clearly in these two fields that educational preparation at all levels and pro-

---

[16]Bureau of Social Science Research, *Two Years After the College Degree: Work and Further Study Patterns* (Washington, D. C.: U.S. Government Printing Office, 1963), pp. 54-62.

fessional requirements have achieved the highest level of congruence, as judged from the reports of recent graduates.

At the other end of the continuum are the two fields where the relationship between higher education and professional work seems more marginal — business administration and engineering. Even here, successful integration is more often the rule than the exception. Thus almost everywhere higher education and the professional world seem to be meshing and functioning hand-in-glove, which emphasizes that they are not separate watertight compartments in the lives of our college graduates.

The growing cooperation between the academic world and the world of work — for example, the spread of contract research on campus and the consulting roles of professors in industry and government — is often thought to interfere with the orderly process of education. More likely, the advantages of these arrangements outweigh the disadvantages in terms of improving the professional preparations of many students, and providing the linkages that are needed for updating the educational scene.

In areas where the fit between education and job requirements is poorer, such as business and engineering, there is a greater tendency for offering noninstitutional training, usually given in an employment setting. The need for this training no doubt arises precisely because of the less adequate fit between formal preparation and job requirements in these fields. Specialized education in nonacademic institutions is becoming a fairly widespread practice: In the B.A. group, 37 percent of the men and 25 percent of the women took such courses within five years after graduating. The basic reason for this development is the growing technical complexities and the high degree of specialization that characterizes both scientific and nonscientific fields.

But one can also speculate that training in noninstitutional settings is of particular interest to students who do not undertake graduate studies, either because they do not have access to graduate schools or because they found their undergraduate program difficult or troublesome. Our data show that those who had never been graduate degree students more often had some additional nonacademic training, in contrast to those graduates who went on for another degree.[17]

## Job Stability

One might have expected recent college graduates to change jobs quite often during the first few years in search of the right niche. And although this seems especially likely during periods of prosperity and opportunity, as were

[17]Similar findings for a sample of engineers and scientists are found in Seymour Warkov and John Marsh, *The Education and Training of American Scientists and Engineers: 1962* (Chicago: National Opinion Research Center, 1965), p. 145.

the early 1960's, it is not the case with our cohort of graduates. Five years after college graduation, a high proportion of the young men and women in our cohort were well established in their career fields. This pattern of stability is measured in terms of job and occupational retention (Table 4.17). Over the three-year period between our two surveys in 1960 and 1963, the overwhelming majority of students did not change their occupation.

In this respect, cohorts of college graduates who have entered the labor market in recent years exhibit very similar behavior. A recent study of the class of 1961 also singles out early occupational stability as characteristic of this cohort.[18] Although there is a fair amount of job changing and experimentation in the early career stages, for a surprisingly large number of persons the first occupational commitment is apparently a very meaningful career decision.

Occupations that are professional at the bachelor level show a greater holding power than occupations requiring graduate or professional study, or those that are professionally marginal. For men, the highest retention rates are in engineering (84 percent), health professions (83 percent), and teaching (80 percent). Among natural and social scientists, many of whom go on to graduate school, there is considerable turnover; only 59 percent of the natural scientists and 30 percent of the social scientists remained in their field. This highlights the occupational marginality of social scientists without a graduate degree.

Because so many women move out of the labor force, it appears that they are much less occupationally stable than men. The highest retention is in teaching; 57 percent of those who taught in 1960 were still in this work in 1963. Only 39 percent of the teachers left the labor force over this three-year period, while close to half of the women in almost every other field stopped working.

The high level of occupational stability is also suggested by long-range career plans. A majority — 83 percent of the men and 71 percent of the women — indicated a continuing commitment to their occupation. Only those graduates in semiprofessional, technical, clerical, and sales jobs expected to change occupations to a noteworthy degree.

This stability is noted not only for occupations but also for place of employment. Over half of the graduates had both the same occupation and employer in 1960 and 1963. The most stable groups were engineers and teachers: 64 percent of the engineers and 60 percent of the teachers stayed with their employers over the three-year period. But employer shifts do

[18] Joe L. Spaeth and Norman Miller, *Trends in the Career Plans and Activities of June 1961 College Graduates* (Chicago: National Opinion Research Center, March 1965), p. 62.

not represent changes in occupation; they often merely involve a change in working conditions, location, or salary.

Table 4.17. Occupational Retention, 1960-63 (1958 B.A. Recipients)

*(percentages)*

| 1963 Occupation | Total | 1960 Occupation | | | | | | | | | | | |
|---|---|---|---|---|---|---|---|---|---|---|---|---|---|
| | | Natural scientist | Engineer | Social scientist | Humanistic professional | Health professional | Teacher | Business and managerial | Other professional | Semiprofessional | Clerical and sales | Other nonprofessional and no answer | Not employed full-time in 1960 |
| **Men** | | | | | | | | | | | | | |
| Natural scientist | 5.4 | *58.5* | 1.2 | 1.2 | 0.5 | 0.7 | 1.3 | 1.3 | 1.9 | 9.7 | 1.3 | 5.8 | 6.8 |
| Engineer | 17.1 | 8.9 | *83.9* | 9.3 | 2.2 | 2.0 | 0.6 | 5.6 | 6.7 | 10.9 | 2.0 | 11.9 | 8.6 |
| Social scientist | 1.0 | 0.7 | 0.1 | *30.2* | 1.0 | 1.0 | 0.8 | 0.4 | 0.5 | 2.4 | 0.2 | 1.1 | 1.6 |
| Humanistic professional | 4.7 | 0.2 | 0.4 | – | *67.1* | 0.3 | 2.8 | 0.6 | 2.4 | 2.9 | 1.5 | 2.7 | 6.7 |
| Health professional | 5.3 | 2.0 | – | – | 0.5 | *83.4* | 0.3 | 0.2 | – | 4.1 | 1.6 | 1.6 | 10.7 |
| Teacher | 19.6 | 3.6 | 1.1 | – | 4.2 | 3.3 | *79.7* | 5.3 | 12.9 | 5.6 | 3.7 | 10.8 | 12.9 |
| Business and managerial | 19.7 | 5.7 | 5.4 | 27.9 | 9.6 | 3.0 | 3.9 | *70.5* | 8.1 | 10.4 | 32.8 | 19.7 | 11.9 |
| Other professional | 6.8 | 4.3 | 1.0 | 11.6 | 2.2 | 0.7 | 1.0 | 1.4 | *48.1* | 11.4 | 3.2 | 15.0 | 14.2 |
| Semiprofessional | 1.4 | 2.0 | 0.3 | – | 1.0 | – | 0.4 | 0.2 | 1.9 | *18.4* | 0.7 | 4.7 | 1.6 |
| Clerical and sales | 6.6 | 2.6 | 1.6 | 3.5 | 2.9 | 1.0 | 1.2 | 7.7 | 5.2 | 6.1 | *46.3* | 1.6 | 4.3 |
| Other nonprofessional and no answer | 3.2 | 5.6 | 2.1 | 7.0 | 2.2 | 0.7 | 1.1 | 3.3 | 8.6 | 10.7 | 2.8 | *19.0* | 2.1 |
| Not employed full-time in 1963 | 9.1 | 6.1 | 3.0 | 9.3 | 6.6 | 4.0 | 6.9 | 3.5 | 3.8 | 7.5 | 3.9 | 6.1 | *18.6* |
| Total percent | 99.9 | 100.2 | 100.1 | 100.0 | 100.0 | 100.1 | 100.0 | 100.0 | 100.1 | 100.1 | 100.0 | 100.0 | 100.0 |
| (Total number) | (16,293) | (609) | (2,361) | (86) | (408) | (302) | (2,752) | (2,472) | (210) | (413) | (1,117) | (554) | (5,009) |
| **Women** | | | | | | | | | | | | | |
| Natural scientist | 0.6 | *17.5* | – | 4.8 | – | 0.4 | 0.1 | – | – | 3.7 | 0.7 | – | 0.3 |
| Engineer | 0.2 | 3.5 | *45.5* | – | 0.4 | – | – | – | 0.5 | – | 0.2 | – | 0.1 |
| Social scientist | 0.3 | 0.9 | – | *19.0* | 0.4 | – | 0.1 | 2.9 | 0.5 | 2.3 | 0.2 | – | 0.2 |
| Humanistic professional | 2.5 | 0.9 | – | 4.8 | *26.8* | 0.4 | 1.4 | 2.9 | 5.9 | 6.9 | 3.7 | – | 1.4 |
| Health professional | 2.9 | – | – | – | 0.4 | *31.2* | 0.7 | – | 0.5 | 11.2 | 0.2 | – | 1.8 |
| Teacher | 31.3 | 6.1 | 9.1 | – | 13.4 | 8.6 | *56.5* | 6.8 | 4.5 | 2.9 | 10.4 | 33.3 | 11.6 |
| Business and managerial | 1.7 | – | – | – | 3.0 | 0.4 | 0.4 | *29.3* | 3.6 | 1.4 | 7.2 | – | 0.7 |
| Other professional | 2.9 | 5.3 | 18.2 | 23.8 | – | 7.8 | 0.9 | 2.9 | *30.2* | 0.3 | 1.7 | 4.5 | 3.3 |
| Semiprofessional | 1.3 | 5.3 | – | – | – | 1.7 | 0.1 | 0.5 | 0.9 | *21.8* | 1.1 | – | 0.7 |
| Clerical and sales | 2.0 | – | – | 4.8 | 0.9 | – | 0.4 | 5.4 | 3.2 | 1.4 | *21.2* | – | 1.0 |
| Other nonprofessional and no answer | 1.0 | 0.9 | – | 4.8 | 4.8 | 0.4 | 0.5 | 1.0 | 4.1 | 1.7 | 0.4 | *27.3* | 0.7 |
| Not employed full-time in 1963 | 53.3 | 59.6 | 27.3 | 38.1 | 49.8 | 48.9 | 38.8 | 48.3 | 46.4 | 46.3 | 53.0 | 34.8 | *78.2* |
| Total percent | 100.0 | 100.0 | 100.1 | 100.1 | 99.9 | 99.8 | 99.9 | 100.0 | 100.3 | 99.9 | 100.0 | 99.9 | 100.0 |
| (Total number) | (9,290) | (114) | (11) | (21) | (231) | (464) | (4,235) | (205) | (222) | (348) | (538) | (66) | (2,835) |

Women show a greater degree of occupational stability than men (83 percent of the women versus 74 percent of the men remained in the same occupation), yet they tend to change employers more frequently than men. This might be explained by the fact that so many women in our cohort entered the teaching profession at the elementary school level and then moved within the profession to different school systems or to higher teaching positions. Additionally, there are indications that some women teachers from small towns move to larger areas for their first teaching job after college and then move again to school systems in smaller communities.

There is also a high degree of projected stability with respect to type of employer, according to our findings. Close to three-quarters of the men and two-thirds of the women expected to spend the major part of their working life with the type of employer with whom they were associated in 1963; this was true in industry and government, as well as educational or nonprofit institutions. Men who anticipated changes often looked forward to self-employment. However, in conformity with the American experience in the past few decades, our cohort indicates that self-employment is not a popular mode of earning one's living. Five years after college graduation, less than 4 percent of the men and 1 percent of the women were self-employed. Most of the projected changes to self-employment will be in the health fields, where it is often an automatic step as soon as full professional status is reached. The big change for women most often will be to leave the labor force.

Another indication that these graduates are well established in their occupations is their high income level. In 1963, the median salaries for full-time employed men and women B.A. recipients were $7,570 and $5,660, respectively (Table 4.12). These median salaries reflect a large increase since 1960 — 38 percent for men and 31 percent for women. Although these figures may now appear low since they are more than five years old, they were quite impressive in terms of prevailing income levels among the older college-educated population.[19] It should also be remembered that not all of the graduates were in the labor force for a total of five years after college, owing to military service and graduate school attendance.

Substantial income differentials characterize college graduates in the various occupations, with teachers near the bottom of the scale and male engineers at the top. The initial differential between occupations tends to be

[19] It is difficult to make valid comparisons between these salaries and those of older members of the college-educated population since the occupational mix has changed considerably over the years. A crude comparison can be made with the census category of "professional, technical and kindred workers," which includes persons without a college education. In 1963, the median income in this group was $7,182 for men and $4,163 for women. See U.S., Bureau of the Census, *Current Population Reports* (Series p-60, No. 43; Washington, D. C.: U.S. Department of Commerce, September 29, 1964).

maintained throughout the years. Generally speaking, the gap neither grows nor narrows.[20]

Although it appears that a high proportion of B.A. holders who enter the labor force are well on their way toward life-time careers, professional commitment and career stabilization take a firmer hold five years after the master's.

Statements about long-range occupational plans are chiefly of interest as indicators of the mood of stability and continuity that seems to characterize college graduates who reach the occupational world. Unplanned or unforeseen changes are bound to occur, of course, but it appears that the period of uncertainty and experimentation so characteristic of the undergraduate years — as evidenced by frequent changes in field of study — has been left behind by these graduates. The assumption of adult status seems to minimize the incentive, or even the freedom, to consider major occupational changes.

Perhaps preoccupation with further study and family formation influences this generation to reduce the upheavals created by job changes in the early career stages. Additionally, the recent graduates might see little to be gained, financially or otherwise, from shifting among employers once they have made a well-anchored preference for specific types of work. High incomes clearly are not the result of frequent employer-hopping in search of higher salaries; for example, engineers are both the best paid and most stable employees.

There is also the problem of success-induced inertia. Given the unprecedented and growing opportunities for well-educated young men and women and the rapid promotions often associated with even a few years of experience, a career change early in life represents a much greater sacrifice for many members of this generation than it did years ago when there were fewer rewards and opportunities for young graduates. Shifts will occur, of course, if only as a result of the constantly changing technology and occupational structure that characterize the American economy. But chances are that most of these shifts will occur within narrower occupational realms and more specialized sectors than was the case in the past.

### Geographic Mobility[21]

As the class of 1958 seeks its place in the job world, we see that they conform to the basic United States population movement patterns — into metropolitan areas and into regions of industrial growth.

---

[20]Additional earnings for summer jobs and part-time second jobs, frequently reported by teachers, help to narrow but fail to close the gap.

[21]The relationship between geographic mobility and early occupational and educational careers, while of interest to our study, was not its prime focus. Residential change was observed at only three time points (after high school graduation, at the time of the

Among the men, the most mobile members of the cohort are the human-istic professionals, such as performers, clergymen, writers, and artists. In second place are natural scientists, followed by engineers and social scientists. The mobility for these men can partially be attributed to their tendency to go to graduate school, which in itself often entails mobility. Least mobile are those in business and managerial positions. In fact, change of residence to a different state or city size is least frequent among graduates working in busi-ness and clerical jobs (see Table 4.18). Out-of-state moves were reported by

Table 4.18. Full-Time Occupation and Mobility of College Graduates (1958 B.A. Recipients)

|                                       | Men     |                           | Women  |                           |
|---------------------------------------|---------|---------------------------|--------|---------------------------|
| Occupation                            | Number  | Percent movers[a]         | Number | Percent movers[a]         |
| *Total*                               | *14,812* | *75.7*                   | *4,332* | *75.6*                   |
| Natural scientist                     | 887     | 84.6                      | 54     | 74.1                      |
| Engineer                              | 2,792   | 82.6                      | 15     | 86.7                      |
| Social scientist                      | 169     | 80.5                      | 32     | 87.5                      |
| Humanistic professional               | 761     | 89.2                      | 228    | 75.0                      |
| Health professional                   | 861     | 77.7                      | 267    | 79.4                      |
| Teacher                               | 3,195   | 76.4                      | 2,912  | 75.0                      |
| Business and managerial               | 3,213   | 66.6                      | 153    | 79.7                      |
| Other professional                    | 1,113   | 73.3                      | 269    | 79.9                      |
| Semiprofessional                      | 233     | 69.5                      | 122    | 71.3                      |
| Clerical and sales                    | 1,073   | 71.8                      | 184    | 65.8                      |
| Other nonprofessional and no answer   | 515     | 66.6                      | 96     | 87.5                      |

[a]"Movers" are those who changed residence between high school graduation (1954 or earlier) and 1963, residing in different states or cities of different sizes during this period.

fewer than half of the men who had majored in business, education, or one of the health fields (see Table 4.19).

For women, the patterns are slightly different: Engineers and social scien-tists are the movers, followed by other professionals, such as lawyers, social workers, and dieticians. It should be noted that the mobility of women graduates often is related to other variables, particularly marital status, which may be more crucial than occupation.

As these young college graduates move, they tend to concentrate in selected areas of the country. This concentration, however, does not differ to any great extent from the migration patterns of the rest of the population.

first post-college job, and in 1963), and emphasis was on regional rather than interstate or intrastate mobility. These limitations, no doubt, lead to an understatement of the total amount of geographic mobility experienced by young college graduates.

Table 4.19. Change of State Residence by Undergraduate Major Field (1958 B.A. Recipients)

*(percentages)*

| Undergraduate Major Field | Change of State Residence[a] | | | | | |
|---|---|---|---|---|---|---|
| | Men | | | Women | | |
| | Number | Same state | Different state | Number | Same state | Different state |
| *Total* | *16,293* | *45.0* | *55.0* | *9,290* | *47.5* | *52.5* |
| Natural sciences | 2,607 | 36.0 | 64.0 | 803 | 42.2 | 57.8 |
| Engineering | 3,128 | 35.6 | 64.4 | 45 | 46.7 | 53.3 |
| Social sciences | 3,070 | 46.5 | 53.5 | 1,417 | 43.5 | 56.5 |
| Humanities and arts | 1,743 | 41.5 | 58.5 | 2,014 | 40.6 | 59.4 |
| Health | 302 | 57.0 | 43.0 | 676 | 43.8 | 56.2 |
| Business and commerce | 3,287 | 52.9 | 47.1 | 478 | 50.2 | 49.8 |
| Education | 1,612 | 57.4 | 42.6 | 3,239 | 54.2 | 45.8 |
| Other | 544 | 54.4 | 45.6 | 618 | 53.2 | 46.8 |

[a]State residence at time of high school graduation (1954 or earlier) was compared with state residence in 1963.

This does not mean that there were no differences. This cohort merely presents a slightly inflated version of what happened to the United States as a whole in terms of population movement.

At high school graduation — 1954 for most members of this cohort — the largest proportion of the class of 1958 lived in the Mid-Atlantic and East North Central regions of the country. This was still the case in 1963, although the proportion had become slightly smaller. By 1963, the net migration was out of the Northeast and into the Pacific and South Atlantic regions.

The graduates became increasingly more urban with the passage of time, more so than the total population. But movement was not all in the direction of ever-increasing concentration in the largest metropolitan areas. There was a move from the very large centers to those of lesser size. This was especially true of men in the humanities, engineering, and natural sciences. It is possible that some of these graduates were employed as teachers at colleges in smaller cities; engineers might be employed in industries located in smaller communities, which is a growing trend. Both academic and economic opportunity — and perhaps the prospect of more pleasant living conditions — clearly attract some of those who grew up in the super-cities to urban areas of less formidable size.[22] Additional moves are noted overseas. Compared to 1960 more than double the number of men and women were living

[22]One must realize that we are dealing here with crude measures. If a graduate lived in a city of a million or more in population at high school graduation and changed to a smaller city, he may still be living in a major center with a total area population of 500,000 to one million.

abroad by 1963. This primarily reflects military and civilian foreign assignments and Peace Corps service.

Although college graduates are obviously highly mobile, our findings suggest much greater regional retention of the highly educated segment of the population than is often assumed by those who talk about the mobility of this group of Americans. When geographic movement is measured by regional shifts, the extent of mobility is much lower. Fewer than 40 percent of the graduates moved from the region in which they were living at high school graduation to another region within five years after college graduation. Although many graduates (54 percent) made interstate moves, the majority did not make a regional move.

The most significant gains are in the Pacific region, which retained the largest proportion of its own graduates and attracted the highest proportion of in-migrants. Eighty-two percent of the men and 88 percent of the women graduates who graduated from high school in this region were still living there in 1963. No doubt, this retention can be attributed to the low-cost college system in California (in 1963, 93 percent of all California residents enrolled in colleges were studying in California), as well as to job opportunities and the power of attraction of the Pacific climate and way of life.

Although movement to the Pacific was popular, regional changes usually involved a move to an adjacent region, rather than a transcontinental shift. New Englanders moved to the Middle Atlantic, and Middle Atlantic residents moved to regions adjacent on all sides — New England, East North Central, and South Atlantic. Even the magnetic Pacific region attracted proportionately more of its in-migrants from the near-by central and mountain states than from the East Coast (see Appendix Table P).

Thus, the widely held stereotype of the highly mobile college graduate who moves easily from New York to Texas or from Georgia to Seattle in response to job opportunities is probably a good description of some segments of the college population: specialized engineers, scientists, writers, or college teachers. But it does not describe the bulk of this population — teachers, those working for business and financial institutions, and many of those in the health or legal professions.[23] While the dominant pattern is indeed one of mobility, it is a mobility to a different city or an adjoining state rather than half-way across the country. The selective migration and mobility among the higher educated Americans has important social and political implications that will be touched upon in the concluding section.

---

[23] For parallel observations about variations in mobility and an interesting typology of professions in relation to migration, see Jack Landinsky, "The Geographic Mobility of Professional and Technical Manpower," *The Journal of Human Resources*, Vol. 2 (Fall 1967), pp. 475-94.

## Career Satisfactions

Career stability and continued commitment to the current occupation and employer emerged as a characteristic of this cohort. We feel that this stability is integrally related to the close fit between education and job.

However, one might ask: Is this stability rooted in positive feelings of satisfaction with the occupations selected and the employment situations encountered? Or is it a somewhat inert reaction, a feeling that the die has been cast and there is not much to be done about it given today's specialized labor market for graduates? In a recent study of Detroit factory workers, the great majority of men in all age and skill groups said they were well satisfied with their jobs. Yet more subtle research instruments and careful analysis led the researchers to the conclusion that many of these workers actually suffered very considerable work-related frustrations that had a marked effect on the level of mental health of the group.[24] Conceivably some of the same findings would emerge for our college cohort if more thorough tests were applied.

However, judging from our studies there is enough evidence to infer that the majority of respondents express stable career interest and occupational loyalty because their jobs satisfy many of their basic values and aspirations. These findings were yielded by a set of job satisfaction/dissatisfaction items used in our survey.[25]

Table 4.20 shows the satisfactory and unsatisfactory aspects of the current job held by the men and women in our survey and how each of these items ranked in terms of its importance to respondents. Although this table is only a crude juxtaposition (it does not show how the three categories were related), the correspondence between satisfaction and value items is evident.

The item selected as the most satisfactory aspect of the job — opportunity to do interesting work — is also the most important career objective. Con-

[24] Arthur Kornhauser, *Mental Health of the Industrial Worker* (New York: John Wiley & Sons, Inc., 1965).

[25] Most of the items selected to measure career values and job satisfactions/dissatisfactions have been adapted from the Cornell Value List developed to measure student values. They fall into three broad categories:

*Self-expression values,* which are goal values with respect to the nature of the work as an end in itself, i.e., work affording opportunity to use one's talents and be creative.

*People-oriented values,* in which the rewards of work consist primarily of opportunities for gratification from interpersonal relations, i.e., opportunity to be helpful to others and to work with people rather than things.

*Extrinsic-reward oriented values,* in which the job is viewed as an instrument for the end of obtaining certain rewards in exchange for one's work, i.e., money or a secure future.

See Rose K. Goldsen *et al., What College Students Think* (Princeton, N. J.: D. Van Nostrand Company, Inc., 1960), and, in particular, Morris Rosenberg, "Choosing a Career," *Occupations and Values* (Glencoe, Ill.: The Free Press, 1957).

Table 4.20.  Career Values and Most and Least Satisfactory Aspects of Current Job
(1958 B.A. Recipients)

*(percentages)*

| Career Values | Chose Item As "Most Satisfactory Aspect of My Job" | | Chose Item as "Least Satisfactory Aspect of My Job" | | Chose Item as "Most Important in Relation to Career Objectives" | |
|---|---|---|---|---|---|---|
| | Men (N=14,812) | Women (N=4,335) | Men | Women | Men | Women |
| *Self-Expression Oriented* | | | | | | |
| Opportunity to do really interesting work | 23.7 | 17.6 | 3.4 | 3.8 | 20.6 | 21.2 |
| Opportunity to use my special talents and abilities | 6.7 | 8.3 | 2.1 | 2.7 | 7.9 | 9.6 |
| Opportunity to use what I learned in college | 1.6 | 2.1 | 3.3 | 2.1 | 1.2 | 1.8 |
| Opportunity to do original and creative work | 4.5 | 3.1 | 5.6 | 4.2 | 5.3 | 3.7 |
| Be free from supervision in my work | 3.1 | 1.0 | 2.6 | 2.5 | 1.2 | 0.5 |
| Opportunity to pursue further studies | 1.4 | 0.9 | 4.6 | 2.7 | 2.3 | 2.5 |
| Opportunity to improve my professional competence | 3.9 | 1.6 | 2.0 | 1.4 | 5.6 | 3.3 |
| *People-Oriented* | | | | | | |
| Opportunity to be helpful to others and to society | 11.9 | 25.1 | 2.8 | 1.0 | 8.5 | 16.5 |
| Opportunity to work with people rather than with things | 8.0 | 14.8 | 1.0 | 0.9 | 4.6 | 7.2 |
| *Extrinsic-Reward Oriented* | | | | | | |
| Yielding a good income | 13.0 | 10.3 | 17.3 | 14.3 | 16.5 | 9.7 |
| Opportunity to travel | 1.0 | 1.3 | 9.2 | 13.9 | 0.4 | 1.8 |
| Opportunity to function in a supervisory capacity | 3.2 | 0.7 | 5.0 | 3.9 | 4.9 | 1.2 |
| Opportunity to get ahead rapidly | 3.0 | 0.2 | 8.9 | 9.8 | 4.4 | 1.3 |
| Enable me to look forward to a stable, secure future | 6.5 | 3.3 | 3.9 | 2.1 | 6.2 | 6.1 |
| Have enough time for my family, my outside interests and my hobbies | 2.7 | 2.7 | 15.0 | 18.2 | 2.6 | 3.4 |
| No Answer | 5.7 | 7.0 | 12.2 | 16.5 | 7.8 | 10.3 |

versely, high dissatisfaction items, such as insufficient time for family and outside interests or inadequate opportunity to travel, have low salience with respect to career importance. We know from other studies that for persons in professional and managerial occupations, intrinsic values (interesting work, use of one's talent or training) are the more important ones in determining job satisfaction.[26] It appears, therefore, that the impression suggested by the data — of considerable satisfaction with the jobs held — is solidly rooted.

[26] See, for example, Richard Centers and Daphne E. Bugental, "Intrinsic and Extrinsic Job Motivations Among Different Segments of the Working Population," *Journal of Applied Psychology* (June 1966), pp. 193-97, and Norman M. Bradburn and David Caplovitz, *Reports on Happiness* (Chicago: Aldine Publishing Company, 1965), pp. 34-41.

Although income is not as central a value for most professionals, it still ranks high. This is probably because, for the professional, income is also a common measure for recognition and esteem. Not surprisingly, data obtained in the surveys relating to income are ambiguous. For men, income ranks high in career importance, high as a satisfactory job aspect, and even higher as an unsatisfactory aspect of the job. Income is obviously the main area where there is a conflict between aspiration and the limitations encountered in a chosen field, especially in the early stages of one's career. However, we feel that while dissatisfaction with income might lead to a shift in employer, most of the respondents will see little need to change occupations since their work remains basically congenial and satisfactory.

The expected differences in the job-related value systems between men and women are apparent in our analysis. The interpersonal aspects of a job, in terms of career values and objectives, are twice as important for women than for men. These values include the opportunity to be helpful to others and to society, and the opportunity to work with people. Women's greater emphasis on interpersonal factors is a standard finding of value studies. Our study shows that even women scientists – presumably less people-oriented than other professional women – rate these factors higher than their male colleagues.

Although income is a less dominant career objective for women than men, women – like men – are apt to measure their success in relation to pay. Women see low pay as an important source of dissatisfaction, second only to not having enough time for one's family and outside interests. In this respect, the rankings of men and women follow the same pattern.

The congruence between occupational values and job satisfaction (or dissatisfaction) appears much sharper when looking at the profiles of specific occupations (Appendix Table N).

*Engineers*

About 60 percent of this group selected one of the following items as the most important career objective: the opportunity to do really interesting work, good income, the opportunity to function in a supervisory capacity, and the opportunity to improve one's professional competence. Almost the same proportion chose those items as the most satisfactory aspect of the current job, thus showing a high degree of congruence between aspirations and attributes of the job held. But this did not hold true throughout the group. It appears that dissatisfaction is associated with lack of supervisory responsibility and lack of opportunity to get ahead, both of which are fairly important to the group. From these data, the tendency of engineers to defect from the field can be explained in terms of their seeking extrinsic work rewards, particularly the opportunity to attain executive responsibilities which are usually found in managerial positions.

*Natural Scientists*

The dominant values for this group are associated with creative talent — the opportunity to do interesting, creative, and original work. Supervisory responsibility and the opportunity to get ahead rapidly are of little importance. In most respects, this group is well pleased with the jobs held. Negative votes, however, are concentrated on income, which may explain the shift into industrial employment by a minority of the natural scientists.

*Social Scientists*

This profile is similar to that for natural scientists, but there is a greater emphasis on the people-oriented nature of the work (opportunity to be helpful to others and society, working with people rather than things). Current jobs seem to satisfy this to a considerable degree. Also of interest and satisfaction to this group are the intrinsic aspects of work, such as job interest, creativity, and the use of one's special talent. While income is more often a source of dissatisfaction for them than for any other group except teachers, none of the other extrinsic rewards rank high among the career values of social scientists.

*Humanistic Occupations*

This group, which includes creative artists as well as clergymen, emphasizes both creative and people-oriented values. Since these values seem to be amply satisfied, the prospects of professional defection are minimal. This group ranked income lower in terms of career values than any other group of professionals.

*Teaching*

This is the only group where dissatisfaction focuses on a single item: income. Nearly 40 percent of the male teachers expressed dissatisfaction with their salaries. For women income was not as important as their concern with advancement and supervisory opportunity; this concern was more evident for teachers than for other professional women, perhaps because of their greater long-term career commitment.

*Business and Administrative Occupations*

Men in this group rank income as the most important career objective, followed by opportunity to do interesting work. In general, they find their jobs satisfactory. Businesswomen, however, are more concerned with having interesting work, and many feel that their jobs may be lacking in the opportunity to do creative and original work.

In brief, the job satisfaction/dissatisfaction items indicate that in the great majority of cases, these college graduates had jobs that were congruent with their values. One is led to conclude that these men and women will find little occasion to reject the occupation they have entered in their early careers. This belief is further strengthened by data pertaining to the older men and women who were holders of the master's degree in 1958. At the master's level, there is a strengthening of professionally relevant values, and a corresponding decline in nonrelevant values. With higher educational achievement, the opportunity to do original and creative work becomes more important. Most interesting in this respect is the decline in the importance rating of income. Only businessmen, for whom this is the approved professional norm, showed an increase in the proportion choosing this answer between the B.A. and M.A. level.

Furthermore, the jobs held by the master's group turn out to be uniformly more satisfactory with respect to important career objectives than at the B.A. level (Appendix Table O). For example, 9 percent of the B.A. natural scientists said the most satisfactory aspect of their job was the opportunity to do original and creative work; 11 percent chose this as the most important career objective. The corresponding choices among M.A. natural scientists were 19 percent for the most satisfactory aspect of the job, 15 percent for the most important career objective. In every occupation, a higher proportion of the master's group than the bachelor's group felt that the best feature of their job was that it provided the opportunity to do really interesting work. The smallest increment in this category from B.A. to M.A. levels was found among the engineers.

Deviations from the general pattern are found chiefly among the teachers. A smaller percentage of the master's group than the bachelor's chose people-oriented responses as satisfactory career objectives. A possible explanation is that, at the M.A. level, the teacher category includes a good many administrators who are less oriented toward the interpersonal aspect of this work than are classroom teachers.

## Conclusions

It appears that graduates today are fairly able to get into the jobs that correspond to their preferences, values, and aspirations. The main impression conveyed by the employment histories was that of a thoroughly professionalized and occupationally committed group. Their primary ambitions are not for material rewards or rapid advancement; neither are they concerned about a secure future, which they obviously take for granted. They seek to make a good living while performing interesting, useful, and responsible work, as well as having time for study and family life. To some extent the data foreshadow some of the more extreme attitudes which seem to characterize more recent cohorts of college students, who put increasing emphasis on nonmaterial work rewards and show great concern with developing a life style and professional commitment in line with a diminished belief in the virtues of a competitive society.

This does not mean that areas of conflict do not exist, or will not emerge in the future. Teachers, for example, are dissatisfied with their low rank on the income scale. Engineers would like to have better opportunities for advancement, and social scientists complain about the limited opportunities to do original or creative work in the early stage of their careers. But because the occupations selected by the majority of graduates appear to satisfy their basic values and aspirations, it seems likely that they will seek to improve their employment situations rather than seek new careers.

# V

---

## THE ROLE OF MILITARY SERVICE
## IN THE CAREERS OF COLLEGE GRADUATES

**B**eginning with World War II, the nexus between college careers and military service has been a strong one. On the one hand, unprecedented numbers of young men who otherwise might not have been able to do so received a free college education as a result of veterans benefits. On the other hand, graduates eager to enter upon orderly civilian careers found their plans disrupted by military service. Fear of the draft also affected the timing of graduate studies, which until 1968 usually led to draft deferment.

Although military service considerations were perhaps not as salient for the class of 1958 as they were for subsequent cohorts who graduated after the outbreak of the Vietnam war, our data provided unusual opportunities for an exploration of the interaction between service in the armed forces and subsequent life-cycle events. Through the experiences of our 1958 cohort of male college graduates,[1] we analyzed the effects of military service on career development, occupational interests, graduate school enrollment, degree attainment, marital status, and parenthood. Our purpose was to determine the extent to which military service makes either a positive or negative contribution to career development.

The regulations governing military service that affected this cohort are found in the Selective Service Act of 1948 and the Universal Military Training and Service Act of 1951. According to these laws, all men eighteen and one-half to twenty-six years of age were candidates for military service for two years. The exceptions to these rules, however, tend to cloud the picture. In addition to student deferments, there were some sixty programs in various

---

[1] This is based on the experiences of 15,365 men. It excludes 938 men from the total group because they did not give complete information.

branches of the armed forces that were available to the young men in this cohort. These programs may alter the pattern of time spent in the service and affect life patterns accordingly. For example, one plan, established by the Reserve Forces Act of 1955, calls for a six-month training period; this is followed by participation in reserve meetings and duties for a specific number of years. In this program, only a six-month block of time is devoted to actual military service. The interruption of civilian life and career development is minimized, although one's military obligation is fulfilled. No doubt, this Reserve plan was attractive to some of the men in the 1958 sample, but because of data collection procedures we were not able to separate them from other enlisted men who served two years or less.

A sizable percentage of the men in our survey probably benefited from the GI Bill of Rights. This Bill made available one and one-half months of educational training (not to exceed thirty-six months) for every month of service for veterans of World War II and the Korean conflict. The GI Bill was in effect up to 1955, one year after most of the 1958 graduates entered college.

### Early, Late, and Nonservers

With respect to military service, the men in our survey divided rather neatly into three groups. Slightly more than one-third served in the armed forces before they obtained their college degree; after graduation in 1958, they entered the civilian work force. Another third received a bachelor's degree in 1958, completed military service after graduating, and then began civilian careers. The final third had not served in the armed forces at the time of the study in 1963; after graduating from college in 1958, these men either went on to graduate study or entered the labor force (Table 5.1). Of course as sketched here, these are pure types of life situations. In actuality there were considerable variations; no doubt, there are men in the survey whose lives followed less orderly patterns. Some of these men may have interrupted their

Table 5.1. Military Experience of 1958 Male College Graduates (1958 B.A. Recipients)

| Service History | Number | | Percent | |
|---|---|---|---|---|
| Never in service | 5,217 | | 34.0 | |
| Pre-1958 | 5,569 | | 36.2 | |
|    Enlisted men | | 5,133 | | 33.4 |
|    Officers | | 436 | | 2.8 |
| Post-1958 | 4,579 | | 29.8 | |
|    Enlisted men | | 2,231 | | 14.5 |
|    Officers | | 2,348 | | 15.3 |
|      Total | 15,365 | | 100.0 | |

college education before graduation, enrolled for military service midway through college, and subsequently gone back to obtain their degrees. However, we feel that most of the men's lives are described by the three basic types.

In general, the early servers were older, academically less talented, and more settled in family situations. They spend more time in the service and were more undecided about career choices when they entered the service. Those who went into the military after receiving their degrees were younger; they included a slightly higher proportion of superior students with firmer career objectives. The nonservers also tended to be younger, had the highest grades, and were the most committed to advanced academic and professional studies.

The age of the men in the three groups proved to be an important finding, relevant for almost all of the following analysis. As one would expect, the men under twenty-five were those who had not yet served or those who served after graduating from college. The older men, mostly in the twenty-seven to twenty-nine age group, were those who served before college. The high proportion of older students in this group is due to the Korean war veterans who went to college with the help of the GI Bill. It would be rare to find a recent college graduating class with such a large number of older students. It is possible, however, that this pattern may reoccur in the future.

Our analysis reveals a direct relationship between age and length of service. Those who were older at graduation tended to spend more time in the service than their younger fellow students. This pattern is repeated even among those who deferred military service until after college. Although officers in all age groups tend to serve longer than enlisted men, those who were older at graduation and then obtained commissions stayed considerably longer than the younger graduates. The average time spent in the military by all those who saw a period of service was two years or less.

Age is also a major factor in the relationship between marital status and military status. As men grow older, the likelihood that they will be married and have children increases, regardless of factors such as graduate school enrollment or military service. This does not mean that these factors do not affect marital status, or that marital status does not affect them; they are intervening rather than independent variables. Increases in the dissolution of marriage through divorce or death are also a function of age. Our data predictably show that the older men who served before graduating from college were most often married, were more likely to be parents, and were more apt to be widowed, separated, or divorced than the younger men – those never in service or those who served after college. For example, more than three-quarters of those who served before 1958 were parents by 1963 versus only half of the post-1958 servers.

The relatively large proportion of single men within the group of post-1958 enlisted men suggests that they were more vulnerable to the draft because they had not married or enrolled in graduate school. We know that not enrolling in graduate school is partially the result of low academic achievement in college. The fact that more than one-fourth of this group were still unmarried in 1963, when most were over twenty-seven, is another indicator of marginal economic and personal status, which we found to be characteristic of men who served as enlistees after graduating from college. (Of the total cohort of male 1958 graduates, only 17 percent were unmarried in 1963.)

### The College Experience:  Undergraduate Major, Academic Achievement, and Military Service

Academic achievement and military experience are clearly related. Graduates who had not served have substantially higher scholastic records than those who served: 30 percent of the nonservers were in the high GPA group, while the proportions were consistently lower among servers (Table 5.2). As previously discussed, students with the highest GPA's most often go to graduate or professional school and therefore obtain deferment status.[2] By 1963, more than half of the nonservers had enrolled for an advanced degree, 15

Table 5.2. Military Status and Grade Point Average[a] (1958 B.A. Recipients)

*(percentages)*

| Military Status | Number | | Grade Point Average | | | | Total Percent |
|---|---|---|---|---|---|---|---|
| | | | Low | Medium | High | Not available | |
| *Total* | *15,365* | | *36.5* | *28.5* | *23.4* | *11.6* | *100.0* |
| Never in service | 5,217 | | 31.3 | 27.3 | 29.7 | 11.8 | 100.1 |
| Pre-1958 | 5,569 | | 39.3 | 30.3 | 18.5 | 11.9 | 100.1 |
| Enlisted men | | 5,133 | 39.4 | 30.2 | 18.3 | 12.1 | 100.0 |
| Officers | | 436 | 38.1 | 31.9 | 20.2 | 9.9 | 100.1 |
| Post-1958 | 4,579 | | 39.0 | 27.6 | 22.2 | 11.1 | 99.9 |
| Enlisted men | | 2,231 | 45.2 | 26.4 | 19.1 | 9.3 | 100.0 |
| Officers | | 2,348 | 33.2 | 28.8 | 25.2 | 12.8 | 100.0 |

[a] For cut-off points of low, medium, and high GPA groups see p. 19.

[2] For an explanation of GPA as used in the follow-up study of college graduates see Chapter III, p. 19.

percent had received a professional degree and 5 percent the Ph.D. In effect, they selected themselves out of the draft by going to graduate school.

Among servers, it is the post-1958 officers who did best in college; the post-1958 enlisted men included the highest proportion of students with poor academic records. For many of these enlisted men, the graduate school deferment alternative was either unavailable or distasteful, given their academic experience. But in general, among those who served before graduating from college (both officers and enlisted men) there were fewer men with high GPA's than among those serving after college.

Academic achievement is not the only screening mechanism in relation to military service; in fact, the differences in academic achievement between servers and nonservers are not as great as one might have anticipated. The choice of undergraduate major, so crucial as a predictor of future occupations and as a determining factor of graduate or professional school attendance, also plays a major role with respect to military service. Certain majors have the effect of removing graduates from the eligible draft pool — at least for a while. Men who major in the natural sciences or humanities and arts, for example, have a propensity not to serve in the armed forces. This primarily reflects the increasing realization that an advanced degree in these fields is necessary; however, it may also reflect a low interest in military service or a determination to avoid it, as well as occupational deferments for doctors and clergymen.

Business and commerce majors, on the other hand, rarely go on immediately to full-time graduate study, since an advanced degree is usually not a requirement for employment in these fields. Therefore, it is not surprising to find a high rate of military service among business and commerce majors, of whom 79 percent served versus 54 percent of the humanities and arts majors (Table 5.3). Furthermore, the fields of business and commerce, as well as

Table 5.3. Military Status by Undergraduate Major Field (1958 B.A. Recipients)

*(percentages)*

| Major Field | Number | Never in Service | Pre-1958 Enlisted men | Pre-1958 Officers | Post-1958 Enlisted men | Post-1958 Officers | Total Percent |
|---|---|---|---|---|---|---|---|
| *Total* | *15,365* | *34.0* | *33.4* | *2.8* | *14.5* | *15.3* | *100.0* |
| Natural sciences | 2,457 | 44.3 | 24.8 | 2.1 | 10.5 | 18.3 | 100.0 |
| Engineering | 2,983 | 31.8 | 33.9 | 3.5 | 11.6 | 19.2 | 100.0 |
| Social sciences | 2,897 | 33.7 | 29.9 | 2.0 | 18.1 | 16.3 | 100.0 |
| Humanities and arts | 1,621 | 46.3 | 27.1 | 1.9 | 13.1 | 11.7 | 100.1 |
| Health | 278 | 35.3 | 34.5 | 1.4 | 19.1 | 9.7 | 100.0 |
| Business and commerce | 3,142 | 21.5 | 40.8 | 4.5 | 18.5 | 14.7 | 100.0 |
| Education | 1,481 | 34.6 | 46.0 | 1.6 | 11.1 | 6.6 | 99.9 |
| Other fields | 506 | 32.6 | 29.1 | 4.3 | 18.2 | 15.8 | 100.0 |

education, attracted nearly half of the men who served prior to 1958. The
selection of business as a major for this group may indicate that they developed managerial career objectives while in the service. More likely, however, it can be explained in terms of academic ability and socioeconomic
origin. We have already seen that servers are less likely to be high academic
performers. There are also strong indications that these pre-college servers are
more likely to be of lower socioeconomic origin than late servers or nonservers. In general, the fields of education and business attract higher proportions of men of working class and lower middle class origin, and below
average proportions of the academically talented.[3] The prospects of post-
service financial benefits, especially the GI Bill, may have been a motivating
factor in the early enlistment decisions of these men.

Social science majors follow a slightly different pattern from men who
majored in other fields. While their participation rate in military service is
close to average, they were more likely to serve after graduation rather than
before. This seems to suggest once again the precarious occupational status of
a college graduate with only a bachelor's degree in a social science field. As
shown in Chapter IV, fewer than 5 percent of the total 1963 sample of male
social science majors held positions as social scientists in 1963. This was
undoubtedly due to the lack of jobs in this area for which graduates with
only a B.A. in the social sciences are qualified. Since employment providing
draft-deferred status was usually not available for the social science majors,
they had two choices: to enroll in graduate school and be deferred, or to
serve in the armed forces. Nearly 20 percent chose the latter alternative. Their
subsequent employment record suggests that those who served as enlisted
men came out of the total education/service experience as low men on the
totem pole.

### Military Service and Graduate Education

It is clear from the discussion so far that as the system has operated in the
past, graduate education and military service tended to be mutually exclusive
because men best equipped for graduate study selected themselves out of the
pool of military eligibles. Obviously, no system is so tight as not to leave
room for exceptions and deviant cases. There were, no doubt, a number of
able students who majored in one of the undergraduate fields commonly
leading to graduate enrollment who served in the armed forces and who
subsequently enrolled for graduate study, just like their classmates who never
served.

[3] Bureau of Social Science Research, *Two Years After the College Degree: Work and
Further Study Patterns* (National Science Foundation Report, NSF 63-26; Washington,
D. C.: U.S. Government Printing Office, 1963), p. 22; and James A. Davis, *Undergraduate
Career Decisions* (Chicago: Aldine Publishing Company, 1965), pp. 70 and 98.

However, speaking in broader statistical terms, we can see by looking at Table 5.4 that only 44 percent of those who never served failed to enroll for an advanced degree, compared to 69 percent of the early servers and 64 percent of most who served after college. And while it has been shown that academic aptitude is an important intervening variable here, more rigorous analysis shows that military service after graduating makes subsequent graduate study less likely, regardless of academic performance.

Table 5.4.  Graduate Student Status by Military Status (1958 B.A. Recipients)

*(percentages)*

| Military Status | Number | Never in school | Some school | Degree candidate[a] | M.A. recipient, not candidate | M.A. recipient and candidate[b] | Professional degree recipient | Ph.D. recipient | Total Percent |
|---|---|---|---|---|---|---|---|---|---|
| *Total* | *15,365* | | *39.4* | *19.6* | *12.8* | *12.1* | *4.6* | *9.4* | *2.1* | *100.0* |
| Never in service | 5,217 | | 25.3 | 18.9 | 15.4 | 12.8 | 7.8 | 14.9 | 4.9 | 100.0 |
| Pre-1958 | 5,569 | | 46.4 | 22.4 | 10.0 | 13.5 | 3.8 | 3.3 | 0.7 | 100.1 |
| Enlisted men | | 5,133 | 45.8 | 22.3 | 10.2 | 13.7 | 3.4 | 3.9 | 0.7 | 100.0 |
| Officers | | 436 | 53.4 | 22.9 | 7.8 | 11.0 | 1.6 | 2.5 | 0.7 | 99.9 |
| Post-1958 | 4,579 | | 47.0 | 17.2 | 13.4 | 9.6 | 9.8 | 2.6 | 0.4 | 100.0 |
| Enlisted men | | 2,231 | 49.7 | 20.7 | 13.9 | 9.1 | 2.2 | 4.3 | 0.2 | 100.1 |
| Officers | | 2,348 | 44.3 | 13.8 | 12.9 | 10.1 | 3.0 | 15.1 | 0.7 | 99.9 |

[a] Candidate for M.A., Ph.D., or professional degree.
[b] For Ph.D. or professional degree.

Assessing the relationship between military service after college graduation and graduate school enrollment more specifically by regression analysis, we sought to determine the relative importance of age, race (white-nonwhite), marital status in 1958, presence or absence of children in 1960, military service (number of years), ROTC training, and GPA in relation to graduate enrollment. Of the several variables studied, the most significant was GPA.[4] This implies that, with all the other variables taken into account, the single most important predictor or determinant of entrance into graduate school is the student's previous academic record. Of second importance, but of primary interest to the discussion at hand, is the negative effect of service in the

[4] For a more detailed discussion and presentation of data, see Laure M. Sharp and Rebecca Krasnegor "College Students and Military Service," *Sociology of Education*, Vol. 41, No. 4 (Fall 1968), pp. 390-400.

armed forces, which shows a greater "deterrent" effect than, for example, marriage or parenthood. The most likely explanation here is that military service has meant the postponement of family formation and career plans for many of these young men. Once finished with their military obligations, they want to begin "catching up" with their contemporaries, rather than devote more time to schooling.

### Economic Consequences of Military Service

It can be argued that postponement or elimination of graduate studies will ultimately result in economic disadvantages for graduates who served in the military. In the meantime, our five-year follow-up study shows the more immediate economic effects of post-college service with respect to the earnings of graduates. It is readily apparent that the timing of military service – early versus late – has an obvious effect on subsequent earnings. By 1963, men who served before graduating from college and who spent five years in the labor force following graduation had better incomes than those who served after graduation and who, accordingly, spent less time in the labor force. To some extent the older ages of the pre-college servers, or the skills and experience acquired while they were in the service, may also have been a factor. But it is clear that the major key to understanding the differences in median income is the amount of time spent in the labor force.

To illustrate this, engineers who served before college did substantially better than their later serving colleagues: $9,758 for the early servers, $8,810 for the later servers. The engineers who served after 1958 show a clear income loss. As Table 5.5 indicates, similar findings exist for businessmen. Both of these fields usually do not require graduate education. In fields where graduate education is more often a requirement for professional employment, the income picture is less clear; still, the men who served in the enlisted ranks after college are most often at a distinct disadvantage.

In the short run, then, it appears that an interruption of one's education by service in the armed forces is less disruptive when it occurs between high school and college graduation, because the man who has worked five years is in a much better financial position than the man who has only worked for two or three years. We also suspect (although we have no data to support this contention) that direct placement out of college or university leads to more desirable jobs. But it is quite conceivable that over time, the gap between early and late servers will be closed and that after, say, fifteen years in the labor force, their incomes will not differ as much as they did in 1963. At the same time, it seems likely that in the long run, the graduates who never served will have the highest incomes, because of the greater likelihood that these men obtained additional education in graduate or professional school.

Table 5.5. Median Income in 1963 by Occupation and Military Status of 1958 B.A. Recipients

| Occupation | Never in Service | Pre-1958 | | Post-1958 | |
|---|---|---|---|---|---|
| | | Enlisted men | Officers | Enlisted men | Officers |
| *Total[a]* | *$7,310* | *$7,805* | *$ 9,490* | *$7,140* | *$8,020* |
| Natural scientist | 8,630 | 7,920 | 8,100 | 7,135 | 7,750 |
| Engineer | 9,750 | 9,860 | 9,656 | 8,720 | 8,900 |
| Social scientist | 8,210 | 7,570 | 9,250 | 6,810 | 6,415 |
| Humanistic professional | 5,335 | 6,250 | 7,250 | 6,310 | 7,335 |
| Health professional | 4,190 | 8,715 | 11,750[b] | 8,715 | 8,870 |
| Teacher | 6,195 | 6,455 | 6,530 | 5,835 | 6,160 |
| Business | 8,135 | 8,105 | 10,090 | 7,790 | 7,695 |
| Other professional | 7,595 | 6,950 | 12,335[c] | 6,565 | 8,285 |
| Semiprofessional | 6,590 | 7,275 | - | 6,390 | 7,000 |
| Clerical and sales | 8,920 | 7,535 | 10,240 | 7,480 | 8,660 |

[a]"Other occupations" and no answers eliminated.
[b]N = 17
[c]N = 20

## College Degrees and Military Duties

The preceding discussion suggests in effect that for most occupations the military experience — especially at the enlisted level — is not seen by employers of college graduates as having provided work experience equivalent to time spent in a civilian job. Our survey data suggest that there is considerable basis for this judgment. The division of our sample into early and late servers provided much meaningful data on the uses to which college graduates are put when serving in the military. One might assume that college graduates are assigned tasks different from those given to men who served without the college experience. The data on both pre-college and post-college servers show, however, that most military tasks performed by the men in this cohort did not require college training. The post-1958 officers are the clear exception (Tables 5.6 and 5.7). In general, the early servers more often had technical jobs, while the late servers — college graduates — had clerical duties. Two-thirds of the pre-1958 officers performed primarily military duties (no doubt as a result of serving during the Korean conflict) versus fewer than 40 percent of the post-1958 officers. Most of the post-1958 officers were assigned "professional" duties.

Jobs requiring college degrees were most often assigned to post-1958 officers who had majored in the natural sciences and health fields (Table 5.7). Business and education majors, on the other hand, were least likely to use their college training during their military service. In the post-1958 enlisted

Table 5.6. Military Duties Performed by Pre-1958 Enlisted Men
and Officers by Undergraduate Major Field

*(percentages)*

| Major Field | Number | Clerical Non-College | Technical Non-College | Requiring College | Military | No Answer | Total Percent |
|---|---|---|---|---|---|---|---|
| | | | Pre-1958 Enlisted Men | | | | |
| *Total* | *5,133* | *26.6* | *37.9* | *7.6* | *26.3* | *1.6* | *100.0* |
| Natural sciences | 609 | 20.4 | 45.5 | 8.5 | 24.5 | 1.1 | 100.0 |
| Engineering | 1,010 | 14.6 | 53.7 | 6.1 | 24.3 | 1.4 | 100.1 |
| Social sciences | 867 | 34.9 | 26.8 | 8.4 | 28.1 | 1.7 | 99.9 |
| Humanities and arts | 440 | 26.6 | 40.0 | 8.4 | 22.7 | 2.3 | 100.0 |
| Health | 96 | 20.8 | 41.7 | 15.6 | 21.9 | – | 100.0 |
| Business and commerce | 1,282 | 36.0 | 28.7 | 4.8 | 28.6 | 1.8 | 99.9 |
| Education | 682 | 23.0 | 38.9 | 10.3 | 26.2 | 1.6 | 100.0 |
| Other fields | 147 | 23.8 | 32.0 | 12.9 | 31.3 | – | 100.0 |
| | | | Pre-1958 Officers | | | | |
| *Total* | *436* | *3.2* | *6.4* | *24.5* | *65.4* | *0.5* | *100.0* |
| Natural sciences | 52 | 1.9 | 7.7 | 34.6 | 55.8 | – | 100.0 |
| Engineering | 105 | 1.0 | 16.2 | 32.4 | 49.5 | 1.0 | 100.1 |
| Social sciences | 58 | 10.3 | 6.9 | 37.9 | 44.8 | – | 99.9 |
| Humanities and arts | 30 | 16.7 | 6.7 | 50.0 | 26.7 | – | 100.1 |
| Health | 4 | – | 25.0 | 50.0 | 25.0 | – | 100.0 |
| Business and commerce | 141 | – | – | – | 100.0 | – | 100.0 |
| Education | 24 | – | – | 45.8 | 54.2 | – | 100.0 |
| Other fields | 22 | 4.5 | – | 22.7 | 68.2 | 4.5 | 99.9 |

men's group, only those who majored in health fields performed duties requiring a college education with any degree of frequency.

It is worth noting that 25 percent of the pre-1958 officers performed duties that required a college education even though they did not possess a bachelor's degree at the time. In contrast, only 14 percent of the post-1958 enlisted men who had college degrees performed duties that required a college education.[5] The early servers, of course, did go on to college, which indicates that they were "college material" at the time they were drafted. This fact, no doubt, is reflected in their military test scores. Furthermore, it turns out that the pre-1958 officers who performed college background duties were more likely to major in a related area when they finally did go to college. Almost one-third of these officers who performed technical or professional college-level jobs in the military went on to major in engineering; additionally, nearly two-thirds of those performing technical noncollege duties were attracted to

[5]This figure may be exceptionally low because of the inclusion of men who were part of the six-month program — a period too short to allow for the utilization of the skills of these men.

Table 5.7. Military Duties Performed by Post-1958 Enlisted Men
and Officers by Undergraduate Major Field

*(percentages)*

| Major Field | Number | Clerical Non-College | Technical Non-College | Requiring College | Military | No Answer | Total Percent |
|---|---|---|---|---|---|---|---|
| | | | Post-1958 Enlisted Men | | | | |
| *Total* | *2,231* | *33.4* | *15.8* | *13.9* | *32.9* | *4.0* | *100.0* |
| Natural sciences | 259 | 21.6 | 22.4 | 22.0 | 30.9 | 3.1 | 100.0 |
| Engineering | 346 | 11.0 | 16.2 | 15.9 | 48.0 | 9.0 | 100.1 |
| Social sciences | 523 | 39.2 | 15.1 | 12.4 | 31.7 | 1.5 | 99.9 |
| Humanities and arts | 212 | 38.7 | 16.0 | 18.9 | 19.8 | 6.6 | 100.0 |
| Health | 53 | 3.8 | 17.0 | 39.6 | 34.0 | 5.7 | 100.1 |
| Business and commerce | 581 | 50.1 | 8.4 | 10.3 | 28.2 | 2.9 | 99.9 |
| Education | 165 | 20.6 | 26.7 | 7.3 | 41.2 | 4.2 | 100.0 |
| Other fields | 92 | 40.2 | 25.0 | – | 32.6 | 2.2 | 100.0 |
| | | | Post-1958 Officers | | | | |
| *Total* | *2,348* | *5.5* | *7.7* | *46.1* | *38.9* | *1.8* | *100.0* |
| Natural sciences | 449 | 3.6 | 3.1 | 64.1 | 27.2 | 2.0 | 100.0 |
| Engineering | 572 | 5.4 | 11.4 | 43.9 | 37.9 | 1.4 | 100.0 |
| Social sciences | 472 | 4.4 | 3.8 | 46.0 | 43.2 | 2.5 | 99.9 |
| Humanities and arts | 189 | 2.6 | 7.4 | 46.0 | 41.8 | 2.1 | 99.9 |
| Health | 27 | – | 11.1 | 63.0 | 25.9 | – | 100.0 |
| Business and commerce | 461 | 11.5 | 12.4 | 32.5 | 43.6 | – | 100.0 |
| Education | 98 | 2.0 | 4.1 | 43.9 | 44.9 | 5.1 | 100.0 |
| Other fields | 80 | 1.2 | 7.5 | 37.5 | 48.7 | 5.0 | 99.9 |

the engineering major. Military duties (including managerial tasks) were most frequently reported by officers who subsequently majored in business and commerce. The same trends are evident for the pre-1958 enlisted men.

## Occupational Carryover: Differences between Officers and Enlisted Men.

The objective differences between ranks in the utilization of college graduates is reflected in the perceptions and judgments of the graduates when asked to rate their military experience.

Officers (both early and late servers) tend to view their military experience in positive terms; nearly three-fourths felt it made an important contribution to their career. In contrast, fewer than half of the enlisted men felt this way. It is specifically among the post-1958 enlisted men where dissatisfaction is greatest; the great majority were, in fact, extraordinarily negative about their military experience. They disagreed that the time spent in the service gave them new ideas for careers (78 percent), new skills (69 percent), time to think about a career (68 percent), achievement of work-related experience (82 percent), or made important contributions to their careers (80 percent). Furthermore, 69 percent felt that the time spent in the service had been wasteful and delayed their careers. No doubt, we can attribute many of these negative responses largely to feelings of status deprivation, to which underutilization of college-acquired skills further contributed.

The marginal status of these post-1958 enlisted men already has been intimated. Five years after graduation, 27 percent of these men (versus only 17 percent for the entire cohort) were still not married. Additionally, this group had done more poorly in college than any other group in the study; nearly one-half had low GPA scores. It is not surprising that we found among them a higher proportion of salesmen and clerical workers than in any other group. It becomes evident that for these men military service was one more input into a gradual deprofessionalization process, which seems to characterize this small group of marginal, unsuccessful college graduates. It will be interesting to see what the reaction to the military experience will be in the future, when the draftees include many more able students, for whom the draft represents an even more severe career disruption, not to mention ideological conflict.

In great contrast to the enlisted men, officers found the period of military service quite productive, regardless of when they served. This positive approach is no doubt rooted in attitudes toward the military: Since their commission-status is the result of some form of voluntary behavior, the students who become officers probably had fewer negative feelings about the military than other students. Furthermore, in objective terms, service as an officer is more comfortable than service as an enlisted man and entails no status deprivation for a college graduate. The prevalence of occupational carry-over from the military to subsequent civilian careers is another major plus-factor. Close to 70 percent of the officers claimed that the service had given them skills which are helpful in their civilian careers, and close to 45 percent felt it had provided a useful working experience; the comparable figures for enlisted men were 45 percent for new skills and 23 percent for working experience. Looking at Table 5.8, it is clear from the point of view of one's future civilian career that commission-status was especially helpful to scientists, engineers, and those in business occupations. In almost every category, however, the difference between enlisted men and officers is clear-cut.

Officers pay a price for the greater advantages they derive from the service. They tend to stay in for longer periods of time than enlisted men. No doubt the longer service period experienced by officers is partially due to three year voluntary enlistments. A longer tour of duty is also one of the obligations often assumed in exchange for educational benefits received through the service (particularly the various Navy and Air Force programs).

Table 5.8. Officers and Enlisted Men within Selected Occupations Agreeing with Positive Statements About Time Spent in the Armed Forces in Terms of Career Objectives[a] (1958 B.A. Recipients)

*(percentages)*

| Full-Time Occupation | Enlisted Men | | | Officers | | |
|---|---|---|---|---|---|---|
| | Number | New skills | Working experience | Number | New skills | Working experience |
| *Total* | *7,061* | *44.9* | *23.2* | *2,267* | *68.5* | *44.4* |
| Agricultural scientist | 130 | 13.1 | 6.2 | 29 | 14.5 | 31.0 |
| Chemist | 82 | 6.1 | 14.6 | 16 | 50.0 | 25.0 |
| Civil engineer | 166 | 6.0 | 16.9 | 91 | 63.7 | 45.0 |
| Electrical engineer | 381 | 3.4 | 63.3 | 99 | 75.8 | 50.5 |
| Mechanical engineer | 256 | 8.6 | 16.8 | 101 | 67.3 | 43.6 |
| Industrial engineer | 132 | 8.3 | 27.3 | 94 | 81.9 | 47.8 |
| Psychologist | 34 | 8.8 | 11.8 | 3[b] | | |
| Clergyman | 95 | 5.2 | 27.4 | 7[b] | | |
| Writer | 85 | 24.7 | 43.5 | 21 | 52.9 | 14.3 |
| Pharmacist | 133 | 45.1 | 38.3 | 17[b] | | |
| M.D. in training | 22 | 36.4 | 18.2 | 27 | 55.5 | 63.0 |
| College teacher | 149 | 49.7 | 23.5 | 22 | 50.0 | 22.7 |
| High school teacher | 980 | 44.8 | 29.9 | 124 | 61.3 | 40.3 |
| Elementary school teacher | 250 | 40.4 | 18.0 | 19 | 52.6 | 26.3 |
| Accountant | 292 | 31.2 | 28.8 | 47 | 59.6 | 42.5 |
| Businessman | 1,603 | 31.5 | 16.7 | 489 | 77.9 | 44.0 |
| Lawyer | 164 | 21.9 | 4.9 | 91 | 71.4 | 42.8 |
| Social worker | 109 | 29.4 | 17.4 | 14[b] | | |
| Salesman | 488 | 29.9 | 8.8 | 197 | 63.5 | 29.9 |

[a] Agreed "strongly or somewhat" with the following statements: (1) During the service in the armed forces I acquired new skills which are (will be) helpful in my civilian occupation; and (2) Service in the armed forces gave me working experience in my chosen career field.
[b] Cases too few to compute percent.

One of the traditional routes to commission-status is participation in ROTC programs, but our survey shows that these are of value only to students participating for three or more years. Men who participated in ROTC for one to two years were no more likely to receive a commission than their nonparticipating fellow students. However, over 90 percent of those in ROTC for three or more years entered the service, almost always as commissioned officers. The proportion participating for one to two years merely reflects the compulsory ROTC participation required by many colleges, and subsequent withdrawal or screen-outs. Those who never served in ROTC units were just about as likely to obtain a commission as those with one or two years of service.

### Service as a Maturing and Decision-Making Stage

Since the military service occupies an increasingly important period in young men's lives (which apparently fewer and fewer men will be able to avoid altogether), it is instructive to analyze the military experience as a factor in the career-decision process. The experiences of the 1958 cohort show that the men who entered military service before college were largely undecided about a career. Most of the college graduates, on the other hand, had at least made some tentative decision about what career to follow before they entered the service.

For men entering the military prior to obtaining their B.A., the military service provided some career ideas and job skills; it also gave them time to think about an occupation before an actual career commitment had to be made. We have already indicated that some officers enroll in college after completing their military obligations because of their exposure to managerial occupations while in the service. In these cases, service fulfilled a career-choice function and had a positive, although delaying, effect. Judging from the survey findings, this respite from decision-making is frequently needed and appreciated by young men. Generally, the pre-1958 servers were slower in making career decisions. They may have chosen longer service periods to further postpone definitive career choices. In many cases, the area of indecision may have involved military versus civilian careers. Although only 5 percent of all the 1958 graduates entered the military with the thought of pursuing it as a career, a fair number of both early- and late-serving officers went through a prolonged period of indecision about switching from a military to a civilian career. This is reflected in the relatively large number of nonmilitary career men who served more than four years.

It appears that the most positive function of the military is that it offers a useful and legitimate respite from decision-making for men serving before college; it does not fulfill a comparable function for the college graduates. Thus, the experience of the class of 1958 confirms what is the prevailing campus belief today: For enlisted men the disadvantages of military service generally outbalance the advantages. Leaving aside ideological considerations, which are probably salient for only some groups of students, the career interruption and — perhaps more serious in the long run — the probable loss of graduate studies outweigh the advantages that time in the service might confer in terms of skill acquisition or experience. It is apparent from the experience of the college men in our study that the military establishment not only showed little interest in utilizing the skills of college-educated draftees and enlistees, but also did not offer them opportunities for training and work commensurate with their educational status.

# VI

## THE NATURE OF THE
## UNDERGRADUATE INSTITUTION

**W**e have seen throughout the preceding discussions that the overwhelming majority of college graduates found that their undergraduate degrees opened the door to occupations and careers which would not have been accessible had they not gone to college. Increasingly a college education is seen as the key to the successful acquisition of the most desirable positions in our society, at least in the view of the great majority of Americans who continue to adhere to the more traditional beliefs concerning personal achievement and success.

At the same time, the emphasis has shifted to some extent from going to college to going to the "right" college. In past generations, this concern chiefly affected the social elite. But now, many middle-class high school students and their families are embroiled in a familiar struggle to get into the "right" college, because of the commonly held belief that success – defined in occupational, economic, and social terms – depends on where one's college education was acquired. Anxious students across the country are wondering if going to a "better" school improves their chances in life. Is it easier to get into a graduate or professional school as an alumnus of a "high-quality" college? Are better, more professional, and higher paying jobs available because of the prestige of one's alma mater? Does the likelihood of an early or late marriage depend on the type of school attended?

From the point of view of personality development and acquisition of a life style, the role of the specific college that a student attends for all or most of his undergraduate studies cannot be discounted (although the few systematic studies which have been conducted suggest that this role may be smaller than is generally assumed).[1] But from the point of view of one's occupational and

[1] Among the most frequently cited earlier studies are those of Bennington students, reported in Theodore M. Newcomb, *Personality and Social Change* (New York: Dryden

graduate school careers, the character and quality of the undergraduate institution attended seem to have a minimal impact. The early careers of graduates from the class of 1958 seemed to reveal only minor inter-school differences. It should be noted that while popular belief in the importance of the type of school attended runs high, the downgrading of institutional differences suggested by our data is in line with other research findings. After studying the 1961 National Merit Scholarship semifinalists and winners, Alexander W. Astin observed that "the college actually attended by the student of high ability appears to make only a slight difference in his eventual career choice, academic and extracurricular achievements during college, academic ability, persistence in college, and the eventual level of education that he obtains."[2] More recent studies by Astin and his colleagues based on a representative cross section of college students further confirm this statement.[3]

In our study of recent college graduates we examined the impact of the undergraduate institution on three areas: graduate study, occupational outcome, and marital status. The institutions were classified by various categories: by type of control (private, public), by sex (coeducational, one-sex), by level (four-year, five-year, university), and by quality. To measure the quality of an institution, we used two procedures. One measure involves a ratio of the number of applicants to the number accepted by the college and is referred to as *selectivity*. The second measure is called *prestige* and is based on the total number of academically talented high school students who want to enroll at a specific college divided by the number of freshmen admitted by that college.[4] There is, of course, some overlap between schools in the high and low categories in both groupings.

In evaluating our findings it is essential to keep in mind that no matter what system of classification is used, all college or university groupings are imperfect. Furthermore, generalizations of the kind made here always

Press, 1943), and those based on studies done at Cornell and discussed in Philip E. Jacobs, *Changing Values in College* (New York: Harper & Row, Publishers, 1958). For more recent and ongoing studies, see Nevitt Stanford (ed.), *The American College* (New York: John Wiley & Sons, Inc., 1962).

[2] Alexander W. Astin, *Who Goes Where to College?* (Chicago: Science Research Associates, Inc., 1965).

[3] Alexander W. Astin and Robert J. Panos, *The Educational and Vocational Development of American College Students* (Washington, D. C.: American Council on Education, 1969).

[4] For the selectivity measure, see Jane Z. Hauser and Paul F. Lazarsfeld, *The Admissions Officer in the American College: An Occupation Under Change* (New York: College Entrance Examination Board, 1964), pp. 1,2 and 6. For the prestige measure, see Astin, *Who Goes Where to College?*

oversimplify; no doubt, within each of the categories discussed, there are colleges and universities whose graduates deviate significantly from our norms. It should also be stressed that the methodology used in our study focussed on what happens to *students* from colleges having certain sets of characteristics, not on the relative number of students from various types of colleges who obtain post-graduate degrees. There is no doubt that the proportion of alumni who obtain post-graduate degrees differs greatly from one institution to another. It is necessary, however, to discriminate between institutional factors (those attributable to the college environment) and predisposing factors (student characteristics, such as social class and academic ability). This distinction is basic to the discussion throughout this chapter and will be raised frequently in the sections which follow.

### Graduate Enrollment

With the growing emphasis on graduate education in terms of individual career outcome and our society's demand for highly trained and specialized professionals, many educators and social scientists have been interested to see why certain types of undergraduate schools seem to foster high rates of graduate study among the student body. A common, but essentially oversimplified belief is that, relative to their total enrollment, the elite undergraduate institutions produce the largest numbers of future Ph.D.'s and other professional men and women and that the proclivity of their graduates to undertake further study can be attributed to the high standards and value systems characteristic of these institutions. This has been challenged by more sophisticated research techniques.[5] Some investigators were able to identify other institutions with less prestige as high Ph.D. producers; others have shown that it is the caliber and predisposition of the entering student that accounts for his subsequent interest in graduate education. Last but not least, the rapid changes taking place on the educational scene, of which the over-all growth of graduate education is the most relevant here, result in the rapid obsolescence of study findings and evaluative judgments.

Because the students with the best high school credentials seek and obtain access to the most selective undergraduate schools, and because these same students are most likely to enter graduate or professional schools, some institutional differences will exist with respect to post-graduate and professional school attendance. In addition, the graduate study data shown here must be cautiously interpreted. In many fields, especially in education,

[5] See, for example, R. H. Knapp and J. J. Greenbaum, *The Younger American Scholar* (Chicago: University of Chicago Press, 1953); Alexander W. Astin "Re-examination of College Productivity," *Journal of Educational Psychology* (June 1961), pp. 173-78; and Alexander W. Astin, "Productivity of Undergraduate Institutions," *Science* (April 13, 1962), pp. 129-35.

the growth of graduate study since World War II has led to a considerable expansion in relatively weak programs. Furthermore, there is undoubtedly a good deal of internal differentiation within a given occupation, with the highest prestige jobs going to persons who went to the better colleges and from there to the better graduate or professional schools.[6] Nevertheless, we feel that there is enough flexibility in the system — with undergraduates from elite schools taking graduate work in unselective graduate schools and vice versa — to justify the broad approach used in our study, which has the further advantage of coming to grips with the magnitude of post-college education at all quality levels.

Important factors in predicting graduate school attendance seem to be personal ones, such as age, marital status, parenthood, and especially undergraduate performance (Appendix Table Q). As discussed in Chapter III, age and parenthood appear to have inhibited the decision for graduate school enrollment for the men in our cohort, while marriage, and not parenthood or age, was the restricting factor for women.

The most significant personal factor determining graduate school attendance is the raw GPA, which is a measure of a graduate's personal academic achievement regardless of the quality or character of the undergraduate institution attended. No doubt the requirement of having a high GPA for admission to graduate school is reflected here. But furthermore, we believe that graduates with low GPA's — even those from the elite schools — select themselves out of the running for graduate school admission. The reason why many undergraduates with high ability but with poor performance records in a highly selective college fail to seek careers requiring a high performance level in graduate or professional school may be based on the relative deprivation mechanism. Through this process, students compare themselves with their more successful classmates and develop feelings of inadequacy concerning their academic ability.[7] As a result, they do not seek the careers that they associate with a need for high-level academic performance, even though C+ students from Ivy League schools, for example, rank among the top in a national distribution. Of course, it is also reasonable to assume that students who did poorly at the undergraduate level do not wish to expose themselves to further classroom experiences.

Since these findings point to the overwhelming importance of undergraduate grades as a predictor of graduate school attendance, they suggest that graduate and professional schools recruit those students who may

[6] Joe L. Spaeth, "Occupational Prestige Expectations Among College Male Graduates," *American Journal of Sociology*, Vol. 73, No. 5 (March 1968), p. 558.

[7] James A. Davis, "The Campus as a Frog Pond: An Application of Theory of Relative Deprivation to Career Decisions of College Men," *American Journal of Sociology*, Vol. 72, No. 1 (July 1966), pp. 17-31.

have worked the hardest and have perhaps been able to make the best personal adjustments during their undergraduate lives. This, of course, excludes many of the most talented members of a given cohort. In brief, it would appear that graduate school admission boards are not as interested in the quality of undergraduate colleges as is commonly thought, which implies that one need not have graduated from a high prestige school in order to get into graduate or professional school.

Using our broad definition of graduate enrollment, we found that graduates of highly selective institutions are only slightly more likely to go to graduate school than graduates of less selective colleges — though they may be more likely to go to the "best" graduate schools. Our findings also show that there is little difference between graduates of public and private coeducational schools and private all-male colleges as far as graduate study is concerned. The major difference seems to be that both men and women from the most selective schools are more likely to have received professional degrees (rather than M.A.'s or Ph.D.'s) and to be further advanced in graduate study than those from less selective schools (Table 6.1).

Table 6.1.  Graduate School Enrollment and Degree Recipiency by Selectivity of Undergraduate Institution[a] (1958 B.A. Recipients)

*(percentages)*

| Selectivity | Number | Never enrolled | Took courses only | Degree candidate | M.A. recipient, not a candidate | Professional degree recipient | M.A. recipient and candidate | Ph.D. recipient | Total Percent |
|---|---|---|---|---|---|---|---|---|---|
| | | | | | **Men** | | | | |
| *Total[b]* | *10,797* | *40.0* | *19.6* | *12.5* | *11.6* | *9.6* | *4.6* | *2.0* | *99.9* |
| High | 2,681 | 32.8 | 19.8 | 13.8 | 11.6 | 13.0 | 5.7 | 3.3 | 100.0 |
| Medium | 5,543 | 41.9 | 19.1 | 12.6 | 11.5 | 8.9 | 4.3 | 1.7 | 100.0 |
| Low | 2,573 | 43.5 | 20.7 | 11.0 | 11.9 | 7.5 | 4.0 | 1.4 | 100.0 |
| | | | | | **Women** | | | | |
| *Total[b]* | *5,834* | *48.4* | *28.7* | *8.7* | *11.9* | *0.7* | *1.3* | *0.2* | *99.9* |
| High | 1,218 | 42.4 | 31.2 | 8.5 | 14.8 | 1.2 | 1.6 | 0.2 | 99.9 |
| Medium | 3,035 | 49.8 | 28.5 | 8.6 | 11.0 | 0.5 | 1.4 | 0.2 | 100.0 |
| Low | 1,581 | 50.2 | 27.2 | 9.1 | 11.5 | 0.6 | 1.1 | 0.1 | 99.8 |

[a] For method of classifying institutions by selectivity, see Jane Z. Hauser and Paul F. Lazarsfeld, *The Admissions Officer in the American College: An Occupation Under Change*, Appendix B (New York: College Entrance Examination Board, 1964), p. 2.

[b] Excludes graduates (5,496 men and 3,456 women) who graduated from institutions for which data was not available for selectivity classification.

If, instead of selectivity, we use the prestige ratings of colleges, which perhaps represent a more updated version of the quality structure, the findings become more meaningful. The relationship between high prestige schools and graduate enrollment is more pronounced, as Table 6.2 illustrates. Slightly more than 50 percent of the men from the highest prestige school had been enrolled as a graduate degree candidate in the five years since college graduation versus 37 percent from an average prestige school. Also within that period, the graduates from the highest prestige schools received nearly twice as many professional degrees and Ph.D.'s as those from the schools of average prestige.

The greater number of professional degrees among these students may well be related to their socioeconomic background, which propels them in the direction of the professions. Others, with both high grades and a high prestige school background behind them, are more likely to receive the limited financial aid available to Ph.D. candidates. With fellowships and other

Table 6.2. Graduate School Enrollment and Degree Recipiency by National Merit Scholar Prestige of Undergraduate Institution[a] (1958 B.A. Recipients)

*(percentages)*

| National Merit Scholar Prestige | Number | Never enrolled | Took courses only | Degree candidate | M.A. recipient, not a candidate | Professional degree recipient | M.A. recipient and candidate | Ph.D. recipient | Total Percent |
|---|---|---|---|---|---|---|---|---|---|
| | | | | | Men | | | | |
| Total[b] | 14,836 | 39.7 | 19.2 | 12.7 | 12.1 | 9.7 | 4.5 | 2.1 | 100.0 |
| Highest prestige | 3,593 | 34.7 | 14.6 | 13.4 | 11.9 | 14.7 | 6.7 | 4.0 | 100.0 |
| Very high prestige | 5,645 | 43.0 | 19.6 | 11.8 | 10.7 | 9.1 | 4.3 | 1.3 | 99.9 |
| Average prestige | 3,121 | 41.4 | 21.5 | 12.9 | 10.2 | 8.3 | 3.6 | 2.0 | 99.9 |
| Below average prestige | 1,299 | 35.0 | 22.1 | 13.6 | 17.6 | 6.7 | 3.6 | 1.4 | 100.0 |
| Low prestige | 1,178 | 39.6 | 22.3 | 13.5 | 17.7 | 4.2 | 2.2 | 0.4 | 99.9 |
| | | | | | Women | | | | |
| Total[b] | 8,212 | 52.8 | 32.7 | 7.9 | 11.3 | 0.7 | 1.4 | 0.2 | 100.0 |
| Highest prestige | 1,785 | 47.5 | 29.6 | 5.5 | 13.0 | 1.5 | 2.5 | 0.4 | 99.9 |
| Very high prestige | 2,729 | 49.5 | 30.2 | 7.5 | 10.9 | 0.6 | 1.1 | 0.2 | 100.0 |
| Average prestige | 1,846 | 48.4 | 32.1 | 9.3 | 8.8 | 0.5 | 0.7 | 0.2 | 100.0 |
| Below average prestige | 896 | 43.6 | 29.8 | 11.7 | 13.4 | 0.2 | 1.1 | 0.1 | 99.9 |
| Low prestige | 956 | 50.3 | 28.5 | 7.3 | 12.0 | 0.1 | 1.8 | – | 100.0 |

[a] For method of classifying institutions by prestige, see Alexander W. Astin, *Who Goes Where to College?* (Chicago Science Research Associates Inc., 1965).
[b] Excludes 1,457 men and 1,078 women who graduated from institutions not classified by Astin.

financial aid, students can more often continue with their graduate studies on a full-time basis, as noted in Chapter III.

These data are confirmed by looking at the class of 1958 through different measures — private versus public, all-male (or all-female) versus coeducational schools. The graduates of private all-male colleges, which include some of the most prestigious schools, are the most likely to have enrolled in graduate school and to have received a professional degree five years after college graduation (Table 6.3).

Professional degree recipiency appears to be the great differentiator: 16 percent of the all-male private college graduates received a professional degree, 13 percent from the private coeducational schools and only 6 percent from the public coeducational schools. The greater professional orientation of

Table 6.3.  Graduate School Enrollment and Degree Recipiency by Type of Control and Sex of Undergraduate Institution (1958 B.A. Recipients)

*(percentages)*

| Graduate School Enrollment | Men | | | | |
| | Public | | Private | | |
| | All-male | Co-ed | All-male | Co-ed | Total |
| --- | --- | --- | --- | --- | --- |
| Never enrolled | 66.7 | 42.4 | 30.8 | 37.1 | 39.3 |
| Took courses only | 8.9 | 20.7 | 18.4 | 19.1 | 19.7 |
| Degree candidate | 7.4 | 12.2 | 14.1 | 12.9 | 12.6 |
| M.A. recipient, not a candidate | 9.6 | 13.2 | 11.8 | 10.8 | 12.2 |
| Professional degree recipient | 3.0 | 5.8 | 16.2 | 12.7 | 9.5 |
| M.A. recipient and candidate | 4.4 | 4.1 | 6.0 | 4.8 | 4.6 |
| Ph.D. recipient | – | 1.5 | 2.7 | 2.6 | 2.1 |
| Total percent | 100.0 | 99.9 | 100.0 | 100.0 | 100.1 |
| (Total number) | (135) | (8,276) | (1,829) | (6,049) | (16,289[a]) |

| Graduate School Enrollment | Women | | | | |
| | Public | | Private | | |
| | All-female | Co-ed | All-female | Co-ed | Total |
| --- | --- | --- | --- | --- | --- |
| Never enrolled | 54.2 | 46.0 | 50.1 | 47.7 | 47.2 |
| Took courses only | 34.5 | 32.6 | 26.8 | 29.3 | 30.7 |
| Degree candidate | – | 9.6 | 7.5 | 8.2 | 8.7 |
| M.A. recipient, not a candidate | 9.9 | 10.6 | 12.2 | 11.9 | 11.2 |
| Professional degree recipient | – | 0.3 | 1.1 | 1.0 | 0.7 |
| M.A. recipient and candidate | 1.4 | 0.9 | 2.0 | 1.7 | 1.3 |
| Ph.D. recipient | – | 0.1 | 0.3 | 0.3 | 0.2 |
| Total percent | 100.0 | 100.1 | 100.1 | 100.1 | 100.0 |
| (Total number) | (142) | (4,672) | (1,408) | (3,050) | (9,272[b]) |

[a] Excludes three graduates who graduated from private all-female colleges and one graduate who graduated from an uncodable institution.

[b] Excludes ten graduates who graduated from private, all-male colleges and eight graduates who graduated from uncodable institutions.

graduates of private institutions no doubt reflects the higher socioeconomic status of many of the graduates, as well as their family backgrounds in law, medicine, and related areas. However, it may also be that these institutions stress their role as prep schools for professional schools and accordingly exert some influence on student career selection.

Graduates from liberal arts colleges tend to go to graduate school to a greater degree than graduates from occupationally oriented schools such as technical institutions (Appendix Table R). No doubt this is because the traditionally broad education received in the liberal arts colleges often does not prepare students for occupations that can be entered directly after graduation without further schooling.

The strong relationship between the college major and graduate degree enrollment has already been documented in Chapter III. We know, for example, that majoring in the natural sciences, the humanities and arts, and the social sciences often leads to graduate study. These are the very areas of study that enroll large proportions of the students at the top prestige colleges. As the prestige of a school increases, the proportion of education majors decreases. Among graduates of the top schools, only 2 percent of the men and 17 percent of the women majored in education versus 12 percent of the men and 38 percent of the women from schools with average prestige. Instead, social science and engineering among the men and social science and humanities and arts among the women were the popular fields for students who attended the most prestigious schools (Appendix Table S).

The type of school attended seems to have a slight bearing on whether one goes on to graduate school. Students who graduated from institutions where advanced degrees are conferred are more likely to have enrolled for a graduate degree and to have progressed further in graduate education. Whether students from institutions with graduate programs have been motivated by the institution or whether they were already predisposed when they applied for admission to these institutions cannot be determined from our study. But we feel that exposure to a graduate school during one's undergraduate years makes graduate enrollment more likely.

In general, our data on women are inconclusive and sketchy at best. Women from the highest prestige colleges (and from the overlapping group, private all-female schools) were enrolled in graduate schools less often than their cohorts from the less prestigious coeducational schools. Yet when the women from the "best" schools did continue with their education, they included the highest proportion of M.A. recipients and Ph.D. candidates. Their counterparts at public and private coeducational schools and at the schools of average prestige continued their education more often, but many were education majors, who are great course-takers rather than recipients of advanced degrees.[8] As was shown in Chapter III, women's interest and progress in graduate school is greatly affected by their marital status. The more refined analysis (shown in Appendix Table Q) further strengthens this point. Our data also suggest that graduates of women's colleges (which include some very high prestige colleges) are less likely to combine marriage and graduate study than women who attended coeducational and lower prestige schools. No doubt the socioeconomic background factors offer the most potent explanation for this differential behavior, but there are also some indications throughout our survey findings that women's colleges influence their graduates in the direction of adhering to more traditional female roles, devoting themselves either full-time to marriage and motherhood or full-time to careers while remaining single.

In summary, these data strongly suggest that academic achievement at the undergraduate level, occupational goals, and personal characteristics rather than institutional factors are of primary importance when it comes to the pursuit of graduate work. Graduates from the high prestige undergraduate schools will progress faster and are more likely to go on to study for the traditional professions, such as law and medicine, but students who attended the less prestigious schools are clearly not handicapped in the pursuit of graduate degrees which are in line with their professional goals.

### Occupational Outcome

Given the tremendous demand for college graduates in every sector of society, it was to be expected that where one went to college has only a minimal impact on whether one works or not. In the class of 1958, almost all of the men were employed full-time five years after college graduation, regardless of where they went to college. There was more of a difference with respect to the careers of those *not* in the labor force. More men in our cohort from the highest prestige schools, for example, were in the armed forces in 1963 than from any other group (2.6 percent versus 1.4 percent from the lowest prestige schools). This can be attributed to the relatively high degree of graduate school enrollment among these graduates, which allowed them to be deferred until after they received their graduate or professional degree. At the other end of the scale, men from the least prestigious schools tended to serve right after college graduation or, as in the case of the Korean War veterans, before going to college.

---

[8] In our study we viewed graduate school attendance as a continuum, ranging from never enrolled in graduate school to Ph.D. recipiency. As such, graduates who have taken some courses without being enrolled for a graduate or professional degree are classified as having had some graduate study.

For women, the type of school attended appears to have a more important effect on subsequent employment. Yet we feel that the determining factors are personal traits or predispositions — which probably account for the choice of college in the first place — rather than true institutional influences.

From Table 6.4 we learn that women graduates from the least prestigious schools were most likely to be employed full-time and least likely to be housewives only. For example, 67 percent of the women from the low prestige schools worked full-time, compared to 33 percent from the highest prestige schools. Conversely, 51 percent of those from the "top" schools were full-time housewives, compared to only 24 percent from the less prestigious

Table 6.4. Employment Status by National Merit Scholar Prestige[a] (1958 B.A. Recipients)

*(percentages)*

| National Merit Scholar Prestige | Number | Employed full-time | Employed part-time | Unemployed | Student | Armed forces | Housewife | Other | No answer | Total Percent |
|---|---|---|---|---|---|---|---|---|---|---|
| | | | | | **Men** | | | | | |
| *Total[b]* | *14,836* | *90.9* | *2.7* | *0.5* | *3.3* | *2.2* | *–* | *0.2* | *0.2* | *100.0* |
| Highest prestige | 3,593 | 87.0 | 3.8 | 0.5 | 5.4 | 2.6 | – | 0.3 | 0.3 | 99.9 |
| Very high prestige | 5,645 | 91.2 | 2.6 | 0.5 | 3.3 | 2.2 | – | 0.2 | 0.1 | 100.1 |
| Average prestige | 3,121 | 92.3 | 2.1 | 0.6 | 2.2 | 2.2 | – | 0.1 | 0.4 | 99.9 |
| Below average prestige | 1,299 | 92.6 | 2.2 | 0.8 | 2.5 | 1.7 | – | – | 0.2 | 100.0 |
| Low prestige | 1,178 | 95.2 | 1.4 | 0.3 | 1.2 | 1.4 | – | 0.3 | 0.3 | 100.1 |
| | | | | | **Women** | | | | | |
| *Total[b]* | *8,212* | *45.0* | *10.1* | *0.6* | *1.8* | *–* | *41.4* | *0.4* | *0.6* | *99.9* |
| Highest prestige | 1,785 | 32.9 | 11.8 | 0.6 | 2.9 | – | 51.1 | 0.3 | 0.4 | 100.0 |
| Very high prestige | 2,729 | 40.6 | 12.6 | 0.6 | 1.9 | – | 42.7 | 0.8 | 0.7 | 99.9 |
| Average prestige | 1,846 | 45.0 | 8.0 | 0.6 | 1.8 | – | 43.7 | 0.2 | 0.7 | 100.0 |
| Below average prestige | 896 | 59.2 | 6.2 | 0.7 | 0.4 | – | 32.6 | – | 0.9 | 100.0 |
| Low prestige | 956 | 67.3 | 7.4 | 0.4 | 0.8 | – | 23.7 | 0.2 | 0.1 | 99.9 |

[a] For method of classifying institutions by prestige, see Alexander W. Astin, *Who Goes Where to College?* (Chicago: Science Research Associates Inc., 1965).
[b] Excludes 1,457 men, 1,078 women who graduated from institutions not classified by Astin.

schools. Personal factors at play here might very well center on the fact that the predominant undergraduate major field for women from low prestige colleges is education, and that jobs which are compatible with domestic responsibilities are more readily available for education majors than for women who majored in the arts or humanities, for example. Because many of the lower prestige schools are public institutions, finances also play a role here. It is possible that women who selected these schools were predisposed to major in education for the precise reason that work would be readily available after college. Age, too, comes into the picture, because relatively few older (married) women attended private and high prestige schools; typically, women who seek to obtain or complete their education relatively late in life do so at public institutions. Thus, the many public and low prestige institutions graduate women positively oriented toward employment because of financial and life-cycle reasons. On the other hand, women who attended the most prestigious schools are less likely to be oriented toward careers, at least during the child-rearing years following graduation.

Furthermore, we see that women from the high prestige, private, all-female schools are statistically the strongest adherents of the traditional female role of full-time housewife (50 percent versus 38 percent for the private coeducational school graduates), and women from coeducational institutions are more likely to work full- or part-time (58 percent versus 46 percent for the private all-female school graduate as shown in Appendix Table T).

Insofar as there is a trend toward greater work or career orientation on the part of college women, it is most clearly manifested by the graduates from coeducational schools (who more often combined marriage and career roles) and by women who graduated from the less prestigious schools and whose occupational orientation toward the traditional teaching role may be prompted by their lesser affluence.

The relationship between jobs held five years after graduation and the type of undergraduate school attended once again shows the strong role of the undergraduate major. As expected, the graduates in our cohort from the more occupationally oriented colleges are committed to the occupations for which they have been trained. From Table 6.5 we see that 65 percent of the graduates from technical institutions became engineers and more than 60 percent of the graduates of teachers colleges became teachers. Differences in teaching careers can be traced to the type of institution attended. Again looking at Table 6.5 we learn that graduates of teachers colleges were more likely to be elementary and high school teachers, whereas graduates of universities and liberal arts colleges were a bit more likely to teach in colleges.

Male graduates from universities and liberal arts colleges scattered themselves in varied occupations. University graduates clustered somewhat in engineering, business, and managerial occupations, while liberal arts graduates

Table 6.5. Full-Time Occupation by Type of Undergraduate Institution and Highest Degrees Offered
(1958 B.A. Recipients)

*(percentages)*

| Full-Time Occupation | University | | Liberal Arts College | | Teachers College | | Technical Institute | | |
|---|---|---|---|---|---|---|---|---|---|
| | M.A. | Ph.D. | B.A. | M.A. or Ph.D. | B.A. | M.A. or Ph.D. | B.A. | M.A. | Ph.D. |
| **Men** | | | | | | | | | |
| Natural scientist | 4.0 | 6.6 | 6.3 | 5.1 | 2.3 | 5.4 | 6.5 | 3.9 | 5.1 |
| Engineer | 21.1 | 22.8 | 6.4 | 10.7 | 3.4 | 1.0 | 64.5 | 63.0 | 69.3 |
| Social scientist | 0.8 | 1.2 | 1.4 | 1.4 | 0.4 | 1.1 | - | - | 0.4 |
| Humanistic professional | 2.9 | 3.2 | 9.9 | 7.0 | 3.0 | 3.5 | - | 7.1 | 1.5 |
| Health professional | 6.3 | 7.1 | 5.3 | 5.6 | 1.1 | 0.9 | - | 0.8 | 0.4 |
| Teacher, college | 1.5 | 3.4 | 2.9 | 5.6 | 2.7 | 2.2 | 6.5 | 1.6 | 2.7 |
| Teacher, other | 10.0 | 9.9 | 24.0 | 21.4 | 65.8 | 58.2 | - | 7.1 | 0.6 |
| Business and management | 33.2 | 23.3 | 19.5 | 24.8 | 13.7 | 15.7 | 9.7 | 2.4 | 11.2 |
| Other professional | 8.1 | 8.3 | 8.9 | 8.6 | 3.4 | 2.7 | 12.9 | 3.9 | 3.6 |
| Semiskilled and technical | 1.7 | 1.8 | 2.2 | 1.3 | - | 1.3 | - | 0.8 | - |
| Clerical and sales | 7.3 | 9.0 | 9.0 | 5.1 | 1.5 | 3.7 | - | 2.4 | 4.0 |
| Other unskilled and no answer | 3.1 | 3.5 | 4.2 | 3.4 | 2.7 | 4.2 | - | 7.1 | 1.3 |
| Total percent | 100.0 | 100.1 | 100.0 | 100.0 | 100.0 | 99.9 | 100.1 | 100.1 | 100.1 |
| (Total number) | (521) | (6,819) | (1,967) | (2,136) | (263) | (979) | (31) | (127) | (475) |

| Full-Time Occupation | University | | Liberal Arts College | | Teachers College | |
|---|---|---|---|---|---|---|
| | M.A. | Ph.D. | B.A. | M.A. or Ph.D. | B.A. | M.A. or Ph.D. |
| **Women** | | | | | | |
| Natural scientist | 0.8 | 1.4 | 1.8 | 1.4 | 0.8 | 0.4 |
| Engineer | - | 0.7 | 0.5 | 0.1 | - | - |
| Social scientist | 0.8 | 0.6 | 0.8 | 1.9 | - | - |
| Humanistic professional | 5.6 | 6.1 | 5.3 | 3.1 | 7.4 | 5.3 |
| Health professional | 5.6 | 10.9 | 4.5 | 5.0 | 0.8 | 2.4 |
| Teacher, college | 7.1 | 4.4 | 3.4 | 3.6 | - | 2.2 |
| Teacher, other | 66.7 | 55.3 | 60.1 | 63.6 | 87.7 | 82.8 |
| Business and management | 1.6 | 3.9 | 4.1 | 4.9 | - | 0.6 |
| Other professional | 2.4 | 6.6 | 6.0 | 7.2 | 0.8 | 3.0 |
| Semiskilled and technical | 5.6 | 2.8 | 5.1 | 2.6 | 0.8 | 0.2 |
| Clerical and sales | 4.0 | 5.1 | 4.9 | 4.0 | - | 2.4 |
| Other unskilled and no answer | - | 2.4 | 3.4 | 2.6 | 1.6 | 0.6 |
| Total percent | 100.2 | 100.2 | 99.9 | 100.0 | 99.9 | 99.9 |
| (Total number) | (126) | (1,267) | (870) | (852) | (122) | (494) |

more often sought careers in the humanistic professions and high school
teaching.

From a perusal of Table 6.6 more meaningful relationships can be detected
between occupational outcome and the prestige of the undergraduate institutions. As the prestige increases so do the proportions of men employed as
engineers, health professionals, businessmen, and managers. Conversely, as the

Table 6.6. Full-Time Occupation by National Merit Scholar Prestige
(1958 B.A. Recipients)

*(percentages)*

| Full-Time Occupation | Highest Prestige | Very High Prestige | Average Prestige | Below Average Prestige | Low Prestige |
|---|---|---|---|---|---|
| **Men** | | | | | |
| Natural scientist | 5.0 | 5.9 | 6.8 | 6.6 | 6.8 |
| Engineer | 23.3 | 21.4 | 18.2 | 10.1 | 3.8 |
| Social scientist | 1.9 | 0.9 | 0.9 | 1.2 | 0.8 |
| Humanistic professional | 4.6 | 4.4 | 5.9 | 5.9 | 4.2 |
| Health professional | 8.1 | 6.1 | 4.6 | 3.7 | 2.7 |
| Teacher, college | 5.0 | 3.0 | 3.5 | 3.2 | 1.7 |
| Teacher, other | 6.0 | 12.7 | 22.0 | 33.1 | 43.7 |
| Business and management | 23.8 | 24.6 | 20.5 | 15.2 | 19.0 |
| Other professional | 10.5 | 7.7 | 6.7 | 4.7 | 6.1 |
| Semiskilled and technical | 1.1 | 1.4 | 2.2 | 1.7 | 2.0 |
| Clerical and sales | 8.5 | 8.8 | 5.6 | 7.3 | 3.7 |
| Other unskilled and no answer | 2.3 | 3.2 | 3.0 | 7.2 | 5.6 |
| Total percent | 100.1 | 100.1 | 99.9 | 99.9 | 100.1 |
| (Total number) | (3,125) | (5,151) | (2,882) | (1,203) | (1,121) |
| **Women** | | | | | |
| Natural scientist | 1.5 | 1.6 | 1.8 | 0.8 | 0.8 |
| Engineer | 1.0 | 0.4 | 0.5 | 0.2 | – |
| Social scientist | 2.0 | 1.0 | 0.5 | 0.8 | – |
| Humanistic professional | 7.5 | 6.4 | 2.4 | 5.5 | 4.8 |
| Health professional | 9.7 | 8.3 | 7.5 | 3.0 | 3.0 |
| Teacher, college | 5.6 | 3.7 | 4.5 | 2.1 | 2.5 |
| Teacher, other | 42.0 | 58.1 | 66.3 | 74.9 | 73.6 |
| Business and management | 7.3 | 5.0 | 1.8 | 0.9 | 2.3 |
| Other professional | 9.4 | 5.7 | 5.7 | 1.9 | 6.2 |
| Semiskilled and technical | 5.1 | 2.8 | 3.7 | 2.1 | 1.3 |
| Clerical and sales | 6.1 | 4.6 | 3.4 | 4.9 | 3.4 |
| Other unskilled and no answer | 2.7 | 2.4 | 2.0 | 2.8 | 2.0 |
| Total percent | 99.9 | 100.0 | 100.1 | 99.9 | 100.0 |
| (Total number) | (588) | (1,109) | (831) | (527) | (643) |

prestige ranking decreases there is an increase in the number of men employed as teachers. Some of these differences, however, are due to the type of institution classified in each level. Teachers colleges tend to be the least prestigious and technical institutions more often top-rated.[9]

[9]The method of constructing the prestige index tends to "discriminate" in favor of technical schools, because the index is affected by the number of institutions in each category available for choice by the high school students. Thus, if a student planned to become an engineer, he would be more likely to choose a higher rated school than a student who wanted to become a teacher. The number of schools spreads the number of choices. Furthermore, National Merit semifinalists interested in teaching careers are unlikely to seek admission to teachers colleges; they are more likely to seek a liberal arts degree as background for future teaching careers. Thus the implication that students who want to become teachers are generally of low academic ability does not necessarily hold, although in the aggregate fewer graduates of high-prestige institutions enter teaching.

Among the women, we find that about 75 percent of those who had graduated from the least prestigious colleges became teachers, compared to less than half of the graduates from the most prestigious colleges. Girls who graduated from high prestige schools more often found jobs on a professional level (in the social sciences, humanities, natural sciences, for example) than did girls from lower rated schools. This can be partly attributed to the wider selection of undergraduate major fields and courses offered at high-level institutions than at lower-level ones. At the same time, the data in Table 6.6 also suggest a somewhat higher concentration of women from top-rated institutions in traditional female and clearly nonprofessional jobs (semi-skilled, technical, clerical, and sales work).

In the world of business it appears that where one goes to school still plays more of a role than in other areas of employment. For example, women who graduated from high prestige colleges were more often employed in business and managerial positions than any other female graduates (6 percent for the above-average prestige school graduates versus less than 2 percent for others). This suggests that the prestige of that type of schooling continues to carry weight in private industry and merchandising fields. For men we also see a slightly greater tendency for prestige school graduates to go into business and sales (33 percent for the highest prestige groups and 22 percent from schools with below average prestige). The apparent success of business in recruiting graduates from elite institutions suggests that the complaints of the business community about the reluctance of the best qualified young graduates to enter the world of business do not seem to be well-founded.

On closer examination and over a longer period of time, the preferences of business employers for graduates of prestige schools may lead to significantly greater career "success" for the graduates of elite schools, in terms of income and leadership. In other fields, however, there are no indications of future significant advantages for graduates from the more prestigious colleges.

As far as salaries are concerned, there is a surprisingly low correspondence between type of college and earnings five years later. Age at that stage in life seems to play a much greater role in predicting salary than does one's alma mater. According to our data, even going to graduate school has little effect on salary, but five years after receiving the B.A. is simply too short a time span to sort out the effects of graduate education versus job experience. Getting the best grades — which we have seen plays an important role in graduate school acceptance — also has little effect on getting the best salary. In the world of work, the best students do not necessarily reap superior rewards. At least in the early career stages, work experience seems more important.

Only in the world of business are there some indications that graduates of the more prestigious colleges tend to make higher salaries than graduates from other schools. Business and managerial positions paid an average of $8,435 in 1963 to men graduates from elite schools and $7,640 to graduates from average schools. In other areas, although there are some slight salary advantages offered to recent college graduates from the high prestige schools (in the natural and social sciences for men, health and teaching professions for women), the differences are slight, and the progression of increases is not orderly enough for meaningful analysis (Table 6.7).

Table 6.7.  Median Salary by Full-Time Occupation and National Merit Scholar Prestige, 1963
(1958 B.A. Recipients)

*(dollars)*

| Full-Time Occupation | Highest Prestige | Very High Prestige | Average Prestige | Below Average Prestige | Low Prestige |
|---|---|---|---|---|---|
| **Men** | | | | | |
| Natural scientist | 8,690 | 7,765 | 8,020 | 7,600 | 8,070 |
| Engineer | 9,630 | 9,285 | 9,245 | 9,820 | 9,190 |
| Social scientist | 8,150 | 7,625 | 7,690 | *a* | *a* |
| Humanistic professional | 5,999 | 6,420 | 5,455 | 5,410 | 4,765 |
| Health professional | 3,999 | 8,345 | 7,350 | 8,220 | 7,400 |
| Teacher, college | 6,940 | 6,790 | 6,735 | 6,580 | 6,215 |
| Teacher, other | 6,025 | 6,225 | 6,140 | 6,140 | 5,380 |
| Business and management | 8,435 | 7,300 | 7,640 | 6,980 | 7,105 |
| Other professional | 7,560 | 7,070 | 8,275 | 6,500 | 7,700 |
| Semiprofessional | 6,635 | 6,780 | 7,100 | 6,625 | 6,400 |
| Clerical and sales | 8,275 | 8,210 | 7,380 | 5,655 | 7,250 |
| **Women** | | | | | |
| Humanistic professional | 5,655 | 5,405 | 4,670 | 6,250 | 5,345 |
| Health professional | 5,715 | 5,695 | 5,575 | 5,999 | 4,560 |
| Teacher, college | 6,530 | 6,355 | 6,095 | *a* | 5,855 |
| Teacher, other | 5,775 | 6,405 | 5,760 | 5,845 | 4,980 |
| Business and management | 5,440 | 5,930 | *a* | *a* | *a* |
| Other professional | 6,440 | 5,860 | 6,525 | *a* | 5,405 |
| Semiprofessional | 5,750 | 5,555 | 6,070 | *a* | *a* |
| Clerical and sales | 4,915 | 4,535 | 3,930 | 4,410 | 3,855 |

*a* Too few cases to compute median salary (N <16).

On the whole, differences in salary appear to depend more on the occupation itself than on the institution which prepared the graduate for the occupation. In the long run, the salary differentials between graduates in the same field but from different institutions may widen as more professional and graduate degree holders fill the labor force. But from the vantage point of five years after college, it appears that the expansion in higher education and the unprecedented demand for college graduates has greatly narrowed the earnings gap between those who went to the most prestigious schools and those who got their education in less exclusive surroundings.

## Marital Status

As demographers have long noted, the highest educated segment of our population have consistently married later than members of their age group with less schooling. But the general feeling is that college education tends to delay marriage rather than to cause permanent spinsterhood or bachelorhood. It was not too long ago, after all, that most institutions did not permit full-time students to be married. Aside from these formal prohibitions, the norms during the first half of this century called for completion of college — and often graduate and professional school as well — prior to marriage.

Today, the idea of student marriages has taken a strong hold on campuses across the country. Among the cohort of 1958 graduates, more than 25 percent of the men and between 15 and 20 percent of the women were married before they graduated. Even though our group includes some older men and women who most likely were married before 1954 and had inter-

Table 6.8. Marital Status in 1963 by Type of Control and Sex Composition of Undergraduate Institution (1958 B.A. Recipients)

*(percentages)*

| Marital Status (With Year of Marriage) | Men | | | | Total |
|---|---|---|---|---|---|
| | Public | | Private | | |
| | All-male | Co-ed | All-male | Co-ed | |
| *Never married* | *9.6* | *14.6* | *24.2* | *17.2* | *16.6* |
| *Married, no children* | *13.3* | *14.3* | *16.6* | *16.0* | *15.2* |
| 1935-53 | – | 0.7 | 0.4 | 0.2 | 0.4 |
| 1954-57 | 0.7 | 1.1 | 0.2 | 0.7 | 0.9 |
| 1958 | 0.7 | 1.5 | 0.5 | 1.2 | 1.3 |
| 1959-64 | 5.8 | 5.0 | 5.6 | 6.9 | 5.8 |
| No answer | 5.9 | 5.9 | 10.1 | 7.0 | 6.8 |
| *Married, children* | *73.3* | *68.1* | *57.0* | *64.0* | *65.4* |
| 1935-53 | 6.7 | 9.3 | 4.0 | 8.0 | 8.2 |
| 1954-57 | 28.9 | 18.6 | 8.1 | 13.1 | 15.5 |
| 1958 | 11.9 | 10.3 | 10.1 | 11.1 | 10.6 |
| 1959-64 | 14.7 | 14.4 | 19.4 | 14.9 | 15.2 |
| No answer | 11.1 | 15.6 | 15.5 | 16.5 | 15.9 |
| *Widowed, separated, divorced* | – | *1.3* | *1.1* | *1.1* | *1.2* |
| 1935-53 | – | 0.2 | 0.1 | 0.2 | 0.2 |
| 1954-57 | – | 0.4 | 0.1 | 0.3 | 0.3 |
| 1958 | – | 0.3 | 0.2 | 0.1 | 0.2 |
| 1959-64 | – | 0.3 | 0.4 | 0.4 | 0.4 |
| No answer | – | 0.1 | 0.2 | 0.1 | 0.1 |
| *No answer* | *3.7* | *1.7* | *1.1* | *1.7* | *1.6* |
| Total percent | 99.9 | 100.0 | 100.0 | 100.0 | 100.0 |
| (Total number[a]) | (135) | (8,276) | (1,829) | (6,049) | (16,289) |

rupted their studies at some point before graduating in 1958, we can estimate that as many as 15 percent of the men and 10 percent of the women got married some time between their freshman and senior years.

A multitude of personality types with probably as many different attitudes toward marriage are attracted to the wide variety of U.S. colleges and universities. But in spite of personal factors, one cannot overlook the role played by situational factors in the marital status of recent college graduates. In fact, this is the one area where we get a sense of important institutional difference.

Our data show that graduates of all-male colleges stay single to a much greater extent than those who attend coeducational schools. More than 24 percent of the men who attended all-male schools were still not married five years after graduation, as opposed to 17 percent of all men in the cohort (Table 6.8). One might speculate that these men, who have shown through their occupational choices a stronger adherence to traditional male roles than

Table 6.8. (Continued)

| Marital Status (With Year of Marriage) | Women | | | | Total |
| | Public | | Private | | |
| | All-female | Co-ed | All-female | Co-ed | |
|---|---|---|---|---|---|
| *Never married* | 16.2 | 16.5 | 25.5 | 22.1 | 19.7 |
| *Married, no children* | 11.3 | 16.5 | 11.9 | 17.0 | 15.9 |
| 1935-53 | - | 0.3 | 0.2 | 0.4 | 0.4 |
| 1954-57 | - | 1.5 | 0.3 | 0.6 | 1.0 |
| 1958 | 1.4 | 1.9 | 0.9 | 1.7 | 1.7 |
| 1959-64 | 5.6 | 6.8 | 6.4 | 7.6 | 7.0 |
| No answer | 4.2 | 5.8 | 4.1 | 6.7 | 5.8 |
| *Married, children* | 71.1 | 60.9 | 58.0 | 56.3 | 59.1 |
| 1935-53 | 0.7 | 8.1 | 0.6 | 5.4 | 5.9 |
| 1954-57 | 4.2 | 8.8 | 3.1 | 7.5 | 7.4 |
| 1958 | 17.6 | 15.0 | 14.3 | 13.9 | 14.6 |
| 1959-64 | 26.8 | 14.6 | 24.7 | 16.6 | 17.0 |
| No answer | 21.8 | 14.5 | 15.3 | 13.1 | 14.3 |
| *Widowed, separated, divorced* | 0.7 | 3.7 | 2.5 | 2.6 | 3.1 |
| 1935-53 | 0.7 | 2.2 | 0.6 | 1.3 | 1.6 |
| 1954-57 | - | 0.6 | 0.9 | 0.1 | 0.4 |
| 1958 | - | 0.1 | 0.3 | 0.3 | 0.2 |
| 1959-64 | - | 0.5 | 0.7 | 0.5 | 0.5 |
| No answer | - | 0.4 | - | 0.4 | 0.3 |
| *No answer* | 0.7 | 2.4 | 2.1 | 1.9 | 2.1 |
| Total percent | 100.0 | 100.0 | 100.0 | 99.9 | 99.9 |
| (Total number) | (142) | (4,672) | (1,408) | (3,050) | (9,272) |

[a]Excludes four men and eighteen women who attended institutions not classified by control or sex composition.

is the case for other graduates, are less willing to follow the newer flexible patterns of combining marriage and study until they have received their advanced degree.

Women graduates from all-girl schools show themselves to be more traditional too. While they are just as likely to stay single as their age-mates who went to a coeducational school, the all-girl school graduates who marry are more likely to be mothers five years after graduation, as Table 6.8 indicates. This may simply reflect later marriages for the coeducational school graduates, but it is quite possible that here too the graduates from the coeducational institutions are more flexible and will work or study for a while, rather than espouse immediately the more traditional housewife-mother role.

The relationship between marital status, size and type of school, and the degree level offered by the school differs for men and women. Men are more likely to be single longer if they are graduates of a technical institute or an undergraduate school where graduate degrees are offered. Another institutional factor affecting marital status is the size of the college: the larger the undergraduate school, the greater the likelihood that male graduates will not have married.

For women, the relationships are quite different. The larger the college and the higher the degree level offered, the greater the likelihood of getting married. The largest proportion of single women were graduates from colleges with 200-499 students; the group that went to schools with more than 5,000 students seems to have married earlier than girls from smaller colleges. The larger coeducational schools obviously offer more continuous exposure to potential marriage partners. And when the undergraduate school is affiliated with a graduate school, a wider range of slightly older potential marriage partners is offered, which is especially significant for women.

In brief, the single-sex schools seem to foster later marriages for men and a less career-oriented life for women. Graduates from coeducational schools, on the other hand, have adopted more flexible patterns which represent the newer adaption to the needs of combining various roles. From their work, marriage, and study patterns (delayed parenthood, combined work-study periods, types of career choices), these young men and women include the highest proportions of innovators, seeking to develop a new life style appropriate to the demands of a changing society.

With the tremendous growth in the college-student populations, of which only a small proportion will go to the elite schools, it appears that the time has come to focus less on the styles of the traditional schools and more on the flexible, middle-range, coeducational schools at all prestige levels if one seeks to gauge the shape of future developments on the American college scene.

# VII

## CONCLUSION

The early career patterns of recent college graduates provide a unique perspective on what remains — in spite of our recent concern with the many other roles and functions of the university — one of the basic tasks of higher education in American society: the preparation of each new generation for certain important occupational tasks. Some of the more radical critics of the system today challenge the validity of this function, and recommend that the university dissociate itself completely from a work-preparatory role. Taking a different perspective, which implicitly assigns to institutions of higher learning a continuing responsibility for occupational training and socialization, we feel that our colleges and universities have accomplished this task more adequately than some of the other tasks implicitly or explicitly assigned to them — such as the creation of intellectually independent and socially cohesive scholarly communities, and the grooming of young people for elite roles in our society. If the major challenge to education in recent decades is defined as the acceptance on the part of the young and not-so-young of the need for life-time learning in view of rapid and continuing changes in the realm of knowledge, one can only conclude that this message has been well conveyed. The interest in graduate education on the part of recent cohorts and their willingness and ability to combine their study needs with work and family demands seems truly remarkable. Lack of funds does not seem to present the serious obstacles which many policy-makers — perhaps because they themselves grew up at a time when young people operated under much greater financial constraints — see as the greatest impediment to the ever fuller boom in graduate education. Rather, one's greater concern should be with the exclusionary processes which are not rooted in financial factors.

There is first of all the omnipresent sex differential when it comes to participation in the graduate process. This is, of course, only one facet of the unresolved problems of women's study and work roles with which neither the universities nor the women themselves seem ready to come to grips. But furthermore, it is clear that many students — including many with high academic ability — take themselves out of the running for graduate studies because they obtained mediocre grades in college. They thus remove themselves from the graduate study process altogether, despite the fact that the lack of at least some graduate study is bound to impede their professional life. Furthermore, from all we know about the life histories of geniuses and of men and women who chalked up solid professional achievements, it is clear that the undergraduate years are too early a point in the life-cycle for this kind of screening-out, especially in an age of lengthening education processes and shifting adolescent norms. One can only conjecture about the quantity and quality of true talent loss which accrues to society from this drop-out phenomenon, but it appears to be far from negligible. There are many other good arguments against the overemphasis on competitive grading which characterizes undergraduate education in most institutions; the premature discouragement of those potentially able to profit from graduate studies should be added to the list. Obviously there is a need for an ultimate screening process, but if we choose to meet the total educational needs of today's college graduates within the present educational structure, this process must be further postponed.

Along the same lines, our data also suggest that the concern with the quality or prestige of the undergraduate institution, which agitates so many parents, counselors, and policy-makers, is perhaps largely misplaced. Students who graduated from middle-level institutions — where much of the growth in enrollment has taken place in recent years — exhibited impressive post-college career and study patterns. Only the business world — and not for technical personnel, but for future managers and executives — seems to be slow to accept this change; here the recruitment emphasis is still on the high-prestige institution, whose graduates fare better in the business world than men and women who attended middle-level institutions. Given the changing mix of graduates and the personnel needs of industry and financial institutions, it might be advisable for many corporations who complain about the difficulties of recruiting college graduates to turn to newer and growing institutions, whose graduates seem to be doing very well indeed in other sectors.

At the risk of becoming tiresome we find ourselves repeating time and again that it is the undergraduate major rather than the institution attended which has the greatest impact on career outcome. But this is not to say that undergraduate — or even graduate — training is seen as equally appropriate in all fields and for all professions by those who enter the world of work. It appears that by far the best congruence and continuity are achieved by those who choose to become teachers. This is the area where college graduates feel themselves to be best prepared and seem to be operating most effectively in the early stages of their career. The growing popularity of teaching careers — especially, but not exclusively, at the college level — is evident in the long-term aspirations of recent graduates; this further confirms the success of undergraduate and graduate institutions in orienting students toward teaching. But while the need for teachers at all levels will continue to grow, it is perhaps necessary to establish better links between the university and some of the professions whose members do not seem to perceive the same close fit between their undergraduate education and their work roles.

In this respect, the greatest ambivalence was seen in the area of business education. Business majors are least likely to see a connection between their undergraduate studies and the work they do after graduation, and of course they are least likely to seek graduate education. Thus, after they graduate, theirs are the most tenuous intellectual ties with the university world. If we assume that one of the important by-products of a college education is a greater life-long receptivity to new ideas and certain value constellations centered on the importance of knowledge, research, and intellectual integrity, it would seem that the relatively short-term identification with the academic world by many of those who go into the business community is unfortunate. If universities include among their offerings professional preparation for business majors, ways should be sought to achieve a better integration between what the universities have to offer and the post-college needs of these students. Perhaps what is needed above all else is to achieve a more sophisticated understanding on the part of young businessmen of the relevance of the college experience and the desirability of their continuing interaction with the academic community for success in the business community. This sophistication is present in some areas, but it needs further diffusion.

The studies on which our observations are based were designed to measure primarily objective career outcomes. We did not set out to assess the relationships between the college experience and the attitudes and values held by graduates in later years. Yet implied in all discussions of educational achievement and higher education is the assumption that these educational experiences lead to greater and more enlightened interest in social problems, public affairs, or cultural progress. In this light one might look again at the experiences of the class of 1958, particularly the sharp differences that exist between those students who majored in the humanities or sciences and those who majored in business, education, or health fields. The former group was geographically more mobile, more likely to have gone to graduate school, and much less likely to have seen military service. The latter group was likely to have remained in the same region all their lives, with the exception of the time spent in the military. From this configuration of experiences, it would be easy to predict that the outlook of humanities and science majors is considerably more cosmopolitan, while, as a group, business, education, and health majors fit in more closely with the "local orientation" model. Obviously no glib assumptions about the population of college graduates can be made, given these profound differences in rates of exposure to other parts of the country (and by implication to Americans of different backgrounds). There is at this time justifiable concern with the greater polarization in this country between the life styles of college graduates and other affluents compared to those whose education went at most through the twelfth grade. Yet it may not be too farfetched to ponder as well about the deep split within the college segment, which has equally real social and ideological consequences. This polarization is especially noteworthy because of its geographic corollaries. The best educated and most cosmopolitan graduates are increasingly concentrated in the largest metropolitan areas where the presence of the largest and most prestigious universities is directly or indirectly responsible for providing their employment. At the other extreme, those college graduates who live in smaller towns and in educationally less advantaged metropolitan areas are those whose "local" orientation is most clear-cut. One need not push speculation very far to be concerned about the social and political consequences of this kind of internal brain-drain and imbalance. Efforts are currently being made to meet the problem by creating or enlarging universities in areas other than on the two coasts. The data from the college follow-up studies certainly should provide further impetus for such plans.

Current events have pushed to the fore one clearly unresolved problem which until recently our society was largely able to shunt aside. This is the fitting of military service into the lives of college students. It seems clear that only men who served prior to college or those who were inclined toward some form of voluntary service, which in turn conferred officer status, derived any personal advantage or satisfaction from the years spent in the armed forces. It is also clear that graduate school and military service are competitors for crucial life-span periods and that the end of graduate deferments is likely to result in some irretrievable talent losses. Before dismissing the hardship which service constituted for the majority of college graduates as simply their share of a universal citizenship burden, it might be well to consider the matter further. Although there is a paucity of data in this area, recent studies suggest that perhaps the majority of draftees who did not attend college derived some occupational or educational benefit from their period of service. Judging from the results of our survey, apparently this was not the case for the college graduates. It may not be too farfetched to conclude that in terms of equity of sacrifice, the college graduate who serves as an enlisted man pays an exceptionally high price. The provision of alternate service options more likely to provide useful work experience and enable graduates to make a valuable contribution to society commensurate with their education seems particularly desirable in the light of the experiences of recent graduates.

For the men, the colleges and universities have not been of much help in solving the problem of reconciling military obligation, personal values, and career needs. It can be argued that this problem was not within the primary purview of academic institutions. By the same token, it can also be argued that the universities offer the same opportunities to women as they do to men, and that the picture which emerges with depressing regularity from every study — that of women confined to traditional study and work areas, earning lower salaries, undertaking graduate study less frequently than men, and progressing less rapidly when they do — is the result of women's own preferences or priorities and the needs they experience to reconcile diverse roles. Our studies show that a sizable proportion of older women are included among recent cohorts of bachelors and master's degree recipients, which indicates that colleges are increasingly responsive to women's second career needs. Yet one cannot help feeling that the schools might take a more active role in departing from the traditional patterns of course offerings or graduate study requirements and encourage women at all ages to seek out new avenues in which they can combine work and family roles and enter occupations outside of the teaching fields.

One can only welcome the gradual disappearance of the single-sex institutions. Judging from our findings, they are the preservers of dysfunctional traditions that make it especially unlikely that men and women will follow new careers and experiment with innovative combinations of study and work periods while being married and having families. There is little doubt that in the decades to come men will need to enter many of the so-called female occupations (in particular teaching, social work, and the arts and humanities), and women's talents in mathematics and the sciences must be more fully exploited if we are to cope effectively with the problems and challenges of the future.

What applies to women applies to Negroes as well. The colleges have until recently failed to innovate and to promote changes which are clearly necessary. It would be foolhardy to minimize the very real dilemma presented by the introduction of sizable numbers of students who are poorly prepared academically. Yet it would appear that, as a result of political developments in the late 1960's, most colleges are now well into the process of compensating for past inaction with respect to Negro students, including academically disadvantaged ones. One sees little comparable effort on behalf of the women — although the task would be a much easier one. This is probably owing to a less clear perception of need and less unanimity among the women themselves and among those who speak on their behalf.

Most of the challenges to higher education which preoccupy today's educators are outside the realm of the topics discussed here. Our findings suggest, however, that there are other less sensational challenges with respect to those functions where the university's competence is less often questioned. There are sizable groups of graduates whose careers raise questions about the total adequacy of the system as it currently operates. The system has also created geographic imbalances in the population of college graduates with increasing concentrations of certain "cosmopolitan" subgroups in relatively few areas. This is apparently an unfortunate by-product of the processes of professional growth and specialization which have taken place in recent years. One can only hope that the further acceleration of these trends will lead to the involvement of new segments of the population with a consequent leveling of regional differences.

# APPENDIX: METHODOLOGY

The data in this book were derived from two sample surveys of 1958 college graduates.

The initial study was designed to include June 1958 graduates from all four-year, degree granting institutions in the United States. Registrars of the 1,299 institutions eligible to participate were contacted and asked to select a 20 percent sample of bachelor's and first-level professional degree recipients and a 33 percent sample of master's and second-level professional degree recipients. A total of 55,396 first-level names and 10,996 second-level names were supplied by 1,244 schools. Usable questionnaires were received from 32,122 first-level and 9,468 second-level graduates, a 65 percent rate of return.

For the 1963 survey, a more detailed questionnaire was sent to 23,309 of the original respondents, selected through a stratified sampling plan. This questionnaire examined in greater depth factors affecting and attitudes toward graduate study and career outcomes. Usable questionnaires were received from 19,299 persons, an 83 percent rate of return.

Since more than one-third of the 1960 survey did not respond, it would have been desirable to resurvey the entire group for the follow-up survey. This course was not followed since (1) the 1963 questionnaire did not include certain basic data already collected in the 1960 survey, and (2) the 1963 survey used a stratified sampling plan, unlike the initial survey.

The problem of nonresponse was handled through other techniques which will be discussed below.

### The Sample for the 1963 Survey

A stratified sample plan with differential sampling among strata was deemed to be the most efficient approach for the 1963 follow-up survey because of the uneven distribution of graduates across fields of study (over one-third of the B.A. recipients had majored in education or business and commerce) and the importance of this variable as a determinant of extent of graduate study and occupational outcome. The following variables were used as the basis for stratification: level of degree, sex, field of study, and graduate study status in 1960.

A sample of 150 cases in each stratum was selected to provide a standard error of estimate no larger than 4.1 percent and to give a sufficient number of cases to allow the necessary cross-breaks for analysis purposes. Exceptions were made in the natural science, engineering, and social science majors, which constitute high interest fields for the NSF, sponsor of the surveys. In these areas, sampling ratios of 1.00 were used to allow greater reliability and the possibility of more detailed cross-breaks. A somewhat larger number (200) was used for education majors because of NSF's interest in science teaching. Table 1 shows for each field the estimated total populations, sample sizes, and standard error of estimate.

Response rates varied by field, sex, and graduate school status at the bachelor's level. Actual returns were received from 11,177 men and 4,476 women. Each cell was weighted in accordance with ratios derived from Table 1, which yielded a weighted total of 16,293 men and 9,290 women. At the master's level, there were 2,651 actual returns from men and 998 from women; the weighted totals were 3,706 men and 1,736 women.

## The Nonrespondents

The 1960 survey yielded a 65 percent return rate, which raised some questions about possible bias in the product. This would be the case if there were a significant difference in the personal characteristics and the study and work experiences of respondents and nonrespondents.

It was therefore decided to select a special sample from the nonrespondents for intensive follow-up. One thousand two hundred names were selected: 1,000 nonrespondents (those who presumably received the questionnaire but chose not to complete it) and 200 unreached (those whose questionnaires had never been delivered and were eventually returned by the Post Office). An attempt was made to locate those 1,200 individuals through further inquiries to the institutions from which they had graduated and subsequent efforts were made to contact them personally, either by telephone or personal visit. As a result of this intensive follow-up procedure, 697 usable questionnaires were received from this group.

In general few differences were observed between the survey respondents and the special "nonrespondent" sample. Male nonrespondents tended to be less frequently enrolled in graduate study programs and, conversely, were

Table 1. Sample for Five-Year Follow-Up Study of 1958 Graduates

| Field | Sex | Stratum P | Graduate status | T | n | SE |
|---|---|---|---|---|---|---|
| | | **1958 B.A. Recipients** | | | | |
| Agriculture | M | 6,677 | N | 350 | 150 | .041 |
| | | | G | 175 | 150 | .041 |
| | W | 92 | N | 28 | 28 | .094 |
| | | | G | 12 | 12 | .144 |
| Pharmacy | M | 3,391 | N | 275 | 150 | .041 |
| | | | G | 50 | 50 | .071 |
| Home economics | W | 4,276 | N | 475 | 150 | .041 |
| | | | G | 225 | 150 | .041 |
| English, journalism | M | 8,439 | N | 375 | 150 | .041 |
| | | | G | 525 | 150 | .041 |
| | W | 10,796 | N | 675 | 150 | .041 |
| | | | G | 525 | 150 | .041 |
| Fine arts | M | 5,850 | N | 300 | 150 | .041 |
| | | | G | 300 | 150 | .041 |
| | W | 6,402 | N | 475 | 150 | .041 |
| | | | G | 325 | 150 | .041 |
| Foreign language | M | 1,814 | N | 50 | 50 | .071 |
| | | | G | 125 | 125 | .045 |
| | W | 2,689 | N | 150 | 150 | .041 |
| | | | G | 150 | 150 | .041 |
| Religion, philosophy | M | 10,097 | N | 230 | 150 | .041 |
| | | | G | 245 | 150 | .041 |
| | W | 1,714 | N | 130 | 130 | .044 |
| | | | G | 35 | 35 | .085 |
| Education | M | 25,542 | N | 900 | 200 | .035 |
| | | | G | 1,100 | 200 | .035 |
| | W | 57,212 | N | 2,525 | 200 | .035 |
| | | | G | 1,475 | 200 | .035 |
| Business, commerce | M | 47,286 | N | 3,050 | 150 | .041 |
| | | | G | 950 | 150 | .041 |
| | W | 3,968 | N | 450 | 150 | .041 |
| | | | G | 150 | 150 | .041 |
| Nursing | W | 6,003 | N | 400 | 150 | .041 |
| | | | G | 150 | 150 | .041 |
| Health, all other | W | 1,965 | N | 150 | 150 | .041 |
| | | | G | 50 | 50 | .071 |

P: Total degrees conferred in the academic year 1957-58. *Source:* U.S. Office of Education, *Earned Degrees Conferred 1958* (Circular 570; Washington, D.C.: U.S. Government Printing Office, 1959).

T: Total number of 1958 respondents. Figures over 50 are usually rounded to nearest 25, 50, 75, or 00.

n: Number in sample.

SE: Standard error of estimate. (The standard error of estimate is conservative, based upon sampling from an infinite population with a hypothetical proportion of .5).

G: Enrolled for graduate or professional study for one term or more between June 1958 and Summer 1960 (includes nondegree-enrolled students).

N: Never enrolled for graduate or professional study.

Table 1 *(cont.)*

| Field | Sex | Stratum P | Stratum Graduate status | T | n | SE |
|-------|-----|-----------|-------------------------|---|---|-----|
| | | **1958 B.A. Recipients** | | | | |
| General | M | 2,616 | N | 75 | 75 | .058 |
| | | | G | 50 | 50 | .071 |
| | W | 686 | N | 30 | 30 | .091 |
| | | | G | 5 | 5 | .224 |
| Mathematics | M | 4,935 | N | 250 | 250 | .032 |
| | | | G | 350 | 350 | .027 |
| | W | 1,971 | N | 175 | 175 | .038 |
| | | | G | 125 | 125 | .045 |
| Premedicine | M | 3,728 | N | 25 | 25 | .100 |
| | | | G | 325 | 325 | .028 |
| | W | 234 | N | 11 | 11 | .151 |
| | | | G | 22 | 22 | .107 |
| Biology | M | 7,498 | N | 200 | 200 | .035 |
| | | | G | 650 | 650 | .020 |
| | W | 2,948 | N | 200 | 200 | .035 |
| | | | G | 200 | 200 | .035 |
| Chemistry | M | 5,705 | N | 250 | 250 | .032 |
| | | | G | 450 | 450 | .024 |
| | W | 1,305 | N | 110 | 110 | .048 |
| | | | G | 90 | 90 | .053 |
| Earth sciences | M | 3,516 | N | 175 | 175 | .038 |
| | | | G | 125 | 125 | .045 |
| | W | 224 | N | 13 | 13 | .139 |
| | | | G | 12 | 12 | .144 |
| Physics | M | 3,042 | N | 75 | 75 | .058 |
| | | | G | 225 | 225 | .033 |
| | W | 144 | N | 7 | 7 | .189 |
| | | | G | 16 | 16 | .125 |
| Physical science | M | 1,150 | N | 50 | 50 | .071 |
| | | | G | 75 | 75 | .058 |
| Electrical engineering | M | | N | 720 | 720 | .019 |
| | | | G | 280 | 280 | .030 |
| Chemical engineering | M | | N | 175 | 175 | .038 |
| | | | G | 125 | 125 | .045 |
| Civil engineering | M | | N | 375 | 375 | .026 |
| | | | G | 125 | 125 | .045 |
| Mechanical engineering | M | | N | 625 | 625 | .020 |
| | | | G | 375 | 375 | .026 |
| Industrial engineering | M | | N | 300 | 300 | .029 |
| | | | G | 100 | 100 | .050 |

Table 1 *(cont.)*

|  | Stratum | | | T | n | SE |
|---|---|---|---|---|---|---|
| Field | Sex | P | Graduate status | | | |
| **1958 B.A. Recipients** | | | | | | |
| Mining engineering | M | | N | 100 | 100 | .050 |
|  | | | G | 50 | 50 | .071 |
| Engineering, all other | M | | N | 250 | 250 | .032 |
|  | | | G | 125 | 125 | .045 |
| All engineering | M | 35,223 | | | | |
|  | W | 109 | N | 35 | 35 | .085 |
|  | | | G | 20 | 20 | .112 |
| Sociology, anthropology | M | 3,181 | N | 150 | 150 | .041 |
|  | | | G | 175 | 175 | .038 |
|  | W | 3,761 | N | 250 | 250 | .032 |
|  | | | G | 150 | 150 | .041 |
| Economics | M | 8,671 | N | 525 | 525 | .022 |
|  | | | G | 325 | 325 | .028 |
|  | W | 647 | N | 50 | 50 | .071 |
|  | | | G | 50 | 50 | .071 |
| History | M | 9,031 | N | 300 | 300 | .029 |
|  | | | G | 600 | 600 | .020 |
|  | W | 3,852 | N | 175 | 175 | .038 |
|  | | | G | 225 | 225 | .033 |
| Political science | M | 5,811 | N | 225 | 225 | .033 |
|  | | | G | 325 | 325 | .028 |
|  | W | 1,244 | N | 75 | 75 | .058 |
|  | | | G | 75 | 75 | .058 |
| Social science, all other | M | 6,956 | N | 300 | 300 | .029 |
|  | | | G | 400 | 400 | .025 |
|  | W | 3,008 | N | 200 | 200 | .035 |
|  | | | G | 175 | 175 | .038 |
| Psychology | M | 4,063 | N | 175 | 175 | .038 |
|  | | | G | 300 | 300 | .029 |
|  | W | 2,867 | N | 175 | 175 | .038 |
|  | | | G | 150 | 150 | .041 |
| **1958 M.A. Recipients** | | | | | | |
| Education | M | 16,479 | N | 1,000 | 200 | .035 |
|  | | | G | 300 | 200 | .035 |
|  | W | 14,633 | N | 1,000 | 200 | .035 |
|  | | | G | 150 | 150 | .041 |
| Business and commerce | M | 3,896 | N | 500 | 150 | .041 |
|  | | | G | 100 | 100 | .050 |
|  | W | 145 | N | 15 | 15 | .129 |
|  | | | G | – | – | – |

All other fields:  universe of 1958 respondents included (all strata too small for subsampling).

more often found in the labor force. This seemed to be a result of the fact that nonresponse was relatively high among men who had majored in education and business. Also noted was the difference between women respondents and nonrespondents with respect to marital status and employment status. The sample slightly underestimated the number of married women with children and, conversely, slightly overestimated the number of women employed.

An effort was made in the 1963 survey to include these 697 special survey nonrespondents because we wanted to secure broad-gauged indications of the direction and extent to which the slight bias introduced by the exclusion of the 1960 nonrespondents may have affected the 1963 survey results. Responses from this hard-to-reach segment continued to be difficult to obtain. Only 287 usable questionnaires were returned by this group: 233 from the original nonrespondent group and 54 from the unreached group. These numbers are so small as not to allow a very effective analysis. Yet we found that the distribution by field of study of this group was similar enough to that of the total nonresponsive sample (and also the 1963 respondent sample) to let us use the available data, meager as they were.

The results of this special survey corroborate the findings of the 1960 special survey and add no new evidence that serious bias exists due to nonresponse. In both 1960 and 1963 there were only few differences between the survey respondents and the nonrespondent sample.

How does the special nonrespondent group differ? In terms of graduate degree enrollment, we found that there was less exposure to graduate school. Furthermore, the nonresponsive B.A. men who went to graduate school were less likely to have studied for a professional degree than the survey participants. The two groups, however, did not differ in their plans for future enrollment for graduate study.

There were some differences in the employment picture between respondents and nonrespondents, as Table 2 shows. Nonrespondent men were more likely to be employed full-time than respondents; among women, however, the reverse was true. Correspondingly, more nonrespondent women were married and had children than their counterparts in the respondent group. There was a similar distribution of jobs held, with slightly larger numbers of nonrespondents in teaching and business (Table 3). Occupational stability, which characterized respondents, was the same, or even slightly greater, for the nonrespondents. Graduates were considered occupationally stable if they had the same occupation and employer in both 1960 and 1963 and if they thought of their current occupation as a permanent one.

Slight differences appeared in how the usefulness of the undergraduate background was rated by both groups. Respondents reported that they made slightly greater use of their training than the nonrespondents. The nonresponsive B.A. men were also more likely to cluster at the extremes when asked

Table 2. Employment Status in 1963

*(percentages)*

| Employment Status | B.A. Men | | | B.A. Women | | M.A. Men | |
|---|---|---|---|---|---|---|---|
| | 1963 respondents (16,293) | Nonresponsive (135) | Unreached (31) | 1963 respondents (9,290) | Nonresponsive (64) | 1963 respondents (3,706) | Nonresponsive (28) |
| Employed full-time | 91 | 98 | 94 | 47 | 34 | 93 | 93 |
| Employed part-time | 4 | 2 | – | 10 | 19 | 5 | 4 |
| Armed forces | 4 | 2 | 7 | 1 | – | 2 | 4 |
| Unemployed, looking for work | 1 | – | 3 | 1 | – | 1 | – |
| Full-time student | 5 | 2 | – | 1 | 2 | 4 | 4 |
| Part-time student | 9 | 10 | 13 | 6 | 6 | 7 | 4 |
| Housewife | – | – | – | 61 | 63 | – | – |
| Retired, disabled, etc. | 1 | – | – | 1 | 2 | 1 | – |
| No answer | 1 | – | – | 1 | – | 1 | – |
| Total percent[a] | 116 | 114 | 117 | 120 | 126 | 114 | 109 |

[a] Add to more than 100 percent because of multiple answers.

Table 3. Occupation in 1963

*(percentages)*

| Occupation | B.A. Men | | | B.A. Women | | M.A. Men | |
|---|---|---|---|---|---|---|---|
| | 1963 respondents (14,812) | Nonresponsive (132) | Unreached (29) | 1963 respondents (4,335) | Nonresponsive (22) | 1963 respondents (3,445) | Nonresponsive (26) |
| Natural scientist | 6 | 5 | 10 | 1 | 5 | 10 | – |
| Engineer | 19 | 16 | 24 | 1 | – | 15 | 8 |
| Social scientist | 1 | 2 | – | 1 | – | 3 | 4 |
| Health professional | 6 | 5 | – | 6 | 5 | 1 | 8 |
| Teacher | 22 | 25 | 10 | 68 | 73 | 45 | 42 |
| Business and commerce | 22 | 23 | 21 | 4 | – | 13 | 19 |
| Other professional | 13 | 10 | 14 | 11 | 9 | 8 | 15 |
| Semiprofessional and technical | 2 | 2 | – | 3 | – | 1 | – |
| Clerical and sales | 7 | 8 | 10 | 4 | 9 | 2 | 4 |
| Other and no answer | 4 | 4 | 10 | 2 | – | 2 | – |
| Total employed full-time | 101 | 100 | 99 | 101 | 101 | 100 | 100 |

about the importance of their undergraduate background as a prerequisite for their current job.

The differences that appear — lower incidence of graduate study, somewhat greater occupational stability, and slightly higher labor force participation — can be explained by the over-representation of education and business majors among nonrespondents.

The only puzzling difference is the slight salary advantage of the nonrespondents, which runs counter to the often-held belief that nonresponse is characteristic of the financially less successful members of a cohort. Among the B.A. men respondents the median salary was $7,550, among the nonresponsive men it was $7,750, and among the unreached it was $8,400. The nonresponsive women, on the other hand, had a somewhat lower median salary — $5,000 versus $5,605 for the respondents.

In brief, several of the most important findings of the study — the long-term commitment to formal education, the importance of the first job as an indicator of longer-term occupational outcome — are not affected by nonresponse bias.

It should be recalled that because both field of study and occupation are such important variables in studying post-graduate study and career outcomes, the bulk of the analysis in the main studies used these variables as controls. This tends to minimize the effect of bias resulting from the slight under-representation of graduates in the education and business fields, which appears to be the most notable effect of nonresponse to the surveys.

# APPENDIX TABLES

Appendix Table A. Enrollment for Graduate and Professional Degrees by Undergraduate Major and Time of First Enrollment (1958 B.A. Recipients)

| Undergraduate Major | Total Degree Enrolled for One Term or More 1958-63 | | Percent Degree Enrolled for the First Time During: | | | | | | | |
|---|---|---|---|---|---|---|---|---|---|---|
| | | | Men | | | | Women | | | |
| | Men | Women | Number | 1958-60 | 1960-63 | Non-speci-fied | Number | 1958-60 | 1960-63 | Non-speci-fied |
| *Total* | *41.0* | *22.1* | *6,672* | *77.9* | *19.3* | *2.7* | *2,051* | *70.2* | *24.8* | *4.9* |
| *Natural Sciences* | *60.0* | *29.3* | *1,564* | *86.0* | *12.7* | *1.3* | *235* | *80.4* | *16.2* | *3.4* |
| Biological science | 69.0 | 28.9 | 476 | 87.1 | 12.2 | 0.8 | 93 | 78.7 | 17.2 | 4.3 |
| Premedicine | 83.0 | 50.0 | 253 | 95.7 | 3.2 | 1.2 | 15 | 100.0 | - | - |
| Chemistry | 58.2 | 25.7 | 327 | 88.7 | 9.8 | 1.5 | 40 | 82.5 | 12.5 | 5.0 |
| Earth science | 36.3 | 11.8 | 89 | 78.6 | 20.2 | 1.1 | 2 | 100.0 | - | - |
| Physics | 62.3 | 47.1 | 157 | 80.9 | 17.2 | 1.9 | 8 | 87.5 | 12.5 | - |
| Other physical sciences | 52.4 | 18.5 | 54 | 81.4 | 14.8 | 3.7 | 5 | 80.0 | - | 20.0 |
| Mathematics | 45.9 | 30.7 | 208 | 76.0 | 22.6 | 1.4 | 72 | 76.4 | 22.2 | 1.4 |
| *Engineering* | *30.9* | *24.4* | *965* | *67.9* | *29.0* | *3.1* | *11* | *63.7* | *36.4* | *-* |
| Chemical | 45.2 | - | 116 | 72.4 | 25.9 | 1.7 | - | - | - | - |
| Civil | 22.7 | - | 97 | 66.0 | 28.9 | 5.2 | - | - | - | - |
| Electrical | 37.1 | - | 309 | 74.4 | 23.6 | 1.9 | - | - | - | - |
| Industrial | 24.1 | - | 82 | 62.2 | 36.6 | 1.2 | - | - | - | - |
| Mechanical | 27.9 | - | 232 | 59.5 | 35.8 | 4.7 | - | - | - | - |
| Mining | 28.7 | - | 39 | 59.0 | 30.8 | 10.3 | - | - | - | - |
| Other | 29.8 | - | 90 | 72.2 | 26.6 | 1.1 | - | - | - | - |
| *Social Sciences* | *52.0* | *28.0* | *1,595* | *81.0* | *16.8* | *2.2* | *397* | *75.6* | *20.1* | *4.0* |
| Economics | 33.5 | 22.8 | 228 | 73.8 | 25.0 | 1.3 | 19 | 68.5 | 21.1 | 10.5 |
| History | 61.0 | 34.9 | 450 | 82.9 | 16.0 | 1.1 | 112 | 75.0 | 22.3 | 1.8 |
| Political science | 57.4 | 29.6 | 250 | 82.8 | 13.2 | 4.0 | 41 | 78.0 | 19.6 | 2.4 |
| Psychology | 61.0 | 27.4 | 241 | 83.7 | 14.0 | 2.1 | 77 | 70.2 | 20.8 | 9.1 |
| Sociology and anthropology | 51.6 | 23.1 | 136 | 78.7 | 16.9 | 4.4 | 71 | 77.5 | 18.2 | 4.2 |
| Other | 51.4 | 26.1 | 290 | 81.1 | 16.9 | 2.1 | 77 | 76.7 | 22.1 | 1.3 |

129

Appendix Table A (cont.)

| Undergraduate Major | Total Degree Enrolled for One Term or More 1958-63 | | Percent Degree Enrolled for the First Time During: | | | | | | | |
| | | | Men | | | | Women | | | |
| | Men | Women | Number | 1958-60 | 1960-63 | Non-specified | Number | 1958-60 | 1960-63 | Non-specified |
|---|---|---|---|---|---|---|---|---|---|---|
| *Humanities and Arts* | *53.3* | *26.3* | *929* | *81.1* | *15.4* | *2.8* | *529* | *72.6* | *24.0* | *3.2* |
| English and journalism | 54.0 | 26.4 | 396 | 79.3 | 18.0 | 2.8 | 264 | 74.9 | 22.0 | 3.0 |
| Fine arts | 43.6 | 22.6 | 220 | 79.1 | 17.2 | 3.6 | 143 | 78.4 | 18.2 | 3.5 |
| Foreign language | 59.2 | 32.0 | 80 | 86.3 | 11.3 | 2.5 | 78 | 65.3 | 32.0 | 2.6 |
| Philosophy | 67.1 | 22.7 | 147 | 91.1 | 8.8 | – | 7 | 42.9 | 57.2 | – |
| Religion | 57.3 | 34.3 | 86 | 80.2 | 13.9 | 5.8 | 37 | 56.7 | 37.8 | 5.4 |
| *Health* | *17.5* | *14.3* | *53* | *84.9* | *13.2* | *1.9* | *97* | *52.6* | *43.3* | *4.1* |
| Nursing | – | 17.7 | – | – | – | – | 83 | 54.2 | 41.0 | 4.8 |
| Pharmacy | 12.1 | – | 31 | 90.4 | 6.4 | 3.2 | – | – | – | – |
| Other | 50.0 | 6.8 | 22 | 77.2 | 22.7 | – | 14 | 42.8 | 57.1 | – |
| Agriculture | 31.5 | – | 143 | 77.0 | 20.3 | 2.8 | – | – | – | – |
| Home economics | – | 14.2 | – | – | – | – | 82 | 69.5 | 23.2 | 7.3 |
| Education | 50.0 | 19.5 | 807 | 68.1 | 28.4 | 3.5 | 632 | 63.7 | 28.6 | 7.8 |
| Business and commerce | 17.3 | 12.1 | 568 | 72.0 | 21.8 | 6.2 | 58 | 79.3 | 20.7 | – |
| General | 54.5 | 22.8 | 48 | 72.8 | 25.0 | 2.1 | 10 | 70.0 | 30.0 | – |

Appendix Table B. How Important Does Your Spouse Think It Is for You to Study for a Graduate Degree? (1958 B.A. Recipients)

*(percentages)*

| Graduate School Attendance | Number of Respondents | Very Important | Somewhat Important | Not Important | Total Percent |
|---|---|---|---|---|---|
| **Men** | | | | | |
| *Total[a]* | *12,884* | *37.2* | *37.7* | *25.1* | *100.0* |
| Never in school | 5,356 | 15.9 | 40.0 | 44.1 | 100.0 |
| Some school | 2,521 | 35.7 | 42.1 | 22.3 | 100.1 |
| Degree candidate | 1,606 | 62.5 | 34.1 | 3.4 | 100.0 |
| M.A. recipient and not candidate | 1,455 | 52.2 | 38.6 | 9.2 | 100.0 |
| Professional degree recipient | 1,153 | 61.1 | 29.9 | 9.0 | 100.0 |
| M.A. recipient and candidate | 536 | 71.5 | 25.9 | 2.6 | 100.0 |
| Ph.D. recipient | 257 | 72.8 | 25.7 | 1.6 | 100.1 |
| **Women** | | | | | |
| *Total[b]* | *6,803* | *15.7* | *36.6* | *47.8* | *100.1* |
| Never in school | 3,693 | 8.4 | 34.3 | 57.3 | 100.0 |
| Some school | 1,979 | 14.1 | 40.6 | 45.2 | 99.9 |
| Degree candidate | 466 | 46.4 | 37.6 | 16.1 | 100.1 |
| M.A. recipient and not candidate | 569 | 38.0 | 35.5 | 26.5 | 100.0 |
| Professional degree recipient | 28 | 50.0 | 35.7 | 14.2 | 99.9 |
| M.A. recipient and candidate | 58 | 46.5 | 41.4 | 12.1 | 100.0 |
| Ph.D. recipient | 10 | 30.0 | 60.0 | 10.0 | 100.0 |

[a] Excludes 2,655 unmarried male graduates and 753 no answers.
[b] Excludes 1,753 unmarried female graduates and 734 no answers.

Appendix Table C. How Important Do Your Parents Think It Is for You to Study
for an Advanced Degree? (1958 B.A. Recipients)

*(percentages)*

| Graduate School Attendance | Number of Respondents | Very Important | Somewhat Important | Not Important | Total Percent |
|---|---|---|---|---|---|
| **Men** | | | | | |
| *Total*[a] | *13,356* | *27.4* | *39.0* | *33.6* | *100.0* |
| Never in school | 5,115 | 9.9 | 32.3 | 57.8 | 100.0 |
| Some school | 2,497 | 24.4 | 45.0 | 30.6 | 100.0 |
| Degree candidate | 1,729 | 43.6 | 46.3 | 10.1 | 100.0 |
| M.A. recipient and not candidate | 1,673 | 36.9 | 46.6 | 16.5 | 100.0 |
| Professional degree recipient | 1,384 | 53.1 | 32.3 | 14.6 | 100.0 |
| M.A. recipient and candidate | 647 | 45.1 | 44.3 | 10.5 | 99.9 |
| Ph.D. recipient | 311 | 49.5 | 37.0 | 13.5 | 100.0 |
| **Women** | | | | | |
| *Total*[b] | *7,454* | *17.4* | *34.1* | *48.5* | *100.0* |
| Never in school | 3,536 | 9.1 | 28.5 | 62.4 | 100.0 |
| Some school | 2,233 | 15.8 | 37.0 | 47.2 | 100.0 |
| Degree candidate | 652 | 40.2 | 41.4 | 18.4 | 100.0 |
| M.A. recipient and not candidate | 868 | 34.4 | 42.5 | 23.0 | 99.9 |
| Professional degree recipient | 55 | 34.5 | 34.5 | 30.9 | 99.9 |
| M.A. recipient and candidate | 95 | 36.8 | 49.4 | 13.7 | 99.9 |
| Ph.D. recipient | 15 | 40.0 | 40.0 | 20.0 | 100.0 |

[a] Excludes 2,272 not applicable (parents deceased, etc.) and 665 no answers.
[b] Excludes 1,274 not applicable (parents deceased, etc.) and 562 no answers.

Appendix Table D.  Degree Status in 1963 by 1958 Graduate Field—Men
(1958 M.A. Recipients)

*(percentages)*

| 1958 M.A. Field | Number | Ph.D. recipient | Candidate for academic degree | Professional degree recipient or candidate | Recipient of second M.A. degree | Candidate for third graduate degree | Total additional graduate degree enrollment | No additional graduate degree work | Total Percent |
|---|---|---|---|---|---|---|---|---|---|
| *Total* | *3,706* | *10.4* | *12.0* | *5.8* | *1.7* | *1.0* | *30.9* | *69.1* | *100.0* |
| *Natural Sciences* | *549* | *29.7* | *16.8* | *3.8* | *0.5* | *1.6* | *52.4* | *47.5* | *99.9* |
| Biological sciences | 142 | 37.3 | 13.4 | 9.2 | 0.7 | 2.8 | 63.4 | 36.6 | 100.0 |
| Chemistry | 91 | 41.8 | 11.0 | 3.3 | – | – | 56.1 | 44.0 | 100.1 |
| Earth sciences | 93 | 19.4 | 17.2 | 1.1 | – | 1.1 | 38.8 | 61.3 | 100.1 |
| Physics | 91 | 33.0 | 22.0 | 3.3 | – | 2.2 | 60.5 | 39.6 | 100.1 |
| Other physical sciences | 22 | 18.2 | 18.2 | 4.5 | 4.5 | 4.5 | 49.9 | 50.0 | 99.9 |
| Mathematics | 110 | 18.2 | 20.9 | – | 0.9 | 0.9 | 40.9 | 59.1 | 100.0 |
| *Engineering* | *570* | *10.5* | *10.9* | *2.3* | *2.3* | *1.4* | *27.4* | *72.6* | *100.0* |
| Chemical | 61 | 24.6 | 19.7 | 1.6 | – | 1.6 | 47.5 | 52.5 | 100.0 |
| Civil | 60 | 6.7 | 16.7 | 3.3 | 1.7 | – | 28.4 | 71.7 | 100.1 |
| Electrical | 155 | 9.7 | 14.2 | 2.6 | 2.6 | 1.3 | 30.4 | 69.7 | 100.1 |
| Industrial | 77 | 1.3 | 2.6 | 2.6 | 2.6 | 1.3 | 10.4 | 89.6 | 100.0 |
| Mechanical | 123 | 8.1 | 6.5 | 0.8 | 3.3 | 1.6 | 20.3 | 79.7 | 100.0 |
| Mining | 27 | 33.3 | 3.7 | 3.7 | 3.7 | 3.7 | 48.1 | 51.9 | 100.0 |
| Other | 67 | 9.0 | 10.4 | 3.0 | 1.5 | 1.5 | 25.4 | 74.6 | 100.0 |
| *Social Sciences* | *393* | *18.3* | *24.9* | *4.6* | *2.5* | *1.8* | *52.1* | *47.8* | *99.9* |
| Economics | 73 | 9.6 | 30.1 | 4.1 | – | – | 43.8 | 56.2 | 100.0 |
| History | 85 | 16.5 | 37.6 | 2.4 | 2.4 | 2.4 | 61.3 | 38.8 | 100.1 |
| Political science | 67 | 17.9 | 20.9 | 1.5 | 3.0 | – | 43.3 | 56.7 | 100.0 |
| Psychology | 94 | 29.8 | 12.8 | 9.6 | 2.1 | 3.2 | 57.5 | 42.6 | 100.1 |
| Sociology and anthropology | 31 | 29.0 | 29.0 | 6.5 | – | – | 64.5 | 35.5 | 100.0 |
| Other | 43 | 4.7 | 20.9 | 2.3 | 9.3 | 4.7 | 41.9 | 58.1 | 100.0 |
| *Humanities and Arts* | *314* | *10.5* | *24.8* | *5.1* | *1.3* | *1.0* | *42.7* | *57.3* | *100.0* |
| English and journalism | 111 | 12.6 | 33.3 | 3.6 | 1.8 | 0.9 | 52.2 | 47.7 | 99.9 |
| Fine arts | 120 | 2.5 | 17.5 | 5.0 | 0.8 | 0.8 | 26.6 | 73.3 | 100.0 |
| Foreign language | 37 | 18.9 | 35.1 | – | – | – | 54.0 | 45.9 | 100.0 |
| Philosophy | 22 | 40.9 | 22.7 | – | – | – | 63.6 | 36.4 | 100.0 |
| Religion | 24 | – | 8.3 | 25.0 | 4.2 | 4.2 | 41.7 | 58.3 | 100.0 |
| Health | 60 | 10.0 | 8.3 | 6.7 | 1.7 | – | 26.7 | 73.3 | 100.0 |
| Agriculture | 77 | 28.6 | 15.6 | 1.3 | – | 1.3 | 46.8 | 53.2 | 100.0 |
| Business and commerce | 505 | 2.2 | 6.5 | 3.4 | 0.2 | 0.4 | 12.7 | 87.3 | 100.0 |
| Education | 1,116 | 1.4 | 5.1 | 10.9 | 2.8 | 0.6 | 20.8 | 79.1 | 99.9 |
| Other fields | 122 | 0.8 | 6.6 | 2.5 | – | – | 9.9 | 90.2 | 100.1 |

Appendix Table E. Degree Status in 1963 by 1958 Graduate Field—Women
(1958 M.A. Recipients)

*(percentages)*

| 1958 M.A. Field | Number | Degree Status in 1963 | | | | | | | Total Percent |
|---|---|---|---|---|---|---|---|---|---|
| | | Ph.D. recipient | Candidate for academic degree | Professional degree recipient or candidate | Recipient of second M.A. degree | Candidate for third graduate degree | Total additional graduate degree enrollment | No additional graduate degree work | |
| *Total* | *1,736* | *2.5* | *5.7* | *2.9* | *0.9* | *0.4* | *12.4* | *87.6* | *100.0* |
| *Natural Sciences* | *96* | *21.9* | *10.4* | *–* | *1.0* | *–* | *33.3* | *66.7* | *100.0* |
| Biological sciences | 43 | 32.6 | 7.0 | – | – | – | 39.6 | 60.5 | 100.1 |
| Chemistry | 18 | 27.8 | 5.6 | – | – | – | 33.4 | 66.7 | 100.1 |
| Earth sciences | 4[a] | | | | | | | | |
| Physics | 4[a] | | | | | | | | |
| Mathematics | 27 | 7.4 | 14.8 | – | 3.7 | – | 25.9 | 74.1 | 100.0 |
| *Engineering* | *1[a]* | | | | | | | | |
| *Social Sciences* | *154* | *7.8* | *15.6* | *3.2* | *3.2* | *1.9* | *31.7* | *68.2* | *99.9* |
| Economics | 8[a] | | | | | | | | |
| History | 31 | 6.5 | 12.9 | – | – | 6.5 | 25.9 | 74.2 | 100.1 |
| Political science | 14 | 7.1 | 14.3 | 7.1 | 7.1 | – | 35.6 | 64.3 | 99.9 |
| Psychology | 53 | 11.3 | 15.1 | 3.8 | 1.9 | 1.9 | 34.0 | 66.0 | 100.0 |
| Sociology and anthropology | 16 | 12.5 | 31.2 | 12.5 | 6.2 | – | 62.4 | 37.5 | 99.9 |
| Other | 32 | – | 12.5 | – | 3.1 | – | 15.6 | 84.4 | 100.0 |
| *Humanities and Arts* | *225* | *3.1* | *12.0* | *0.9* | *2.2* | *0.4* | *18.6* | *81.3* | *99.9* |
| English and journalism | 90 | 5.6 | 12.2 | 1.1 | 2.2 | 1.1 | 22.2 | 77.8 | 100.0 |
| Fine arts | 72 | 1.4 | 16.7 | – | 2.8 | – | 20.9 | 79.2 | 100.1 |
| Foreign language | 30 | 3.3 | 10.0 | 3.3 | 3.3 | – | 19.9 | 80.0 | 99.9 |
| Philosophy | 3[a] | | | | | | | | |
| Religion | 30 | – | 3.3 | – | – | – | 3.3 | 96.7 | 100.0 |
| *Health* | *64* | *–* | *4.7* | *1.6* | *1.6* | *1.6* | *9.5* | *90.6* | *100.1* |
| Nursing | 40 | – | 5.0 | 2.5 | 2.5 | 2.5 | 12.5 | 87.5 | 100.0 |
| Other | 24 | – | 4.2 | – | – | – | 4.2 | 95.8 | 100.0 |
| Education | 961 | 0.2 | 2.6 | 4.3 | 0.4 | 0.1 | 7.6 | 92.4 | 100.0 |
| Home economics | 61 | – | 4.9 | 3.3 | – | – | 8.2 | 91.8 | 100.0 |
| Other fields | 174 | 0.6 | 4.0 | – | – | 0.6 | 5.2 | 94.8 | 100.0 |

[a] Too few cases to compute percent.

Appendix Table F.  Judgment by 1958 M.A. Recipients of Their Completion Rates
of Post-Master Graduate Study

*(percentages)*

|  | Recipients | | Candidates | |
|---|---|---|---|---|
|  | Men | Women | Men | Women |
| *Completion Rate*[a] | | | | |
| Too fast | 2.6 | 2.5 | 1.0 | 8.1 |
| Just right | 64.5 | 60.0 | 28.9 | 24.3 |
| Too slow | 29.9 | 33.8 | 69.0 | 66.2 |
| No answer | 3.0 | 3.8 | 1.2 | 1.5 |
| Total percent | 100.0 | 100.1 | 100.1 | 100.1 |
| (Total number) | (541) | (80) | (603) | (136) |
| *Reason for Slow Completion*[b] | | | | |
| Financial obstacle | 40.7 | 33.3 | 55.0 | 51.1 |
| Course difficulty | 2.5 | – | 1.9 | 1.1 |
| Faculty pressure | 8.0 | 11.1 | 5.0 | 12.2 |
| No push | 21.6 | 14.8 | 13.5 | 8.9 |
| Inconvenient schedule | 2.5 | 7.4 | 2.6 | 3.3 |
| Language requirement | 4.3 | 3.7 | 2.9 | 1.1 |
| Thesis requirement | 9.9 | 7.4 | 6.2 | 3.3 |
| Routine unknown | 2.5 | 3.7 | 3.6 | 6.7 |
| No answer | 8.0 | 18.5 | 9.1 | 12.2 |
| Total percent | 100.0 | 99.9 | 99.8 | 99.9 |
| (Total number) | (162) | (27) | (416) | (90) |

[a] Do you feel that the rate at which you have been, or are, completing graduate study is too fast, just right, or too slow?

[b] If you feel that the rate at which you have been, or are, completing graduate study is too slow, where would you put the blame?

1. Could not afford to study full-time or continuously for financial reasons,

2. Found courses too difficult or the professors too demanding,

3. Pressure from faculty to participate in research work or teaching, thereby postponing completion of thesis,

4. Did not push myself hard enough,

5. Courses were not conveniently scheduled or courses not offered when needed for my program,

6. Had difficulty meeting language requirements,

7. Had difficulty meeting thesis requirements,

8. Was not aware of some academic routines or requirements, and lost time on that account.

Appendix Table G.  Grade Point Average and Graduate School Attendance
(1958 B.A. Recipients)

*(percentages)*

| Graduate School Attendance | Number | GPA[a] | | | | Total Percent |
| | | Low | Medium | High | Not available | |
|---|---|---|---|---|---|---|
| **Men** | | | | | | |
| *Total* | *16,293* | *36.7* | *28.3* | *23.4* | *11.7* | *100.1* |
| Never in school | 6,404 | 46.4 | 28.5 | 13.4 | 11.7 | 100.0 |
| Some school[b] | 3,215 | 42.6 | 28.9 | 18.4 | 10.1 | 100.0 |
| Degree candidate | 2,059 | 34.2 | 31.9 | 25.0 | 8.9 | 100.0 |
| M.A. Recipient and not candidate | 1,980 | 24.2 | 30.4 | 31.5 | 13.9 | 100.0 |
| Professional degree recipient | 1,554 | 21.7 | 23.5 | 43.7 | 11.1 | 100.0 |
| M.A. recipient and candidate | 744 | 12.2 | 25.3 | 45.4 | 17.1 | 100.0 |
| Ph.D. recipient | 335 | 6.6 | 11.6 | 61.5 | 20.3 | 100.0 |
| **Women** | | | | | | |
| *Total* | *9,290* | *21.7* | *30.5* | *35.3* | *12.6* | *100.1* |
| Never in school | 4,389 | 24.7 | 28.7 | 32.4 | 14.2 | 100.0 |
| Some school[b] | 2,850 | 20.9 | 36.2 | 31.2 | 11.7 | 100.0 |
| Degree candidate | 807 | 21.1 | 29.2 | 37.5 | 12.1 | 99.9 |
| M.A. recipient and not candidate | 1,044 | 14.5 | 26.3 | 50.5 | 8.7 | 100.0 |
| Professional degree recipient | 63 | 7.9 | 14.3 | 66.7 | 11.1 | 100.0 |
| M.A. recipient and candidate | 119 | 2.5 | 13.4 | 71.4 | 12.6 | 99.9 |
| Ph.D. recipient | 18 | 11.1 | 16.7 | 50.0 | 22.2 | 100.0 |

[a]For definition of high, medium, and low GPA see p. 19.
[b]Took courses, but not degree enrolled.

Appendix Table H.  Employment Status by Marital Status in 1963 (1958 B.A. Recipients)

*(percentages)*

| Marital Status | Number | Employed full-time | Employed part-time | Full-time student | Part-time student | Employed full-time, full-time student | Employed part-time, full-time student | Employed full-time, part-time student | Employed part-time, part-time student | Housewife only | Other status | Total Percent |
|---|---|---|---|---|---|---|---|---|---|---|---|---|
| **Men** | | | | | | | | | | | | |
| *Total* | *16,293* | *82.5* | *0.7* | *3.3* | *0.2* | *0.5* | *1.4* | *7.9* | *0.5* | *0.1* | *2.8* | *99.9* |
| Never married | 2,705 | 75.3 | 1.1 | 7.7 | 0.4 | 0.5 | 2.6 | 7.1 | 1.0 | - | 4.4 | 100.1 |
| Married, no children | 2,477 | 77.0 | 0.8 | 5.7 | 0.3 | 0.3 | 2.5 | 10.1 | 0.6 | - | 2.6 | 99.9 |
| Married, with children | 10,653 | 85.6 | 0.6 | 1.7 | 0.1 | 0.6 | 0.9 | 7.7 | 0.4 | 0.1 | 2.3 | 100.0 |
| Widowed, etc.,[a] no children | 82 | 69.5 | - | 3.7 | - | - | 8.5 | 9.8 | 2.4 | - | 6.1 | 100.0 |
| Widowed, etc.,[a] children | 109 | 79.8 | 2.8 | 2.8 | - | - | - | 10.1 | - | - | 4.6 | 100.1 |
| No answer | 267 | 87.3 | 0.7 | 1.5 | - | - | 0.4 | 3.4 | 0.4 | - | 6.4 | 100.1 |
| **Women** | | | | | | | | | | | | |
| *Total* | *9,290* | *42.6* | *8.7* | *0.9* | *0.9* | *0.1* | *0.3* | *4.0* | *0.6* | *40.7* | *1.3* | *100.1* |
| Never married | 1,836 | 82.7 | 0.9 | 2.3 | 0.4 | 0.2 | 1.5 | 8.1 | 0.7 | - | 3.3 | 100.1 |
| Married, no children | 1,474 | 61.7 | 9.6 | 1.2 | 1.0 | 0.1 | 0.2 | 8.2 | 1.4 | 15.6 | 0.8 | 99.8 |
| Married, with children | 5,492 | 21.8 | 11.5 | 0.2 | 1.1 | 0.1 | - | 1.5 | 0.4 | 63.0 | 0.5 | 100.1 |
| Widowed, etc.,[a] no children | 67 | 89.6 | - | 3.0 | 1.5 | - | - | 4.5 | 1.5 | - | - | 100.1 |
| Widowed, etc.,[a] children | 223 | 77.6 | 6.7 | 0.4 | 0.4 | 0.4 | 0.4 | 7.2 | 0.4 | 5.8 | 0.4 | 99.7 |
| No answer | 198 | 49.5 | 1.0 | 1.5 | - | - | - | - | - | 40.4 | 7.6 | 100.0 |

[a] "Widowed, etc." categories include persons who are divorced and separated.

Appendix Table I. 1958 M.A. Field and 1963 Occupation (1958 M.A. Recipients)

| Occupation | Total number | Natural science | Engineering | Social science | Humanities and arts | Health | Agriculture or home economics | Education | Business and commerce | Other fields |
|---|---|---|---|---|---|---|---|---|---|---|
| | | | | | | **M.A. Field** | | | | |
| | | | | | **Men** | | | | | |
| *Total number* | *3,445* | *495* | *533* | *353* | *268* | *54* | *72* | *1,067* | *485* | *118* |
| Teacher | 1,533 | 136 | 46 | 149 | 182 | 6 | 16 | 935 | 47 | 16 |
| College | 461 | 97 | 46 | 86 | 121 | 5 | 12 | 56 | 33 | 5 |
| All other^a | 1,072 | 39 | - | 63 | 61 | 1 | 4 | 879 | 14 | 11 |
| Engineer | 527 | 53 | 403 | 7 | 2 | 4 | 2 | 5 | 48 | 3 |
| Natural scientist | 355 | 259 | 25 | 5 | - | 5 | 47 | 8 | 5 | 1 |
| Social scientist | 112 | 2 | 3 | 83 | 3 | - | - | 10 | 11 | - |
| Humanistic professional^b | 105 | 4 | 2 | 8 | 49 | - | - | 20 | 3 | 19 |
| Health professional^c | 45 | 14 | 1 | 6 | - | 20 | - | 3 | 1 | - |
| Social worker | 71 | 2 | - | 4 | 4 | - | - | 6 | - | 55 |
| Other professional^d | 112 | 7 | 21 | 26 | 6 | 2 | 3 | 16 | 17 | 14 |
| Business and managerial | 454 | 2 | 22 | 53 | 12 | 14 | 2 | 28 | 315 | 6 |
| Clerical and sales | 58 | 5 | 2 | 7 | 4 | - | - | 12 | 26 | 2 |
| All other | 45 | 9 | 5 | 4 | 2 | 1 | 2 | 10 | 12 | -- |
| No answer | 28 | 2 | 3 | 1 | 4 | 2 | - | 14 | 1 | 1 |
| | | | | | **Women** | | | | | |
| *Total number* | *1,229* | *59* | *1* | *100* | *131* | *51* | *40* | *729* | *-* | *118* |
| Teacher | 822 | 26 | - | 44 | 99 | 11 | 23 | 602 | - | 17 |
| College | 119 | 13 | - | 13 | 34 | 7 | 7 | 43 | - | 2 |
| All other^a | 703 | 13 | - | 31 | 65 | 4 | 16 | 559 | - | 15 |
| Engineer | 4 | 2 | 1 | - | - | - | 1 | - | - | - |
| Natural scientist | 29 | 16 | - | 1 | - | 4 | - | 6 | - | 2 |
| Social scientist | 21 | - | - | 17 | 1 | - | - | 1 | - | 2 |
| Humanistic professional^b | 85 | 1 | - | 8 | 19 | - | 1 | 25 | - | 31 |
| Health professional^c | 74 | 2 | - | 4 | 2 | 33 | - | 33 | - | - |
| Social worker | 76 | - | - | 10 | 1 | 1 | - | 12 | - | 52 |
| Other professional^d | 36 | 1 | - | 2 | 1 | 2 | 12 | 12 | - | 6 |
| Business and managerial | 9 | - | - | 3 | - | - | - | 1 | - | 5 |
| Clerical and sales | 10 | - | - | 2 | 2 | - | - | 6 | - | - |
| All other | 35 | 10 | - | 7 | 3 | - | 1 | 13 | - | 1 |
| No answer | 28 | 1 | - | 2 | 3 | - | 2 | 18 | - | 2 |

^a Includes private music and art teachers, principals, curriculum supervisors, etc.
^b Includes clergymen, writers, artists, etc.
^c Includes physicians, dentists, pharmacists, physical therapists, etc.
^d Includes social workers, librarians, lawyers, etc.

Appendix Table J.  Use of Graduate Background in Current Occupation in 1963[a]
(1958 B.A. Recipients)[b]

*(percentages)*

| Occupation in 1963 | Number | Considerable use | Needed other courses | Occasional use | No use | Not relevant | No answer | Total Percent |
|---|---|---|---|---|---|---|---|---|
| **Men** | | | | | | | | |
| *Total* | *3,953* | *82.1* | *3.8* | *9.3* | *1.6* | *1.3* | *1.9* | *100.0* |
| Natural scientist | 312 | 80.8 | 7.1 | 9.9 | – | 1.6 | 0.6 | 100.0 |
| Engineer | 387 | 63.0 | 5.4 | 24.0 | 4.4 | 1.8 | 1.3 | 99.9 |
| Social scientist | 98 | 90.8 | 3.1 | 5.1 | 1.0 | – | – | 100.0 |
| Humanistic professional | 377 | 92.6 | 3.2 | 2.4 | 0.8 | – | 1.1 | 100.1 |
| Health professional | 520 | 97.3 | 0.2 | 1.3 | – | – | 1.2 | 100.0 |
| Teacher | 1,288 | 82.2 | 4.9 | 9.1 | 1.4 | 0.8 | 1.6 | 100.0 |
| Business and managerial | 295 | 64.4 | 4.1 | 19.0 | 4.1 | 7.5 | 1.0 | 100.1 |
| Other professional | 543 | 92.6 | 1.3 | 2.9 | 0.9 | 0.7 | 1.5 | 99.9 |
| Semiprofessional | 27 | 63.0 | 3.7 | 11.1 | – | 11.1 | 11.1 | 100.0 |
| Clerical and sales | 34 | 23.5 | 20.6 | 41.2 | 11.8 | 2.9 | – | 100.0 |
| Other | 32 | 43.8 | – | 46.9 | 9.4 | – | – | 100.1 |
| No answer | 40 | 40.0 | – | 2.5 | – | 2.5 | 55.0 | 100.0 |
| **Women** | | | | | | | | |
| *Total* | *871* | *80.3* | *5.3* | *7.8* | *1.6* | *1.7* | *3.3* | *100.0* |
| Natural scientist | 17 | 76.5 | – | 17.6 | – | – | 5.9 | 100.0 |
| Engineer | 1[c] | | | | | | | |
| Social scientist | 10 | 80.0 | – | 20.0 | – | – | – | 100.0 |
| Humanistic professional | 79 | 91.1 | 1.3 | 2.5 | 1.3 | 2.5 | 1.3 | 100.0 |
| Health professional | 53 | 90.6 | 1.9 | 1.9 | – | – | 5.7 | 100.1 |
| Teacher | 594 | 78.6 | 6.6 | 8.6 | 1.9 | 1.3 | 3.0 | 100.0 |
| Business and managerial | 13 | 38.5 | 30.8 | 15.4 | 7.7 | 7.7 | – | 100.1 |
| Other professional | 80 | 90.0 | – | 3.7 | – | 2.5 | 3.7 | 99.9 |
| Semiprofessional | 11 | 63.6 | 9.1 | 27.3 | – | – | – | 100.0 |
| Clerical and sales | 3[c] | | | | | | | |
| Other | 5[c] | | | | | | | |
| No answer | 5[c] | | | | | | | |

[a] Exact wording of questionnaire:

How useful is your educational background in the performance of the work you actually do? We are especially interested in knowing how much use you make of fields of graduate or professional study.

I make considerable use of my knowledge in the field(s) in which I obtained my graduate (or professional) education.

There is need on my job for knowledge in the field(s) in which I studied in graduate (or professional) school, but the courses I took are not the right preparation for the type of work I am called upon to perform.

I make only occasional use of my knowledge in the field(s) I studied in graduate or professional school.

I make practically no use of my knowledge in the field(s) I studied in graduate or professional school.

Graduate or professional training such as I had is not relevant to my job.

[b] Graduate degree holders only.

[c] Too few cases to compute percents.

Appendix Table K. Importance of Graduate Degree as a Prerequisite for Current Job, 1963—Men[a]
(1958 B.A. Recipients)

(percentages)

| Occupation in 1963 | No Graduate Degree Received[b] | | | | | | | Degree Received[c] | | | | | | |
|---|---|---|---|---|---|---|---|---|---|---|---|---|---|---|
| | Number | Degree in field prerequisite | Degree in related field prerequisite | Degree prerequisite | Degree not required | No answer | Total Percent | Number | Degree in field prerequisite | Degree in related field prerequisite | Degree prerequisite | Degree not required | No answer | Total Percent |
| Total | 10,859 | 7.6 | 1.9 | 2.0 | 69.8 | 18.7 | 100.0 | 3,953 | 53.3 | 10.6 | 2.6 | 32.1 | 1.4 | 100.0 |
| Natural scientist | 575 | 6.4 | 2.6 | 0.5 | 72.2 | 18.3 | 100.0 | 312 | 45.5 | 25.3 | 0.6 | 27.6 | 1.0 | 100.0 |
| Engineer | 2,405 | 3.2 | 2.2 | 0.7 | 76.5 | 17.5 | 100.1 | 387 | 18.6 | 14.5 | 3.9 | 62.0 | 1.0 | 100.0 |
| Social scientist | 71 | 25.3 | 9.9 | 2.8 | 54.9 | 7.0 | 99.9 | 98 | 58.2 | 29.6 | 1.0 | 10.2 | 1.0 | 100.0 |
| Humanistic professional | 384 | 15.1 | 1.6 | 2.1 | 69.3 | 12.0 | 100.1 | 377 | 65.5 | 7.2 | 0.5 | 26.5 | 0.3 | 100.0 |
| Health professional | 341 | 39.9 | 0.6 | 0.6 | 35.8 | 23.2 | 100.1 | 520 | 97.5 | 0.2 | 0.2 | 1.7 | 0.4 | 100.0 |
| Teacher | 1,907 | 17.9 | 4.6 | 4.3 | 61.4 | 11.8 | 100.0 | 1,288 | 43.7 | 11.1 | 4.1 | 39.9 | 1.2 | 100.0 |
| Business and managerial | 2,918 | 3.2 | 0.9 | 1.2 | 70.3 | 24.4 | 100.0 | 295 | 8.1 | 17.6 | 6.4 | 66.8 | 1.0 | 99.9 |
| Other professional | 570 | 8.9 | 1.2 | 2.3 | 75.2 | 12.3 | 99.9 | 543 | 85.8 | 4.1 | 0.2 | 9.2 | 0.7 | 100.0 |
| Semiprofessional | 206 | 2.4 | 1.0 | 1.0 | 62.1 | 33.5 | 100.0 | 27 | 8.8 | – | 23.5 | 67.6 | – | 99.9 |
| Clerical and sales | 1,039 | 0.1 | 0.1 | 4.2 | 76.2 | 19.4 | 100.0 | 34 | 13.9 | 6.9 | 1.4 | 50.0 | 27.8 | 100.0 |
| Other | 322 | 1.6 | 0.3 | 1.2 | 82.6 | 14.3 | 100.0 | 32 | 12.5 | 12.5 | 3.1 | 71.9 | – | 100.0 |
| No answer | 121 | 6.6 | 1.7 | 1.7 | 48.8 | 41.3 | 100.1 | 40 | 15.0 | 2.5 | – | 32.5 | 50.0 | 100.0 |

[a]Data for women are not presented because numbers are too small for most cells.
[b]Includes those never in school, in school but never degree enrolled, and degree candidates.
[c]Includes those who have received one or more graduate or professional degrees since 1958.

Appendix Table L. Expected Employer Shifts, by Current Type of Employer, 1963
(1958 B.A. Recipients)

(percentages)

### Men

| Current Employer (1963) | Number[b] | Future Employer[a] | | | | | | | | | | | | | Total Percent |
|---|---|---|---|---|---|---|---|---|---|---|---|---|---|---|---|
| | | Private industry, manufacturing | Private industry, nonmanufacturing | Elementary school | High school | Junior college | College, university | Nonprofit institution | Federal government | Armed forces | State and local government | Two employers | Other | No answer | |
| Total | 1,332 | 16.0 | 15.8 | 0.8 | 6.9 | 3.2 | 28.7 | 3.3 | 3.9 | 1.5 | 2.3 | 0.3 | 0.9 | 16.5 | 100.1 |
| Private industry, manufacturing | 236 | 14.4 | 18.6 | 0.4 | 6.4 | 1.7 | 32.2 | 1.3 | 6.8 | - | 0.8 | - | - | 17.4 | 100.0 |
| Private industry, nonmanufacturing | 218 | 26.1 | 11.9 | 2.8 | 6.4 | 4.1 | 19.7 | 0.9 | 3.2 | 7.8 | 1.8 | - | 1.8 | 13.3 | 99.8 |
| Elementary school | 48 | - | 2.1 | - | 54.2 | 2.1 | 12.5 | 14.6 | 2.1 | - | 2.1 | - | - | 10.4 | 100.1 |
| High school | 265 | 4.5 | 5.3 | - | 6.8 | 8.3 | 48.3 | 2.3 | 3.0 | - | 0.8 | 0.8 | 1.1 | 18.9 | 100.1 |
| Junior college | 24 | - | - | - | - | - | 87.5 | - | - | - | - | - | - | 12.5 | 100.0 |
| College, university | 59 | 33.9 | 18.6 | - | 1.7 | - | 11.9 | 3.4 | 8.5 | - | 1.7 | - | 3.4 | 16.9 | 100.0 |
| Nonprofit institution | 103 | 6.8 | 21.4 | - | 4.9 | - | 20.4 | 1.9 | 6.8 | 1.9 | 6.8 | - | 1.0 | 28.2 | 100.1 |
| Federal government | 166 | 34.9 | 27.7 | - | 4.2 | 1.2 | 18.7 | 1.8 | 1.2 | - | 0.6 | - | 0.6 | 9.0 | 99.9 |
| Armed forces | 43 | 18.6 | 18.6 | - | 9.3 | - | 34.9 | 9.3 | 3.5 | - | 2.3 | - | - | 7.0 | 100.0 |
| State and local government | 115 | 11.3 | 25.2 | 0.9 | 0.9 | - | 17.4 | 9.6 | 3.5 | 0.9 | 8.7 | 1.7 | - | 20.0 | 100.1 |
| Other (including two employers) | 24 | 5.9 | 17.6 | - | 5.9 | - | 23.5 | 5.9 | 5.9 | - | 5.9 | - | 5.9 | 23.5 | 100.0 |
| No answer | 31 | 6.5 | 12.9 | 6.5 | - | 12.9 | 19.4 | 9.7 | 3.2 | - | 3.2 | - | - | 25.8 | 100.1 |

**Women**

| | Total | 3.4 | 7.3 | 8.7 | 8.9 | 4.5 | 24.6 | 9.2 | 8.4 | 1.4 | 2.5 | 0.6 | 0.3 | 20.4 | 100.2 |
|---|---|---|---|---|---|---|---|---|---|---|---|---|---|---|---|
| | 358 | 3.4 | 7.3 | 8.7 | 8.9 | 4.5 | 24.6 | 9.2 | 8.4 | 1.4 | 2.5 | 0.6 | 0.3 | 20.4 | 100.2 |
| Private industry, manufacturing | 14 | 7.1 | 21.4 | – | 14.3 | – | 14.3 | – | 28.6 | – | – | – | – | 14.3 | 100.0 |
| Private industry, nonmanufacturing | 47 | 12.8 | 2.1 | 8.5 | 8.5 | – | 10.6 | 27.7 | 4.3 | – | – | – | – | 25.5 | 100.0 |
| Elementary school | 53 | – | 1.9 | 1.9 | 7.5 | 5.7 | 45.3 | 5.7 | 1.9 | 1.9 | – | – | – | 28.3 | 100.1 |
| High school | 65 | 1.5 | 16.9 | 1.5 | – | 18.5 | 41.5 | 3.1 | 6.2 | 6.2 | – | – | – | 4.6 | 100.0 |
| Junior college | 4[c] | | | | | | | | | | | | | | |
| College, university | 28 | 3.6 | 7.1 | – | 21.4 | 3.6 | 17.9 | 14.3 | 14.3 | – | 3.6 | – | – | 14.3 | 100.1 |
| Nonprofit institution | 62 | – | 3.2 | 17.7 | 8.1 | – | 27.4 | 4.8 | 11.3 | – | 11.3 | – | 1.6 | 14.5 | 99.9 |
| Federal government | 25 | – | 8.0 | 24.0 | 24.0 | – | 16.0 | 16.0 | – | – | – | 4.0 | – | 8.0 | 100.0 |
| Armed forces | 4[c] | | | | | | | | | | | | | | |
| State and local government | 47 | 6.4 | 6.4 | 10.6 | – | – | 4.3 | 8.5 | 14.9 | – | 2.1 | 2.1 | – | 44.7 | 100.0 |
| Other (including two employers) | 4[c] | | | | | | | | | | | | | | |
| No answer | 5[c] | | | | | | | | | | | | | | |

[a]Exact wording of question: "Do you expect to work for this type of employer for the major part of your working life? (If not) which type of employer?"
[b]Limited to respondents who are employed full-time and expect to change type of employer.
[c]Too few cases to compute percents.

Appendix Table M.  Reason for Changing Occupation between 1960 and 1963, by 1963 Occupation
(1958 B.A. Recipients)

*(percentages)*

| 1963 Occupation | Number | Reason[a] | | | | | | | | Total Percent |
|---|---|---|---|---|---|---|---|---|---|---|
| | | Better conditions | Better future | Better use of training | Suits talents | Just temporary | Lost job | Other | No answer | |
| *Total Men* | *3,255* | *15.7* | *30.9* | *5.0* | *21.7* | *8.8* | *1.5* | *10.1* | *6.4* | *100.1* |
| *Total Women* | *684* | *16.2* | *13.9* | *6.6* | *29.2* | *4.4* | *1.2* | *22.1* | *6.4* | *100.0* |
| **Natural Scientist** | | | | | | | | | | |
| Men | 195 | 15.9 | 15.9 | 14.4 | 17.9 | 11.8 | 1.5 | 12.3 | 10.3 | 100.0 |
| **Engineer** | | | | | | | | | | |
| Men | 470 | 15.5 | 40.0 | 5.5 | 16.0 | 8.1 | 1.7 | 10.6 | 2.6 | 100.0 |
| **Social Scientist** | | | | | | | | | | |
| Men | 48 | 4.2 | 25.0 | 12.5 | 25.0 | 10.4 | – | 14.6 | 8.3 | 100.0 |
| **Humanistic Professional** | | | | | | | | | | |
| Men | 173 | 5.8 | 12.1 | 7.5 | 31.8 | 19.7 | 1.2 | 15.0 | 6.9 | 100.0 |
| Women | 108 | 5.6 | 25.9 | 4.6 | 40.7 | 4.6 | – | 17.6 | 0.9 | 99.9 |
| **Health Professional** | | | | | | | | | | |
| Men | 124 | 7.3 | 9.7 | 9.7 | 5.6 | 33.1 | 0.8 | 21.8 | 12.1 | 100.1 |
| Women | 22 | 9.1 | 13.6 | 13.6 | 18.2 | 18.2 | – | 27.3 | – | 100.0 |
| **Teacher** | | | | | | | | | | |
| Men | 487 | 13.3 | 16.0 | 10.5 | 34.3 | 10.1 | 1.4 | 8.4 | 6.0 | 100.0 |
| Women | 264 | 21.1 | 6.1 | 9.5 | 31.1 | 4.2 | 1.5 | 19.3 | 7.2 | 100.1 |
| **Business and Managerial** | | | | | | | | | | |
| Men | 1,002 | 18.0 | 39.8 | 0.9 | 21.8 | 3.5 | 0.9 | 7.3 | 7.9 | 100.1 |
| Women | 49 | 6.1 | 18.4 | – | 28.6 | 4.1 | – | 16.3 | 26.5 | 100.0 |

Appendix Table M. (Continued)

| 1963 Occupation | Number | Reason[a] | | | | | | | | Total Percent |
|---|---|---|---|---|---|---|---|---|---|---|
| | | Better conditions | Better future | Better use of training | Suits talents | Just temporary | Lost job | Other | No answer | |
| **Other Professional** | | | | | | | | | | |
| Men | 238 | 10.9 | 32.4 | 3.8 | 16.4 | 18.5 | 2.1 | 8.8 | 7.1 | 100.0 |
| Women | 85 | 16.5 | 14.1 | 1.2 | 29.4 | 3.5 | 2.4 | 29.4 | 3.5 | 100.0 |
| **Semiprofessional** | | | | | | | | | | |
| Men | 70 | 25.7 | 25.7 | 4.3 | 11.4 | 7.1 | 4.3 | 14.3 | 7.1 | 99.9 |
| Women | 30 | 13.3 | 20.0 | – | 20.0 | 6.7 | 3.3 | 30.0 | 6.7 | 100.0 |
| **Clerical and Sales** | | | | | | | | | | |
| Men | 303 | 16.2 | 48.5 | 1.0 | 18.8 | 2.3 | 1.0 | 8.3 | 4.0 | 100.1 |
| Women | 66 | 16.7 | 15.2 | 7.6 | 10.6 | 4.5 | – | 37.9 | 7.6 | 100.1 |
| **Other Nonprofessional** | | | | | | | | | | |
| Men | 145 | 33.1 | 15.9 | 1.4 | 22.8 | 3.4 | 4.8 | 17.2 | 1.4 | 100.0 |
| Women | 30 | 13.3 | 26.7 | 10.0 | 33.3 | – | – | 13.3 | 3.3 | 99.9 |

[a] Exact wording of answers:
1. New occupation offers better conditions (more pay, more convenient location, more convenient hours or working conditions).
2. New occupation has better future (is more promising, represents career advancement).
3. New occupation makes better use of my undergraduate and/or graduate training.
4. New occupation suits my talents, aptitudes, and interests better.
5. Old job was just temporary.
6. I lost my old job and was unable to find a new job in my old occupation.

*(percentages)*

Appendix Table N. Career Values and Most and Least Satisfactory Aspect of 1963 Job (1958 B.A. Recipients)

| Career Values | Engineers (Men = 2,792, Women = 15) | | | | | | Natural Scientists (Men = 887, Women = 54) | | | | | | Social Scientists (Men = 169, Women = 32) | | | | | |
|---|---|---|---|---|---|---|---|---|---|---|---|---|---|---|---|---|---|---|
| | Chose item as "most satisfactory aspect of my job" | | Chose item as "least satisfactory aspect of my job" | | Chose item as "most important in relation to career objectives" | | Chose item as "most satisfactory aspect of my job" | | Chose item as "least satisfactory aspect of my job" | | Chose item as "most important in relation to career objectives" | | Chose item as "most satisfactory aspect of my job" | | Chose item as "least satisfactory aspect of my job" | | Chose item as "most important in relation to career objectives" | |
| | Men | Women | Men | Women | Men | Women | Men | Women | Men | Women | Men | Women | Men | Women | Men | Women | Men | Women |
| *Self-Expression Oriented* | | | | | | | | | | | | | | | | | | |
| Interesting work | 27.4 | 13.3 | 4.6 | – | 24.2 | 26.7 | 30.3 | 31.5 | 3.9 | – | 26.9 | 29.6 | 29.0 | 37.5 | 2.4 | 25.0 | 26.0 | 43.7 |
| Use special talents | 4.8 | 13.3 | 4.3 | 20.0 | 6.6 | 13.3 | 6.3 | 1.9 | 2.9 | 5.6 | 5.6 | 9.3 | 6.5 | – | 1.2 | – | 10.7 | 6.2 |
| Use college learning | 1.4 | – | 5.4 | – | 1.1 | – | 2.6 | 1.9 | 1.9 | 5.6 | 2.6 | 1.9 | 1.2 | – | 2.4 | – | 0.6 | – |
| Creative work | 6.2 | 13.3 | 6.6 | – | 6.2 | – | 8.7 | 5.6 | 6.4 | 7.4 | 10.6 | 5.6 | 13.0 | – | 10.7 | 3.1 | 8.9 | – |
| No supervision | 3.8 | 13.3 | 2.5 | – | 1.9 | – | 2.0 | 3.7 | 3.8 | 1.9 | 0.7 | 5.6 | – | 3.1 | – | – | 0.6 | – |
| Further studies | 1.6 | – | 5.6 | 6.7 | 1.9 | – | 2.3 | 3.7 | 6.7 | – | 3.4 | 1.9 | 4.1 | 3.1 | 1.2 | – | 7.1 | 3.1 |
| Improve competence | 4.5 | 6.7 | 2.8 | – | 7.6 | 6.7 | 5.7 | 3.7 | 1.7 | – | 6.9 | 1.9 | 4.7 | 3.1 | 2.4 | – | 3.6 | 9.4 |
| *People Oriented* | | | | | | | | | | | | | | | | | | |
| Helpful to others | 1.7 | – | 3.9 | 6.7 | 2.9 | – | 4.3 | 3.7 | 4.7 | 11.1 | 5.7 | 9.3 | 9.5 | 21.9 | 5.3 | 6.2 | 5.9 | 12.5 |
| Work with people | 3.9 | – | 1.7 | – | 1.7 | 6.7 | 2.6 | 3.7 | 2.4 | 9.3 | 1.9 | 1.9 | 6.5 | 6.2 | 0.6 | – | 5.3 | – |
| *Extrinsic Reward Oriented* | | | | | | | | | | | | | | | | | | |
| Good income | 20.0 | 40.0 | 6.6 | – | 17.8 | 13.3 | 14.4 | 16.7 | 12.5 | 3.7 | 12.9 | 18.5 | 9.5 | 18.7 | 15.4 | 15.6 | 13.6 | 18.7 |
| Travel | 1.0 | – | 6.5 | 13.3 | 0.4 | – | 1.4 | 1.9 | 6.0 | 13.0 | 0.5 | – | 1.2 | – | 10.7 | 12.5 | 0.6 | – |
| Supervise others | 4.1 | – | 9.0 | 6.7 | 8.1 | 6.7 | 1.8 | 1.9 | 6.8 | 5.6 | 2.5 | – | 1.2 | – | 8.3 | – | 3.6 | – |
| Get ahead | 3.4 | – | 10.3 | 6.7 | 6.3 | – | 1.9 | – | 9.8 | 9.3 | 3.3 | 1.9 | 1.8 | – | 12.4 | 9.4 | 0.6 | – |
| Secure future | 8.2 | – | 7.8 | 6.7 | 6.6 | 6.7 | 7.0 | 3.7 | 3.3 | 1.9 | 6.8 | 1.9 | 3.0 | – | 6.5 | – | 1.8 | – |
| Time for family and hobbies | 3.6 | – | 11.2 | 6.7 | 2.2 | 20.0 | 4.2 | 7.4 | 12.3 | 5.6 | 2.5 | 1.9 | 2.4 | 3.1 | 6.5 | 28.1 | 4.7 | – |
| No Answer | 4.5 | 9.3 | 14.9 | 20.4 | 7.3 | 9.3 | 4.5 | 9.3 | 14.9 | 20.4 | 7.3 | 9.3 | 6.5 | – | 17.2 | – | 6.5 | 6.2 |

| | Humanistic Professionals Men = 761 Women = 228 | | | | | | Teachers Men = 3,195 Women = 2,912 | | | | | | Business and Managerial Men = 3,213 Women = 156 | | | | | |
|---|---|---|---|---|---|---|---|---|---|---|---|---|---|---|---|---|---|---|
| | Men | Women | Men | Women | Men | Women | Men | Women | Men | Women | Men | Women | Men | Women | Men | Women | Men | Women |
| *Self-Expression Oriented* | | | | | | | | | | | | | | | | | | |
| Interesting work | 15.5 | 21.5 | 1.4 | 8.3 | 10.9 | 26.3 | 19.7 | 15.5 | 1.1 | 2.4 | 18.1 | 18.8 | 27.4 | 17.9 | 4.2 | 4.5 | 18.7 | 29.5 |
| Use special talents | 9.7 | 11.0 | 3.4 | 4.4 | 14.7 | 9.2 | 9.6 | 8.9 | 1.7 | 2.0 | 9.1 | 10.2 | 4.7 | 2.6 | 2.7 | 12.2 | 7.0 | 3.8 |
| Use college learning | 1.2 | 5.3 | 1.3 | 3.1 | 0.9 | 1.3 | 2.3 | 2.1 | 1.2 | 1.6 | 1.7 | 1.7 | 2.1 | - | 3.0 | 2.6 | 0.9 | 0.6 |
| Creative work | 8.0 | 9.6 | 2.9 | 6.6 | 8.8 | 11.4 | 4.0 | 2.6 | 3.6 | 2.7 | 4.6 | 3.0 | 3.6 | 8.3 | 6.8 | 14.1 | 4.5 | 7.7 |
| No supervision | 0.4 | - | 2.4 | - | 0.3 | - | 1.4 | 0.3 | 1.3 | 3.0 | 0.8 | 0.4 | 3.3 | 1.9 | 4.2 | 1.9 | 1.5 | - |
| Further studies | 0.9 | 5.7 | 8.7 | 9.2 | 2.4 | 0.9 | 1.9 | 0.4 | 3.3 | 2.0 | 4.2 | 2.7 | 0.8 | - | 3.2 | 6.4 | 0.6 | - |
| Improve competence | 2.9 | 8.3 | 1.7 | 1.8 | 5.4 | 5.7 | 0.9 | 0.9 | 0.9 | 1.2 | 2.5 | 2.7 | 3.1 | 0.6 | 2.5 | 0.6 | 4.8 | 3.8 |
| *People Oriented* | | | | | | | | | | | | | | | | | | |
| Helpful to others | 37.1 | 10.5 | 1.2 | 0.4 | 29.0 | 13.2 | 28.8 | 30.8 | 0.6 | 0.4 | 15.6 | 19.3 | 2.4 | 10.3 | 3.9 | 1.9 | 3.1 | 3.2 |
| Work with people | 10.2 | 7.5 | 0.1 | 3.1 | 7.9 | 7.5 | 14.3 | 16.1 | 0.1 | 0.1 | 8.7 | 8.0 | 6.0 | 26.3 | 1.2 | - | 2.3 | 4.5 |
| *Extrinsic Reward Oriented* | | | | | | | | | | | | | | | | | | |
| Good income | 3.4 | 10.5 | 13.8 | 22.4 | 7.4 | 2.6 | 3.0 | 7.9 | 38.9 | 14.9 | 13.8 | 9.3 | 17.7 | 21.8 | 11.5 | 5.1 | 21.5 | 14.7 |
| Travel | - | 0.4 | 6.4 | 11.4 | 0.1 | - | 0.5 | 1.2 | 10.9 | 14.2 | 0.7 | 2.3 | 1.2 | - | 9.1 | 9.6 | 0.2 | - |
| Supervise others | 0.5 | - | 2.8 | 0.4 | 0.7 | - | 1.0 | 0.4 | 2.5 | 4.1 | 1.8 | 0.6 | 6.0 | 3.2 | 4.8 | 1.3 | 7.5 | 7.1 |
| Get ahead | 0.9 | - | 6.7 | 7.0 | 0.7 | 3.5 | 0.1 | - | 10.0 | 10.8 | 1.5 | 0.8 | 6.8 | 0.6 | 8.9 | 7.1 | 7.4 | 5.1 |
| Secure future | 1.2 | 0.9 | 5.0 | 2.6 | 0.7 | 10.1 | 4.2 | 3.5 | 2.5 | 1.5 | 5.4 | 6.7 | 8.1 | 1.3 | 3.4 | 3.8 | 8.7 | 3.2 |
| Time for family and hobbies | 0.8 | 2.6 | 25.5 | 11.0 | 2.2 | 0.9 | 2.3 | 2.6 | 10.8 | 20.8 | 3.0 | 3.6 | 2.4 | - | 17.5 | 14.1 | 3.8 | 1.3 |
| *No Answer* | 7.2 | 6.1 | 16.7 | 8.3 | 8.0 | 7.5 | 6.0 | 6.7 | 10.7 | 18.4 | 8.5 | 9.9 | 4.6 | 5.1 | 13.0 | 14.7 | 7.7 | 15.4 |

Appendix Table O.  Career Values and Most Satisfactory Aspect of 1963 Job[a]
(1958 B.A. and M.A. Recipients)

*(percentages)[b]*

| | Men | | | | | | | | | | Women | | | | | |
| --- | --- | --- | --- | --- | --- | --- | --- | --- | --- | --- | --- | --- | --- | --- | --- | --- |
| | Engineers | | Teachers | | Natural scientists | | Social scientists | | Business and managerial | | Teachers | | Natural scientists | | Social scientists | |
| | B.A. | M.A. | B.A. | M.A. | B.A. | M.A. | B.A. | M.A. | B.A. | M.A. | B.A. | M.A. | B.A. | M.A. | B.A. | M.A. |
| *Yielding a Good Income* | | | | | | | | | | | | | | | | |
| Most satisfactory aspect of job | 20.0 | 21.3 | 3.0 | 4.4 | 14.4 | 11.0 | 9.5 | 11.6 | 17.7 | 17.6 | 7.9 | 9.0 | 16.7 | 13.8 | 18.7 | - |
| Most important career value | 17.8 | 13.5 | 13.8 | 10.3 | 12.9 | 7.9 | 13.6 | 8.0 | 21.5 | 24.4 | 9.3 | 14.6 | 18.5 | 27.6 | 18.7 | 9.5 |
| *Opportunity to do Really Interesting Work* | | | | | | | | | | | | | | | | |
| Most satisfactory aspect of job | 27.4 | 28.5 | 19.7 | 26.0 | 30.3 | 32.7 | 29.0 | 34.8 | 27.4 | 33.7 | 15.5 | 16.4 | 31.5 | 31.0 | 37.5 | 28.6 |
| Most important career value | 24.2 | 27.3 | 18.1 | 20.5 | 26.9 | 30.7 | 26.0 | 35.7 | 18.7 | 25.6 | 18.8 | 15.6 | 29.6 | 37.9 | 43.7 | 23.8 |
| *Opportunity to Use My Special Talents and Abilities* | | | | | | | | | | | | | | | | |
| Most satisfactory aspect of job | 4.8 | 6.3 | 9.6 | 8.5 | 6.3 | 8.5 | 6.5 | 4.5 | 4.7 | 2.9 | 8.9 | 10.3 | 1.9 | 13.8 | - | 19.0 |
| Most important career value | 6.6 | 12.9 | 9.1 | 9.1 | 5.6 | 7.6 | 10.7 | 10.7 | 7.0 | 9.9 | 10.2 | 9.2 | 9.3 | 3.4 | 6.2 | 14.3 |
| *Opportunity to be Helpful to Others and to Society* | | | | | | | | | | | | | | | | |
| Most satisfactory aspect of job | 1.7 | 2.8 | 28.8 | 25.6 | 4.3 | 2.3 | 9.5 | 11.6 | 2.4 | 4.4 | 30.8 | 25.8 | 3.7 | - | 21.9 | 9.5 |
| Most important career value | 2.9 | 4.6 | 15.6 | 18.0 | 5.7 | 3.9 | 5.9 | 5.4 | 3.1 | 2.4 | 19.3 | 20.6 | 9.3 | 3.4 | 12.5 | 14.3 |

*Opportunity to Get Ahead Rapidly*

| | | | | | | | | | | | | | | | |
|---|---|---|---|---|---|---|---|---|---|---|---|---|---|---|---|
| Most satisfactory aspect of job | 3.4 | 1.5 | 2.3 | 0.2 | 1.9 | 0.6 | 1.8 | 1.8 | 6.8 | 6.2 | – | 0.1 | – | – | – |
| Most important career value | 6.3 | 4.4 | 1.7 | 1.3 | 3.3 | 5.1 | 0.6 | 0.9 | 7.4 | 6.6 | 0.8 | 0.1 | 1.9 | – | 4.8 |

*Opportunity to Work With People Rather Than Things*

| | | | | | | | | | | | | | | | |
|---|---|---|---|---|---|---|---|---|---|---|---|---|---|---|---|
| Most satisfactory aspect of job | 3.9 | 2.5 | 14.3 | 12.1 | 2.6 | 1.1 | 6.5 | 4.5 | 6.0 | 4.0 | 16.1 | 15.0 | 3.7 | 3.4 | 6.2 | 14.3 |
| Most important career value | 1.7 | 1.7 | 8.7 | 6.1 | 1.9 | 1.4 | 5.3 | 1.8 | 2.3 | 1.5 | 8.0 | 7.9 | 1.9 | – | – | – |

*Opportunity to do Original and Creative Work*

| | | | | | | | | | | | | | | | |
|---|---|---|---|---|---|---|---|---|---|---|---|---|---|---|---|
| Most satisfactory aspect of job | 6.2 | 10.1 | 4.0 | 5.9 | 8.7 | 18.9 | 13.0 | 13.4 | 3.6 | 5.3 | 2.6 | 2.1 | 5.6 | 13.8 | – | 9.5 |
| Most important career value | 6.2 | 9.5 | 4.6 | 9.8 | 10.6 | 15.2 | 8.9 | 4.8 | 4.5 | 5.1 | 3.0 | 5.5 | 5.6 | 6.9 | – | 4.8 |

[a]Selected occupations and selected values only.
[b]Percentages add to less than 100% for each profession/degree group, because not all answer categories are listed.

*(percentages)*

Appendix Table P. Regional Stability and Movement between High School Graduation and 1963
(1958 B.A. Recipients)

| Region[a] at High School Graduation (1954 or Earlier) | Number | Region in 1963 | | | | | | | | | | | Total Percent |
|---|---|---|---|---|---|---|---|---|---|---|---|---|---|
| | | New England | Middle Atlantic | East North Central | West North Central | South Atlantic | East South Central | West South Central | Mountain | Pacific | Puerto Rico | Outside U.S. | |
| **Men** | | | | | | | | | | | | | |
| *Total* | *15,310[b]* | *7.7* | *20.5* | *18.9* | *8.6* | *12.5* | *4.2* | *7.9* | *4.9* | *12.8* | *0.5* | *1.4* | *99.9* |
| New England | 1,252 | 68.1 | 12.7 | 2.8 | 1.1 | 5.8 | 1.9 | 1.1 | 1.0 | 4.7 | - | 0.8 | 100.0 |
| Middle Atlantic | 3,694 | 4.9 | 70.5 | 5.6 | 1.3 | 8.0 | 0.5 | 1.1 | 1.1 | 5.1 | - | 1.9 | 100.0 |
| East North Central | 3,029 | 1.7 | 4.3 | 73.1 | 3.2 | 4.5 | 1.3 | 1.1 | 2.3 | 7.2 | - | 1.4 | 100.1 |
| West North Central | 1,635 | 1.2 | 3.5 | 10.2 | 63.2 | 2.5 | 0.9 | 2.0 | 8.0 | 7.8 | - | 0.8 | 100.1 |
| South Atlantic | 1,577 | 2.3 | 5.1 | 4.7 | 0.8 | 72.2 | 5.8 | 3.6 | 0.9 | 3.8 | 0.1 | 0.9 | 100.2 |
| East South Central | 727 | 0.3 | 2.9 | 10.2 | 1.2 | 16.9 | 58.2 | 4.8 | 1.0 | 3.2 | - | 1.4 | 100.1 |
| West South Central | 1,298 | 1.0 | 2.2 | 4.1 | 4.3 | 3.2 | 1.5 | 73.2 | 4.2 | 5.3 | - | 1.0 | 100.0 |
| Mountain | 658 | 0.8 | 2.3 | 3.3 | 2.4 | 5.0 | 0.5 | 4.7 | 55.9 | 24.2 | - | 0.9 | 100.0 |
| Pacific | 1,260 | 0.9 | 1.5 | 3.0 | 2.5 | 2.1 | 0.6 | 1.5 | 3.7 | 82.0 | - | 2.2 | 100.0 |
| Puerto Rico | 79 | 1.3 | 1.3 | 1.3 | - | - | - | - | - | - | 96.1 | - | 100.0 |
| Outside U.S. | 101 | 6.9 | 17.8 | 14.0 | 4.0 | 10.9 | 4.0 | 2.0 | 7.9 | 27.7 | - | 5.0 | 100.2 |

**Women**

| | Number | New England | Middle Atlantic | East North Central | West North Central | South Atlantic | East South Central | West South Central | Mountain | Pacific | Puerto Rico | Outside U.S. | Total |
|---|---|---|---|---|---|---|---|---|---|---|---|---|---|
| *Total* | 8,650[b] | 8.1 | 20.1 | 20.7 | 7.7 | 12.2 | 3.5 | 8.0 | 4.3 | 14.0 | 0.5 | 1.0 | 100.1 |
| New England | 687 | 68.8 | 13.7 | 3.3 | 0.1 | 5.4 | 0.1 | 0.4 | 0.9 | 4.9 | - | 2.5 | 100.1 |
| Middle Atlantic | 1,979 | 5.8 | 70.8 | 5.3 | 1.9 | 7.9 | 0.3 | 0.7 | 0.6 | 5.5 | - | 1.3 | 100.1 |
| East North Central | 1,969 | 3.0 | 3.6 | 73.4 | 4.3 | 4.4 | 1.1 | 1.5 | 1.8 | 6.4 | - | 0.6 | 100.1 |
| West North Central | 824 | 1.3 | 1.8 | 9.3 | 59.3 | 2.3 | 0.5 | 3.3 | 6.9 | 13.3 | - | 1.8 | 99.8 |
| South Atlantic | 915 | 2.5 | 11.6 | 4.5 | 0.5 | 69.5 | 2.6 | 3.8 | 0.7 | 3.9 | - | 0.3 | 99.9 |
| East South Central | 390 | 1.5 | 1.3 | 8.7 | 3.3 | 16.2 | 58.5 | 5.1 | 1.0 | 4.0 | - | 0.3 | 99.9 |
| West South Central | 700 | 0.3 | 1.7 | 3.7 | 3.1 | 4.6 | 1.1 | 77.5 | 2.1 | 5.6 | 0.1 | - | 99.8 |
| Mountain | 409 | 0.2 | 3.9 | 4.2 | 2.4 | 1.5 | 0.5 | 3.4 | 55.0 | 28.6 | - | 0.2 | 99.9 |
| Pacific | 698 | 1.3 | 1.9 | 2.9 | 0.7 | 1.9 | 0.4 | 0.9 | 1.7 | 87.6 | - | 0.7 | 100.0 |
| Puerto Rico | 46 | - | 8.7 | - | - | 2.2 | - | - | - | 4.3 | 84.7 | - | 99.9 |
| Outside U.S. | 33 | 3.0 | 12.1 | 15.2 | 9.1 | 12.1 | 6.1 | 3.0 | 3.0 | 15.2 | 3.0 | 18.2 | 100.0 |

[a] The states are distributed in these regions as follows:
New England: Maine, New Hampshire, Vermont, Massachusetts, Rhode Island, Connecticut.
Middle Atlantic: New York, New Jersey, Pennsylvania.
East North Central: Ohio, Indiana, Illinois, Michigan, Wisconsin.
West North Central: Minnesota, Iowa, Missouri, North Dakota, South Dakota, Nebraska, Kansas.
South Atlantic: Delaware, Maryland, District of Columbia, Virginia, West Virginia, North Carolina, South Carolina, Georgia, Florida.
East South Central: Kentucky, Tennessee, Alabama, Mississippi.
West South Central: Arkansas, Louisiana, Oklahoma, Texas.
Mountain: Montana, Idaho, Wyoming, Colorado, New Mexico, Arizona, Utah, Nevada.
Pacific: Washington, Oregon, California, Alaska, Hawaii.
[b] Excludes no answers.

Appendix Table Q.  Intercorrelations and Beta Weights of Variables and Graduate School Attendance, 1958-63[a] (1958 B.A. Recipients)

| Variables | Institutional Size | Public vs. Private Control | GPA Adjustment Factor | Selectivity | National Merit Scholar Prestige | College Endowment per Student | College Income per Student | Age | Children | GPA-Raw | Marital Status |
|---|---|---|---|---|---|---|---|---|---|---|---|
| **Men** | | | | | | | | | | | |
| Institutional size | | | | | | | | .07 | .00 | | |
| Public vs. private control | .40 | | | | | | | .19 | .11 | | |
| GPA adjustment factor | .05 | .43 | | | | | | .22 | .14 | .00 | |
| Selectivity | .00 | .17 | .23 | | | | | .11 | .08 | -.01 | |
| National Merit Scholar prestige | .29 | -.34 | -.69 | -.18 | | | | -.22 | -.13 | .01 | |
| College endowment per student | -.12 | -.36 | -.66 | -.24 | .53 | | | -.19 | -.11 | .01 | -.11 |
| College income per student | .15 | -.10 | -.58 | -.17 | .53 | .72 | | -.14 | -.07 | .00 | -.07 |
| Age | | | | | | | | | | | |
| Children | | | | | | | | .35 | | | |
| GPA-raw | -.02 | -.04 | | | | | | -.10 | -.04 | | |
| Marital status | .03 | .14 | .14 | .08 | -.13 | | | .36 | .77 | -.02 | |
| Graduate school attendance | -.07 | -.14 | -.11 | -.05 | .07 | .11 | 0.6 | -.22 | -.18 | .33 | -.15 |
| Beta weight  R = .41 | -.03 | -.06 | -.05 | .00 | -.03 | .03 | .00 | -.13 | -.11 | .31 | .00 |
| **Women** | | | | | | | | | | | |
| Institutional size | | | | | | | | .08 | .02 | | |
| Public vs. public control | .52 | | | | | | | .03 | .04 | | |
| GPA adjustment factor | -.02 | .37 | | | | | | .13 | .03 | .02 | |
| Selectivity | -.05 | .04 | .10 | | | | | .03 | .04 | .01 | |
| National Merit Scholar prestige | .23 | .29 | -.69 | -.14 | | | | -.14 | -.02 | -.05 | |
| College endowment per student | -.15 | -.34 | -.67 | .05 | .55 | | | -.12 | -.01 | -.03 | .02 |
| College income per student | .17 | -.11 | -.60 | .00 | .60 | .59 | | -.13 | .02 | -.02 | .06 |
| Age | | | | | | | | | | | |
| Children | | | | | | | | .11 | | | |
| GPA-raw | -.02 | -.04 | | | | | | -.04 | .02 | | |
| Marital status | .06 | .06 | .00 | .02 | .02 | | | .10 | .61 | .06 | |
| Graduate school attendance | .02 | -.04 | -.07 | -.01 | .05 | .07 | .01 | .05 | -.26 | .19 | -.24 |
| Beta weight  R = .37 | .05 | .00 | -.06 | .00 | .00 | .08 | -.06 | .08 | -.18 | .20 | -.15 |

[a] Graduate school attendance includes degree enrollment (all levels) as well as attendance "for courses only."

*Note:*  Institutional variables selected for this regression analysis are those believed to have some effect on "productivity," of undergraduate institutions. The quality measures used were derived as follows:

*GPA adjustment factor:*  Factor by which grade point average was adjusted to reflect institutional quality. Based on James A. Davis, *Great Aspirations* (Chicago: Aldine Publishing Company, 1964), pp. 27-29.

*Selectivity:*  Ratio of number of applicants to number accepted by college. Based on Jane Z. Hauser and Paul F. Lazarsfeld, *The Admissions Officer in the American College: An Occupation Under Change* (New York: College Entrance Examination Board, 1964), pp. 1, 2, and 6.

*National Merit Scholar prestige:*  Factor based on the total number of highly able students who want to enroll at the college compared to the number of freshmen admitted. Based on Alexander W. Astin, *Who Goes Where to College?* (Chicago: Science Research Associates, Inc., 1965).

Appendix Table R. Graduate School Enrollment and Degree Recipiency between 1958 and 1963 by Type of Undergraduate Institution and Degrees Offered (1958 B.A. Recipients)

*(percentages)*

| Type of Institution and Degrees Offered | Number | Never enrolled | Took courses only | Degree candidate | M.A. recipient, not a candidate | Professional degree candidate | M.A. recipient and candidate | Ph.D. recipient | Total Percent |
|---|---|---|---|---|---|---|---|---|---|
| | | | | Graduate School Enrollment | | | | | |
| **Men** | | | | | | | | | |
| *Total[a]* | 14,844 | 39.5 | 19.6 | 12.8 | 12.1 | 9.6 | 4.5 | 2.0 | 100.1 |
| *University* | 8,054 | 44.2 | 18.1 | 11.0 | 10.6 | 9.4 | 4.4 | 2.2 | 99.9 |
| M.A. | 559 | 40.4 | 25.4 | 12.0 | 7.2 | 9.8 | 3.7 | 1.4 | 99.9 |
| Ph.D. | 7,495 | 44.5 | 17.6 | 10.9 | 10.8 | 9.4 | 4.5 | 2.3 | 100.0 |
| *Liberal arts college* | 4,579 | 33.0 | 21.0 | 14.1 | 12.1 | 13.3 | 4.7 | 1.8 | 100.0 |
| B.A. | 2,172 | 34.7 | 21.3 | 12.6 | 11.6 | 14.0 | 4.3 | 1.6 | 100.1 |
| M.A. and Ph.D. | 2,407 | 31.4 | 20.7 | 15.6 | 12.6 | 12.8 | 5.1 | 1.9 | 100.1 |
| *Teachers college* | 1,305 | 31.6 | 22.1 | 17.9 | 22.0 | 2.3 | 3.1 | 1.0 | 100.0 |
| B.A. | 276 | 28.3 | 30.1 | 20.3 | 16.3 | 1.4 | 3.6 | – | 100.0 |
| M.A. and Ph.D. | 1,029 | 32.5 | 19.9 | 17.3 | 23.5 | 2.5 | 3.0 | 1.3 | 100.0 |
| *Technical institute* | 708 | 42.8 | 19.1 | 14.7 | 11.3 | 2.0 | 6.7 | 3.4 | 100.0 |
| B.A. | 38 | 47.4 | 15.8 | 10.5 | 2.6 | 7.9 | 7.9 | 7.9 | 100.0 |
| M.A. | 142 | 57.0 | 23.9 | 5.6 | 8.5 | 1.4 | 2.8 | 0.7 | 99.9 |
| Ph.D. | 528 | 38.6 | 18.0 | 17.4 | 12.7 | 1.7 | 7.5 | 4.0 | 99.9 |
| *Other* | 198 | 40.4 | 29.8 | 9.6 | 10.1 | 7.1 | 2.5 | 0.5 | 100.0 |
| B.A. | 42 | 23.8 | 28.6 | 9.6 | 7.1 | 23.8 | 4.8 | 2.4 | 100.0 |
| M.A. | 117 | 39.3 | 36.8 | 12.9 | 10.3 | – | 0.9 | – | 100.2 |
| Ph.D. | 39 | 61.5 | 10.3 | – | 12.8 | 10.3 | 5.1 | – | 100.0 |
| **Women** | | | | | | | | | |
| *Total[a]* | 8,218 | 48.0 | 30.2 | 8.3 | 11.2 | 0.7 | 1.3 | 0.2 | 99.9 |
| *University* | 3,295 | 49.5 | 30.7 | 6.8 | 10.7 | 0.8 | 1.2 | 0.2 | 99.9 |
| M.A. | 210 | 48.6 | 32.4 | 3.8 | 14.3 | – | 1.0 | – | 100.1 |
| Ph.D. | 3,085 | 49.6 | 30.6 | 7.0 | 10.5 | 0.9 | 1.2 | 0.3 | 100.1 |
| *Liberal arts college* | 3,718 | 48.6 | 30.2 | 7.3 | 11.5 | 0.7 | 1.6 | 0.2 | 100.1 |
| B.A. | 1,847 | 52.1 | 28.2 | 7.7 | 10.6 | 0.5 | 0.8 | 0.1 | 100.0 |
| M.A. and Ph.D. | 1,871 | 45.2 | 32.1 | 6.9 | 12.3 | 0.9 | 2.3 | 0.3 | 100.0 |
| *Teachers college* | 1,123 | 42.3 | 29.5 | 15.0 | 12.0 | – | 1.2 | 0.1 | 100.1 |
| B.A. | 207 | 31.9 | 36.7 | 20.3 | 11.1 | – | – | – | 100.0 |
| M.A. and Ph.D. | 916 | 44.7 | 27.8 | 13.8 | 12.2 | – | 1.4 | 0.1 | 100.0 |
| *Technical institute* | 32 | 40.6 | 25.0 | 28.1 | – | 6.3 | – | – | 100.0 |
| *Other* | 50 | 34.0 | 24.0 | 26.0 | 16.0 | – | – | – | 100.0 |

[a] Excludes graduates (1,449 men and 1,072 women) who graduated from institutions not classified by this measure.

Appendix Table S.  Undergraduate Major Field by National Merit Scholar Prestige[a]
(1958 B.A. Recipients)

*(percentages)*

| National Merit Scholar Prestige | Number | Natural science | Engineering | Social science | Humanities and arts | Health | Business and commerce | Education | Other | Total Percent |
|---|---|---|---|---|---|---|---|---|---|---|
| **Men** | | | | | | | | | | |
| *Total[b]* | *14,836* | *16.4* | *19.2* | *19.1* | *10.5* | *1.6* | *20.7* | *9.3* | *3.2* | *100.0* |
| Highest prestige | 3,593 | 17.0 | 25.1 | 25.5 | 12.4 | 1.3 | 15.1 | 2.2 | 1.4 | 100.0 |
| Very high prestige | 5,645 | 15.1 | 21.8 | 16.6 | 8.9 | 2.2 | 24.9 | 7.0 | 3.6 | 100.1 |
| Average prestige | 3,121 | 16.8 | 17.5 | 16.9 | 11.2 | 1.6 | 19.9 | 12.1 | 4.1 | 100.1 |
| Below average prestige | 1,299 | 18.8 | 8.7 | 18.6 | 11.9 | 1.2 | 17.9 | 18.7 | 4.2 | 100.0 |
| Low prestige | 1,178 | 17.0 | 4.5 | 18.2 | 9.3 | 0.3 | 22.9 | 24.8 | 3.1 | 100.1 |
| **Women** | | | | | | | | | | |
| *Total[b]* | *8,212* | *9.1* | *0.5* | *15.6* | *22.0* | *7.6* | *5.4* | *33.3* | *6.6* | *100.1* |
| Highest prestige | 1,785 | 10.9 | 0.3 | 24.0 | 30.5 | 10.6 | 3.5 | 16.9 | 3.2 | 99.9 |
| Very high prestige | 2,729 | 8.0 | 0.7 | 16.8 | 22.3 | 9.3 | 5.9 | 30.2 | 6.8 | 100.0 |
| Average prestige | 1,846 | 9.6 | 0.5 | 12.8 | 18.6 | 7.2 | 4.7 | 37.5 | 9.1 | 100.0 |
| Below average prestige | 896 | 7.5 | 0.4 | 8.6 | 14.7 | 2.8 | 7.1 | 52.9 | 5.9 | 99.9 |
| Low prestige | 956 | 9.0 | 0.1 | 8.4 | 18.5 | 2.7 | 7.0 | 46.3 | 7.9 | 99.9 |

[a] See p.98 for further explanation on how measure was obtained and used.
[b] Excludes graduates (1,457 men and 1,078 women) from institutions not classified by this measure.

Appendix Table T.  Employment Status in 1963 by Type of Control and Sex Composition
of Undergraduate Institution (1958 B.A. Recipients)

*(percentages)*

**Men**

| Employment | Public | | Private | |
| Status | All-male | Co-ed | All-male | Co-ed |
|---|---|---|---|---|
| Employed full-time | 88.9 | 92.0 | 88.0 | 90.4 |
| Employed part-time | 1.5 | 2.4 | 3.3 | 2.9 |
| Unemployed | 0.7 | 0.5 | 0.5 | 0.6 |
| Student | 0.7 | 2.7 | 4.9 | 3.6 |
| Armed Forces | 7.4 | 2.0 | 3.0 | 2.0 |
| Other | – | 0.1 | 0.1 | 0.2 |
| No answer | 0.7 | 0.2 | 0.2 | 0.2 |
| Total percent | 99.9 | 99.9 | 100.0 | 99.9 |
| (Total number) | (135) | (8,276) | (1,829) | (6,049) |

**Women**

| | Public | | Private | |
| | All-female | Co-ed | All-female | Co-ed |
|---|---|---|---|---|
| Employed full-time | 50.0 | 48.2 | 38.6 | 47.8 |
| Employed part-time | 5.6 | 9.9 | 7.2 | 10.5 |
| Unemployed | 1.4 | 0.5 | 0.6 | 0.8 |
| Student | 2.1 | 1.3 | 2.5 | 1.8 |
| Housewife | 40.1 | 38.8 | 49.8 | 38.2 |
| Other | – | 0.7 | 0.1 | 0.4 |
| No answer | 0.7 | 0.5 | 1.2 | 0.5 |
| Total percent | 99.9 | 99.9 | 100.0 | 100.0 |
| (Total number) | (142) | (4,672) | (1,408) | (3,050) |

# BIBLIOGRAPHY

*Books and Documents*

Astin, Alexander W. *Who Goes Where to College?* Chicago: Science Research Associates, Inc., 1965.

Astin, Alexander W., and Panos, Robert J. *The Educational and Vocational Development of American College Students.* Washington, D.C.: American Council on Education, 1969.

Becker, Howard S., Greer, Blanche, and Hughes, Everett. *Making the Grade — The Academic Side of College Life.* New York: John Wiley & Sons, Inc., 1968.

Berelson, Bernard. *Graduate Education in the United States.* New York: McGraw-Hill Book Company, 1960.

Berger, Alan S. *Longitudinal Studies on the Class of 1961: The Graduate Science Students.* Chicago: National Opinion Research Center, January 1967.

Bradburn, Norman M., and Caplovitz, David. *Reports on Happiness.* Chicago: Aldine Publishing Company, 1965.

Bureau of Social Science Research. *Two Years After the College Degree: Work and Further Study Patterns.* National Science Foundation Report NSF 63-26. Washington, D.C.: U.S. Government Printing Office, 1963.

Davis, James A. *Great Aspirations.* Chicago: Aldine Publishing Company, 1964.

———. *Undergraduate Career Decisions.* Chicago: Aldine Publishing Company, 1965.

Fichter, Joseph H. *Graduates of Predominantly Negro Colleges, Class of 1964.* Washington, D.C.: U.S. Government Printing Office, 1967.

Goldsen, Rose K., *et al. What College Students Think.* Princeton, N.J.: D. Van Nostrand Co., Inc., 1960.

154

Gossman, Charles S., *et al. Migration of College and University Students in the United States.* Seattle: University of Washington Press, 1968.

Hauser, Jane Z., and Lazarsfeld, Paul F. *The Admissions Officer in the American College: An Occupation Under Change.* New York: College Entrance Examination Board, 1964.

Jacobs, Philip E. *Changing Values in College.* New York: Harper & Row, Publishers, 1958.

Jencks, Christopher, and Riesman, David. *The Academic Revolution.* Garden City, N.Y.: Doubleday & Company, Inc., 1968.

Knapp, R. H., and Greenbaum, J. J. *The Younger American Scholar.* Chicago: University of Chicago Press, 1953.

Kornhauser, Arthur. *Mental Health of the Industrial Worker.* New York: John Wiley & Sons, Inc., 1965.

National Science Foundation. *Graduate Student Support and Manpower Resources in Graduate Science Education (Fall 1965, Fall 1968).* NSF 68-13. Washington, D.C.: U.S. Government Printing Office, June 1968.

_____. *Scientific and Technical Manpower Resources.* NSF 64-28. Washington, D.C.: U.S. Government Printing Office, 1964.

Newcomb, Theodore M. *Personality and Social Change.* New York: Dryden Press, 1943.

Rice, Mabel C., and Mason, Paul L. *Residence and Migration of College Students, Fall 1963.* Washington, D.C.: U.S. Government Printing Office, 1965.

Rosenberg, Morris. *Occupations and Values.* Glencoe, Ill.: The Free Press, 1957.

Schwartz, Mildred A. *The United States College-Education Population: 1960.* Chicago: National Opinion Research Center, 1965.

Sibley, Elbridge. *The Education of Sociologists in the United States.* Washington, D.C.: Russell Sage Foundation, 1963.

Spaeth, Joe L., and Miller, Norman. *Trends in the Career Plans and Activities of the 1961 College Graduates.* Chicago: National Opinion Research Center, March 1965.

Stanford, Nevitt (ed.). *The American College.* New York: John Wiley & Sons, Inc., 1962.

U.S. Bureau of the Census. *Current Population Reports.* Series P-60, No. 43. Washington, D.C.: U.S. Department of Commerce, September 29, 1964.

Wallace, Walter L. *Student Culture.* Chicago: Aldine Publishing Company, 1966.

Warkov, Seymour, and Marsh, John. *The Education and Training of American Scientists and Engineers: 1962.* Chicago: National Opinion Research Center, 1965.

Wilson, Kenneth W. *Of Time and the Doctorate.* SREB Research Monograph, No. 9. Atlanta: Southern Regional Education Board, 1965.

Wolfe, Dael. *America's Resources of Specialized Talent.* New York: Harper and Brothers, 1954.

*Articles*

Astin, Alexander W. "Productivity of Undergraduate Institutions," *Science* (April 13, 1962), 129-35.

\_\_\_\_\_. "Re-examination of College Productivity," *Journal of Educational Psychology* (June 1961), 173-78.

Bayer, Alan E., and Astin, Helen S. "Sex Differences in Academic Rank and Salary Among Science Doctorates in Teaching," *Journal of Human Resources*, Vol. 3 (Spring 1968), 191-200.

Centers, Richard, and Bugental, Daphne E. "Intrinsic and Extrinsic Job Motivations Among Different Segments of the Working Population," *Journal of Applied Psychology* (June 1966), 193-97.

Davis, James A. "The Campus as a Frog Pond: An Application of Theory of Relative Deprivation to Career Decisions of College Men," *American Journal of Sociology*, Vol. 72, No. 1 (July 1966), 17-31.

Ferriss, Abbott L. "Graduate Student Migration and Regional Loss of Talent." Unpublished working paper. Washington, D.C.: Russell Sage Foundation, 1968.

Folger, John K. "Some Relationships Between Ability and Self-Reported Grades," *Sociology of Education*, Vol. 40 (Summer 1967), 270-74.

Holland, John L. "Current Psychological Theories of Occupational Choice and Their Implications for National Planning," *The Journal of Human Resources*, Vol. 2 (Spring 1967), 176-90.

Landinsky, Jack. "The Geographic Mobility of Professional and Technical Manpower," *The Journal of Human Resources*, Vol. 2 (Fall 1967), 475-94.

Schein, Edgar H. "The First Job Dilemma," *Psychology Today* (March 1968), 27-37.

Sharp, Laure M. "The Meaning of the Bachelor's Degree," *Sociology of Education*, Vol. 37 (Winter 1963), 93-109.

Sharp, Laure M., and Krasnegor, Rebecca. "College Students and Military Service," *Sociology of Education*, Vol. 41, No. 4 (Fall 1968), 390-400.

Spaeth, Joe L. "Occupational Prestige Expectations Among College Male Graduates," *American Journal of Sociology*, Vol. 73, No. 5 (March 1968), 558.

Werts, Charles E. "A Comparison of Male vs. Female College Attendance Probabilities," *Sociology of Education*, Vol. 41, No. 1 (Winter 1968), 103-10.

# INDEX

Academic aptitude
  and graduate school, 24, 89, 100
  and military service, 86-87, 89
Academic Performance Index (API), 19*n*, 24
Actors. *See* Humanistic occupations
Agricultural scientists, 37, 56. *See also* Natural scientists
American College Testing Program, 19
Artists. *See* Humanistic occupations
Arts, 15, 16, 37
  financial support, 22
  military service, 87
  prestige schools, 104
Astin, Alexander, W., 98

B.A.
  and government employment, 58
  importance of, 44
  median salary in 1963, 72
  time lag before Ph.D., 26
  use of in job, 68
Berelson, Bernard, 27
Biologists, 41, 56, 57. *See also* Natural scientists
Bureau of Social Science Research (BSSR), 27
Business, field of
  characteristics of majors, 117-18
  geographical influence, 37, 38
  military service, 87-88, 93
Business occupations
  commitment, 51, 54
  degree, use of, 68
  geographic mobility, 74
  importance of income, 54, 80, 81
  and M.A., 15
  and major, 40-41, 52, 68, 69, 117
  for nonmajors, 11-12, 52
  occupational mobility, 53
  popularity of, 52
  recruitment for, 53-54, 116
  salary and school-type, 110-11
  satisfaction/dissatisfaction, 80
  school-type, importance of, 52, 54, 108, 110, 116
  stability, 51-52, 53, 54
  for women, 110

California college system, 76
Campus unrest, 1
  and decline in graduate study, 4
Career commitment
  business, 51, 54
  and occupational stability, 70
  reasons for change, 50
  teaching, 49, 50
  of women, 60, 107

Career satisfaction/dissatisfaction, 77*n*
  and income, 79
  at the M.A. level, 81
  reasons for, 77-79
  and values, 77, 79-81
Chemists, 22, 56, 57, 60. *See also* Natural scientists
Children
  and geographic mobility, 38
  and graduate studies, 29, 30, 33, 100
  and women's employment, 60
Clergymen. *See* Humanistic occupations
Coeducational schools, 98, 101, 103, 104-5, 107, 113, 114
College. *See* Undergraduate institutions
College attendance, 1, 97, 114
College Entrance Examination Board, 19
College major
  change in, 6-8, 12
  change in, at graduate level, 18-19
  choice, timing of, 7
  commitment, early and late, 8
  and community size, 37
  consequences of choice, 8, 10, 12, 39-41
  and geographic region, 37
  and graduate study, 8, 14, 34, 104
  importance of, 44
  and occupational income, 6-8, 10, 39-41, 42-43, 107-8, 116
  and socioeconomic background, 7
  and students' characteristics, 117-18
  use of in job, 67-69
  use of in military service, 91, 92, 94
  *See also* specific disciplines (Business, Education, Engineering, Natural sciences, Social sciences)
College selectivity, 54
  definition, 98
  influence on graduate studies, 101
College teaching. *See* Teaching
Community size
  and choice of major, 37
  and graduate study, 38
  and professionals, 38
  and women, 37
  *See also* Geographic influences on career; Geographic influences on graduate study
Competitive grading, 116
Continuing education, 3, 34
Cosmopolitan orientation group
  career outcome, 38
  characteristics, 38
  geographic mobility, 118, 120

D.D.S., 15. *See also* Health occupations; Professional degree

157